a reason for Science
Hands-On Activities with Scripture Values

   LEVEL **A**

TEACHER GUIDEBOOK

ISBN # 1-58938-208-0

Published by **The Concerned Group, Inc.**
700 East Granite • PO Box 1000 • Siloam Springs, AR 72761

Authors	**Dave & Rozann Seela**
Publisher	**Russ L. Potter, II**
Senior Editor	**Bill Morelan**
Contributing Editor	**Robyn Pryor**
Project Coordinator	**Rocki Vanatta**
Creative Director	**Daniel Potter**
Reading Consultant	**Susan Hancock**
Proofreaders	**Tricia S. Williams & Lou Stewart**
Illustrations	**Josh Ray**
Colorists	**Josh & Aimee Ray**

Printed on recycled paper in the United States

For more information about **A Reason For®** curricula,
write to the address above, call, or visit our website.

www.AReasonFor.com
800.447.4332

TABLE OF CONTENTS

Overview

How To Use This Guidebook

Weekly Lessons

"A sound grounding in science strengthens many of the skills that people use every day, like solving problems creatively, thinking critically, working cooperatively in teams, using technology effectively, and valuing life-long learning."*

*National Science Education Standards, 1999 Washington, D.C.: National Academy Press. (p. ix)

A NEW PARADIGM

A Reason For® Science was designed for children, the handiwork of an infinite God — young minds created with an unlimited capacity to think, to learn, and to discover!

Because of this emphasis on children and how they learn, *A Reason For® Science* is based on a different paradigm from the traditional textbook approach. Why? In an effort to address standards and accountability, many of today's science textbooks seem to get learning backwards. They focus primarily on building a knowledge base, assuming students will later attach meaning to memorized facts. The problem is that few elementary students master information presented this way because they simply never become engaged with the material.

By contrast, *A Reason For® Science* is based on the premise that learning science is an **active** process. It's *"something that students do, not something that is done to them."*[1]

According to the **National Science Education Standards**, *". . . active science learning means shifting emphasis away from teachers presenting information and covering science topics. The perceived need to include all the topics, vocabulary, and information in textbooks is in direct conflict with the central goal of having students learn scientific knowledge with understanding."*[2]

To paraphrase William Butler Yeats: Teaching is not filling a pail. It's lighting a fire!

INQUIRY-BASED LEARNING

A Reason For® Science is designed to teach basic Life, Earth, and Physical Science concepts through fun, hands-on activities linked to meaningful direct instruction.

But a "hands-on" approach alone is not enough. To truly master a concept, students must have a "minds-on" experience as well! This means actively engaging the material through a variety of activities such as group discussion, problem solving, and journaling. It also requires thought-provoking questions that help develop higher-level cognitive skills. The weekly format of *A Reason For® Science* is designed to reflect this inquiry-based model.

According to the **National Science Education Standards**, *"Inquiry is central to science learning. When engaging in inquiry, students describe objects and events, ask questions, construct explanations, test those explanations against current scientific knowledge, and communicate their ideas to others . . . In this way, students actively develop their understanding of science by combining scientific knowledge with reasoning and thinking skills."*[3]

Since different students achieve understanding in different ways and to different degrees, the flexible format of *A Reason For® Science* also encourages multiple learning styles and allows for individual differences. Activities challenge students to develop their own unique skills, and encourage them to come up with creative solutions.

NATIONAL STANDARDS

National standards referred to in **A Reason For® Science** come from the **National Science Education Standards**.[4] More specifically, they reflect the 1st - 4th Science Content Standards (p.121 - 141) and 5th - 8th Science Content Standards (p. 143 - 171).

The Teacher Guidebook gives a list of the specific content standards that relate to each lesson. The references are based on the NSES alphabetic format, plus a numeric code to indicate the bulleted sub-topic. For example, **C1** in a second grade lesson would indicate Content Standard **C** and sub-topic **1**. (This content standard is outlined on page 127 of the **Standards,** and a detailed description can be found on page 129.)

However, lower grade and upper grade standards are found in different sections of the book. The lower grade **C1** reference above, for example, would be found on page 129 ("characteristics of organisms"). By contrast, a **C1** reference for a seventh grade lesson would be found on page 156 ("structure and function in living systems").

METHODOLOGY

Master teachers know that a science curriculum is much more than information in a textbook. It has to do with the way content is organized and presented in the classroom. It is driven by underlying principles, and by attitudes and beliefs about how learning occurs. It is expressed in the practices and procedures used in its implementation.

In other words, textbooks don't teach science — *teachers* do!

That's why it's important for you to understand how this curriculum is designed to be used, and how you can enhance the learning process in your classroom. [5]

Concepts, Not Content

The needs of children in elementary school are very different from high school students, especially when it comes to science education. The presentation of the Periodic Table provides a good example. High school students may find it useful to memorize each element, its atomic weight, and its position on a chart. By contrast, elementary school students must first understand the concept of such a table. What is it? How is it used? Why is it arranged this way? Has it always looked like this? How (and why) has it changed over time?

Such an approach leads to a foundational understanding of a concept, rather than a body of memorized "facts" that may change over time.*

As Nobel prize winner, Dr. Richard Feynman, once said, *"You can know the name of a bird in all the languages of the world, but when you're finished, you'll know absolutely nothing whatever about the bird . . . (that's) the difference between knowing the name of something and knowing something!"*[6]

---

* For example, many students were taught the "fact" that matter has only three states (solid, liquid, and gas). But by 2001, scientists were aware of at least SIX states of matter! There are many such examples in education — including the Periodic Table charts themselves, which are being replaced in many colleges by a new 3D computer model that offers new insights into the relationships between elements.

Multi-Sensory Learning

In addition to focusing on concepts instead of just content, **A Reason For® Science** uses a multi-sensory approach to learning that supports multiple learning styles.

Visual events include watching teacher demonstrations, studying diagrams and illustrations, and reading summaries. **Auditory** events include participating in group discussions with team members, listening to teacher directions and explanations, and hearing the unique sounds that are associated with activities. **Kinesthetic** events include tactile interaction with activity materials and hands-on experimentation, as well as taking notes, writing answers, and drawing diagrams.

Omitting any of these components can significantly weaken the learning process, especially for children with specific learning disabilities.

Student-Driven, Teacher-Directed

As long-time educators, the authors of this series recognize that many elementary teachers don't consider themselves "science people." Therefore, this series avoids unnecessary technical jargon. It deals with complex interactions in simple, easy-to-understand language that's reinforced with concrete, hands-on activities.

The *Teacher Guidebook* is designed to give you the confidence that you need to teach science effectively. In addition to the usual answer keys and explanations, it includes several sections just for teachers.

Additional Comments and **Special Instructions** offer tips and techniques for making each lesson run smoothly. **Teacher to Teacher** provides expanded scientific explanations to increase your understanding. **Extended Teaching** presents a variety of extension ideas for those who wish to go further.

During the first year, we strongly recommend that you try every activity a day or two in advance. Although most activities are relatively simple, this added practice will give you a better feel for any potential problems that might arise.

Most of all, remember that one of the primary goals of this series is to make science *fun* for the participants. And that includes you, too!

COMPONENTS

The following are some of the key components in this series:

Parent Interaction

Positive communication between home and school is essential for optimum success with any curriculum. The "Letter to the Parents" (page 3, Student Worktext) provides a great way to introduce **A Reason For® Science** to parents. It covers the lesson format, safety issues, connections with **Standards**, and the integration of Scripture. Along with the opening sections of the *Teacher Guide*, the parent letter provides information you need to answer common questions about the series.

In addition, the bottom of the "weekly quiz" (see page 12) contains a special section called **To the Parent**. When you send the quiz home, this section helps keep parents informed and involved. It reviews the lesson focus and objective, summarizes the **Standard** covered, and provides follow-up questions to enhance student/parent interaction.

Student Research Teams

A Reason For® Science was created to model the way scientific study works in the adult world. Students are divided into "research teams" to work through activities cooperatively. Ideally, each research team should be composed of three to five students. (Fewer students per team makes monitoring more difficult; more students per team minimizes participation opportunities.) The best groupings combine students with different abilities, complementary personalities, etc. — the same kinds of combinations that make effective teams in the corporate or industrial world.

In addition, **A Reason For® Science** encourages collaboration between the different teams, again modeling the interactions found in the scientific community.

Individual Student Worktexts

Although students collaborate on activities and thought questions, the Student Worktexts provide opportunities for individual reaction and response. The importance of allowing students to write their own response to questions, keep their own notes, and journal about their individual experiences cannot be underestimated. (While collaboration is essential in the scientific community, no true scientist would neglect to keep his/her own personal notes and records!)

Individual Student Worktexts also provide teachers with an objective way to monitor student participation and learning throughout the school year.

Materials Kits

Quality materials are an integral part of any hands-on activity. **A Reason For® Science** offers complete, easy-to-use materials kits for every grade level. With some minor exceptions*, kits contain all the materials and supplies needed by one research team for an entire school year.

Materials for each team come packaged in an attractive, durable storage container. You can choose to restock consumable portions of the kit from local materials, or purchase the convenient refill pack.

(See page 238 for a simple "Shopping List" of non-supplied items.)

* To help minimize expense, kits do not include common classroom supplies (pencils, paper, etc.) and a few large items (soft drink bottles, tin cans, etc.) that are easily obtained by the teacher. Kit and non-kit materials needed for each lesson are clearly marked in this Teacher Guidebook. A "Shopping List" of non-supplied items (other than standard classroom supplies) can be found on page 238.

Personal Science Glossary

A glossary is a common component in many science textbooks, yet students rarely use traditional glossaries except when assigned to "look up" a word by the teacher. Since words and terms used in elementary science are not highly technical, this activity is better served by referring students to a standard dictionary.

A more effective approach to helping students learn science words at this level is to encourage them to develop and maintain a **personal science glossary**. This can be a plain spiral-bound notebook with one page (front and back) dedicated to each letter of the alphabet. Throughout the school year, students continually add new words and definitions — not only from their own reading and research, but from the findings of their team members as well.

FORMAT

The lessons in this edition of **A Reason For® Science** are based on a simple, effective weekly format. The daily headings are: ENGAGE, INFORM, EXPLORE, EXPAND, and ASSESS. (Lessons are very flexible, however, so the suggested sequence can be modified to fit almost any schedule.)

ENGAGE - Day 1

Research strongly supports the value of engaging student interest at the beginning of any new lesson. This helps focus attention on the topic and draws students into the learning process. Here are some helpful tips for Day 1.

As you introduce each section (OBSERVE, DESCRIBE, DISCUSS), read the instructions aloud as students follow along. Be sure to read the instructions slowly and clearly. This support is especially helpful for Emergent readers.

Encourage every student to create a personal "Science Journal" using a clean spiral notebook. Use these to follow-up the DESCRIBE and DISCUSS activities. Use one page (front and back) for each lesson. Have students create simple headings with the lesson's name and the National Standard addressed. In their Science Journal . . .

- **Emergent** readers can draw simple illustrations and label them.
- **Transitional** readers can draw illustrations, label them, then add comments.
- **Fluent** readers can give longer reponses with more detail (including full paragraphs).

This option provides a great cross-curricular connection to both art and language arts.

INFORM - Day 2

Many science programs are either "direct instruction" (text only) or "hands-on" (activities only). Since both of these approaches have their strengths, **A Reason For® Science** provides a unique combination of both. **Read the Story** is the core "direct instruction" component each week. It also provides excellent connections to both reading and writing.

You can make cross-curricular connections to reading with these options:

- **Emergent** readers can read the large colored words aloud with you. (You may also wish to have them point to the pictures as you read each section.)
- **Transitional** readers can read all of the colored words aloud with you.
- **Fluent** readers can read aloud as Transitional readers, then re-read the complete text silently to themselves.

You can make another cross-curricular connection to reading by having student teams read the story aloud together (shared reading). You may wish to have a Fluent reader on each team so they can lead out. (There is a growing body of research that indicates strong positive benefits in the brain from reading aloud — even for adults!)

After reading and discussion, you can make a cross-curricular connection to writing by challenging each team to list key points from the reading. Emergent readers may simply write the "dotted" words from the DISCUSS section. Transitional and Fluent readers should include descriptions of specific things they've learned from the reading. When teams are finished, have them take turns sharing what they've written.

EXPLORE - Day 3

Do the Activity is the core "hands-on" component each week. Be sure to read the activity in advance so you understand it thoroughly. (If time allows, try it out yourself.) Then before students begin, carefully go over the **Safety Concerns** together.

Pass out all materials students need for the activity, then have students follow along as you read the instructions for **Step 1**. Monitor teams closely as they complete this step. (Note: Different degrees of monitoring or assistance may be required depending on developmental and behavioral differences.) Once teams have completed **Step 1**, read the instructions for **Step 2**. Monitor teams as before. Repeat this process for **Step 3** and **Step 4**.

After the activity is completed, allow time for each team to share their observations (what they did, what they saw, what the results were, etc.). To encourage higher-level thinking skills, encourage teams to not only share their observations with each another, but also with other research teams. Conclude by reading **What Happened** to "tell them what you taught them."

You can make a cross-curricular connection to Language Arts by pointing out the **red** words in each sentence. These are the primary verbs. Ask students how these words are different from the other words in the sentence. (They indicate action.)

EXPAND - Day 4

You can expand the lesson by reviewing the activity from **Day 3**, then having students answer the questions from **What I Learned** (part 2). While **What I Learned** (part 1) contains mostly fact-based questions, **What I Learned** (part 2) requires higher-level cognitive responses. Question 1 asks students to *explain* some part of the activity. Question 2 requires them to *compare* and *contrast*. Question 3 asks them to *predict* something based on what they've learned.

Best results are often achieved by letting students discuss each question with their research team before turning away to write the answer in their own words. This forces students to synthesize the information rather than simply copying someone else's answer. If a student has difficulty, they are allowed to ask their team for further input — but must still finish by writing the answer in their own words.

ASSESS - Day 5

Authentic assessment is an important part of any quality curriculum. (For full details on the assessment options available in **A Reason For® Science**, see the "ASSESSMENT METHODS" section on page 12.)

SAFETY ISSUES

When using hands-on science activities, teachers must be constantly aware of the potential for safety problems. Even the simplest activities using the most basic materials can be dangerous when used incorrectly. *Proper monitoring and supervision is required at all times!*

Although the publisher and authors have made every reasonable effort to ensure that all science activities in **A Reason For® Science** are safe when conducted as instructed, neither the publisher nor the authors assume any responsibility for damage or injury resulting from implementation.

It is the responsibility of the school to review available science safety resources and to develop science safety training for their teachers and students, as well as posting safety rules in every classroom.

An excellent source of science safety information is the Council of State Science Supervisors at: **http://csss.enc.org/safety**. The CSSS website offers a FREE, downloadable safety guide, "Science and Safety, Making the Connection." This booklet was created with support from the American Chemical Society, the Eisenhower National Clearinghouse for Mathematics and Science Education, the National Aeronautics and Space Administration, and the National Institutes of Health.

To support appropriate safety instruction, **A Reason For® Science** has developed "Peat the Safety Worm" to warn students of potential hazards. Peat (spelled like the soil in a bog) is featured in a special safety section in the front of each Student Worktext. It is strongly recommended that every teacher verify all students clearly understand all safety information *before* beginning any science activities.

ASSESSMENT METHODS

Authentic assessment is an important part of any quality curriculum. **A Reason For® Science** offers a dual approach to assessment. First, participation, understanding, and higher-level thinking skills can be assessed by periodically collecting and reading students' responses to the essay-style questions in the Student Worktext.

Second, each lesson in the Student Worktext contains a "weekly quiz" called **Show What You Know**. This general assessment is specifically designed to allow you to check a student's understanding of the week's concept regardless of the child's reading level. It can also be removed from the book and sent home to the parents (see **Parent Interaction**, page 7). In addition, you also may wish to give Fluent readers the optional quiz found in the *Teacher Guide*.

Finally, you can use both methods to create a customized quarterly or yearly assessment tool. Simply combine questions from the weekly quizzes with essay-style questions from the Student Worktext.

Reading Levels

If you wish to do further assessment focusing on individual reading levels, the following guidelines may prove helpful. This example (based on the lesson **Plant Parts**) shows some simple modifications that reflect appropriate adjustments for developmental differences.

- **Emergent** readers: Write the following words on the board: plant, roots, stems, leaves. Have each student write one word at the top of a sheet of paper. Next have them draw a picture of what that word represents.

- **Transitional** readers: Give each student a blank sheet of paper. Have them draw a simple picture of a plant. (If desired, you can let them use the plant picture from the general assessment as an example.) Now have them label the plant's three primary parts —roots, stems, leaves.

- **Fluent** readers: Give students the simple 10-point quiz found in the *Teacher Guide*. (Reproducible masters and answer keys are provided for each lesson.) This optional quiz offers a more traditional assessment of science mastery based on fact acquisition. Questions are similar to the type that students might face on any standardized test.

SCRIPTURE CONNECTION

Integrating faith and learning is an essential part of a quality religious education. A unique component of **A Reason For® Science** is the incorporation of Scripture Object Lessons (called **Food for Thought**) into every lesson. As your students discover basic science principles, they are also encouraged to explore various spiritual connections through specific Scripture verses. Since some school systems may prefer one Scripture translation to another, Scriptures are referenced by chapter and verse only, rather than direct quotations in the text.

Creationism

Many people, including many notable scientists, believe that God created the universe and all the processes that resulted in our solar system and life on Earth.

However, advocates of "creation science" hold a variety of viewpoints. Some believe that Earth is relatively young, perhaps only 6,000 years old. Others believe that Earth may have existed for millions of years, but that various organisms (especially humans) could only be the result of divine intervention since they demonstrate "intelligent design."

Within the creation science community, there are dozens of variations on these themes even within specific denominational groups. Instead of promoting one of these specific views, the authors of this series have chosen to focus on the concept that "God created the heavens and the earth," and leave the specifics up to the individual school.

Creationism is a faith-based issue.* As such, every school is strongly urged to have a clear position on this topic, and an understanding of how that belief is to be conveyed to its students.

For that matter, so is the theory of evolution.

Footnotes:

[1] *National Science Education Standards*, 1999 Washington, D.C.: National Academy Press. (p. 2)

[2] *Ibid.* (p. 20)

[3] *Ibid.* (p. 2)

[4] *National Science Education Standards*, 1999 Washington, D.C.: National Academy Press. ISBN 0-309-05326-9

[5] In addition to **Inquiry-Based Learning**, **A Reason For® Science** also supports other highly successful instructional strategies. The use of "research teams" of three to five students is based on **Cooperative Learning** concepts. The weekly science story (adjusted for either Emergent, Transitional, or Fluent readers) supports **Differentiated Instruction**. The multiple "entry points" each lesson takes, allowing students to approach the topic through preferred learning modes, reflects **4MAT**, **Multiple Intellegences**, and general **Constructivist** philosophies. Those familiar with successful "learner-focused" strategies will find many more examples.

[6] Feynman, Richard P. "Science Hobbyist" Website. 10 September 1994. 24 January 2005 <http://www.amasci.com/feynman.html>.

THE TEACHER GUIDEBOOK

The Teacher Guidebook is based on a simple, easy-to-understand format. Lessons throughout the series follow the same pattern, so once you're familiar with the format for one lesson, you can find information quickly for any other lesson. The samples on the following pages explain the purpose of each section.

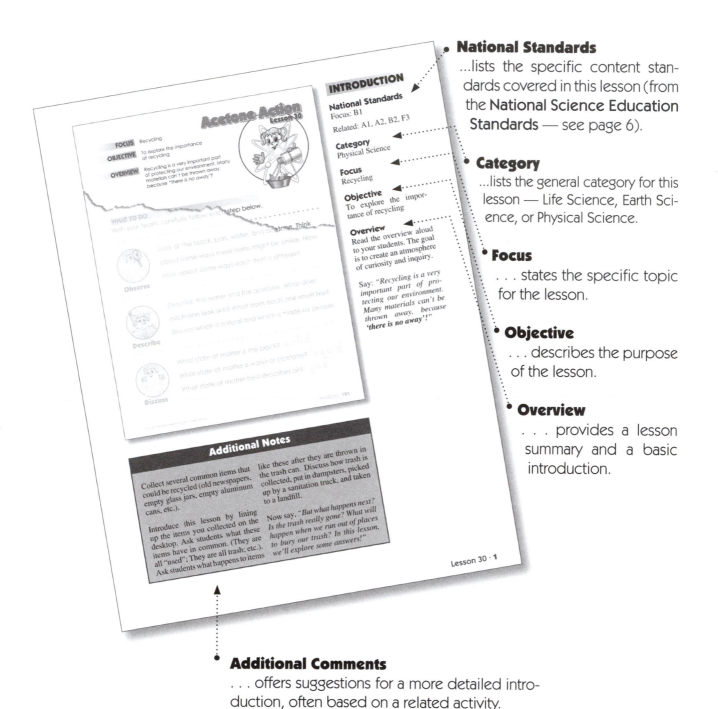

National Standards

...lists the specific content standards covered in this lesson (from the **National Science Education Standards** — see page 6).

Category

...lists the general category for this lesson — Life Science, Earth Science, or Physical Science.

Focus

. . . states the specific topic for the lesson.

Objective

. . . describes the purpose of the lesson.

Overview

. . . provides a lesson summary and a basic introduction.

Additional Comments

. . . offers suggestions for a more detailed introduction, often based on a related activity.

ENGAGE
What To Do •

. . . outlines directions for introductory activities (observe, describe, discuss) that are vital to good scientific study.

Options •

. . . offers alternative procedures for parts of the lesson.

Teacher To Teacher •

. . . provides expanded science explanations to increase the teacher's understanding.

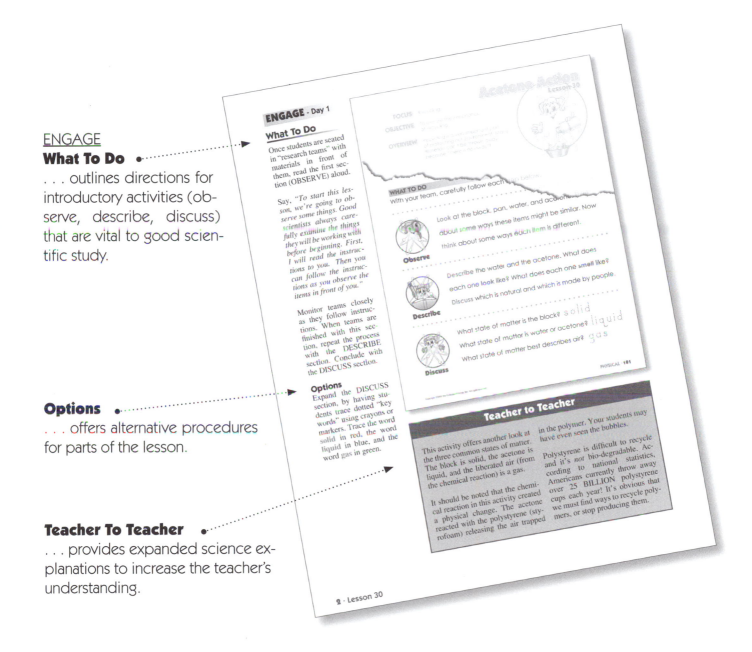

ENGAGE - Day 1

What To Do

Once students are seated in "research teams" with materials in front of them, read the first section (OBSERVE) aloud.

Say, *"To start this lesson, we're going to observe some things. Good scientists always carefully examine the things they will be working with before beginning. First, I will read the instructions to you. Then you can follow the instructions as you observe the items in front of you."*

Monitor teams closely as they follow instructions. When teams are finished with this section, repeat the process with the DESCRIBE section. Conclude with the DISCUSS section.

Options

Expand the DISCUSS section, by having students trace dotted "key words" using crayons or markers. Trace the word solid in red, the word liquid in blue, and the word gas in green.

WHAT TO DO
With your team, carefully follow each step below.

Observe — Look at the block, pan, water, and acetone. Think about some ways these items might be similar. Now think about some ways each item is different.

Describe — Describe the water and the acetone. What does each one look like? What does each one smell like? Discuss which is natural and which is made by people.

Discuss — What state of matter is the block? *solid* What state of matter is water or acetone? *liquid* What state of matter best describes air? *gas*

PHYSICAL · 181

Teacher to Teacher

This activity offers another look at the three common states of matter. The block is solid, the acetone is liquid, and the liberated air (from the chemical reaction) is a gas.

It should be noted that the chemical reaction in this activity created a physical change. The acetone reacted with the polystyrene (styrofoam) releasing the air trapped in the polymer. Your students may have even seen the bubbles.

Polystyrene is difficult to recycle and it's *not* bio-degradable. According to national statistics, Americans currently throw away over 25 BILLION polystyrene cups each year! It's obvious that we must find ways to recycle polymers, or stop producing them.

2 · Lesson 30

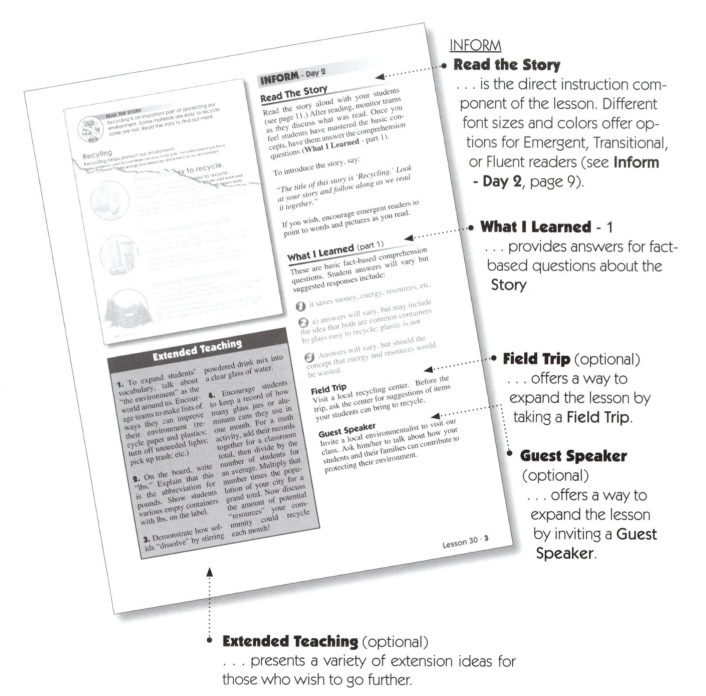

INFORM

- **Read the Story**

  . . . is the direct instruction component of the lesson. Different font sizes and colors offer options for Emergent, Transitional, or Fluent readers (see **Inform - Day 2**, page 9).

- **What I Learned** - 1

  . . . provides answers for fact-based questions about the **Story**

- **Field Trip** (optional)

  . . . offers a way to expand the lesson by taking a **Field Trip**.

- **Guest Speaker** (optional)

  . . . offers a way to expand the lesson by inviting a **Guest Speaker**.

- **Extended Teaching** (optional)

  . . . presents a variety of extension ideas for those who wish to go further.

EXPLORE

Materials Needed
. . . is a comprehensive list of materials used in the lesson. **Bold-faced** words indicate items that are provided in the Materials Kit.

Safety Concerns
. . . describes any potential safety hazards (see **Safety Issues**, page 11).

Do the Activity
. . . is the hands-on component of the lesson. This section provides general instructions for completing the activity.

Special Instructions
. . . lists additional instructions or precautions (if any) for completing the activity.

What Happened?
. . . provides a summary of the activity to *"tell them what you taught them."*

EXPLORE - Day 3

Materials Needed*
polystyrene block   acetone
craft stick   tart pan

Safety Concerns
3. Poison Hazard
Although acetone is a relatively safe chemical (similar to gasoline), no one should handle it at any time except the teacher. The fumes from acetone should not be inhaled.

4. Slipping
There is a potential for spilled liquids. Remind students to exercise caution.

Do the Activity
Read the activity in advance so you understand it thoroughly. (If time allows, try it yourself.) Before students begin, carefully go over the **Safety Concerns** together.

Pass out materials, then have your students follow along as you read the instructions for **Step 1**. Monitor teams closely as they complete this step.

Once teams have completed **Step 1**, read instructions for **Step 2**. Monitor teams as before. Repeat for **Step 3** and **Step 4**.

After the activity, allow time for each team to share their observations. To encourage higher-level thinking, encourage teams to not only share their observations with each other, but also with other teams.

Special Instructions
Step 1 - Demonstrate "wafting". Hold the bottle away from your nose and wave the smell toward you. (For students to waft, the teacher should hold the bottle.) *Never directly smell an unknown substance!*

Step 2 - Pour gently to avoid splatters. Remind students to stay a safe distance away.

Step 3 - Thoroughly wash the "lump" to remove all acetone! Let these polymer lumps dry overnight and they'll become extremely hard. Remind students this ugly lump will still be sitting in a landfill when their grandchildren have grandchildren!

4 · Lesson 30

DO THE ACTIVITY
Working with your research team, carefully follow each step below. Before you start, be sure you know the safety rules for this activity.

What Happened?

Immediately following the activity, help your students understand what they observed.

Say: "This activity demonstrates that many materials cannot be thrown away because there's no such thing as "away." Many kinds of trash remain in the environment for generations.

In **Step 1**, you compared the look and smell of acetone to water.

In **Step 2**, you observed that water does not react

with polystyrene. But in **Step 3**, you saw a significant chemical reaction as the acetone quickly melted the polystyrene.

Finally in **Step 4**, you saw that even chemicals can't completely get rid of polystyrene. A hard, solid leftover material remains, probably to end up in a landfill where it will take up space for centuries.

(Remember, never try an activity like this at home unless an adult is present to help you.)

Bold-faced items supplied in kit.

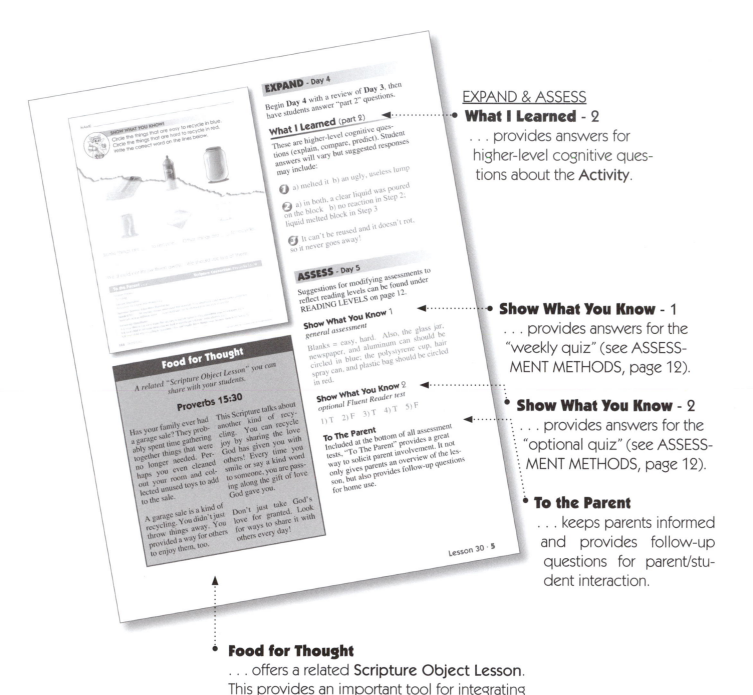

EXPAND - Day 4

Begin **Day 4** with a review of **Day 3**, then have students answer "part 2" questions.

What I Learned (part 2)

These are higher-level cognitive questions (explain, compare, predict). Student answers will vary but suggested responses may include:

1 a) melted it b) an ugly, useless lump

2 a) in both, a clear liquid was poured on the block b) no reaction in Step 2; liquid melted block in Step 3

3 It can't be reused and it doesn't rot, so it never goes away!

ASSESS - Day 5

Suggestions for modifying assessments to reflect reading levels can be found under READING LEVELS on page 12.

Show What You Know 1
general assessment

Blanks = easy, hard. Also, the glass jar, newspaper, and aluminum can should be circled in blue; the polystyrene cup, hair spray can, and plastic bag should be circled in red.

Show What You Know 2
optional Fluent Reader test

1) T   2) F   3) T   4) T   5) F

To The Parent
Included at the bottom of all assessment tests, "To The Parent" provides a great way to solicit parent involvement. It not only gives parents an overview of the lesson, but also provides follow-up questions for home use.

Lesson 30 · 5

Food for Thought

A related "Scripture Object Lesson" you can share with your students.

Proverbs 15:30

Has your family ever had a garage sale? They probably spent time gathering together things that were no longer needed. Perhaps you even cleaned out your room and collected unused toys to add to the sale.

A garage sale is a kind of recycling. You didn't just throw things away. You provided a way for others to enjoy them, too.

This Scripture talks about another kind of recycling. You can recycle joy by sharing the love God has given you with others! Every time you smile or say a kind word to someone, you are passing along the gift of love God gave you.

Don't just take God's love for granted. Look for ways to share it with others every day!

EXPAND & ASSESS

What I Learned - 2
. . . provides answers for higher-level cognitive questions about the **Activity**.

Show What You Know - 1
. . . provides answers for the "weekly quiz" (see ASSESSMENT METHODS, page 12).

Show What You Know - 2
. . . provides answers for the "optional quiz" (see ASSESSMENT METHODS, page 12).

To the Parent
. . . keeps parents informed and provides follow-up questions for parent/student interaction.

Food for Thought
. . . offers a related **Scripture Object Lesson**. This provides an important tool for integrating faith and learning.

Basic Needs
Lesson 1

FOCUS Basic Needs

OBJECTIVE To explore some basic needs of plants and animals

OVERVIEW Plants and animals need certain things in order to "survive and thrive." Some of the most important needs are food, water, air, and sunlight.

WHAT TO DO

With your team, carefully follow each step below.

Observe

Look at the two plants your teacher gives you. Look at the soil they are planted in. Look at their leaves. Think about what these plants might need to live.

Describe

Describe the two plants. What color are they? What shape are the leaves? In what ways are the two plants the same? In what ways are they different?

Discuss

Name one thing a plant might need to live. *food*
Name another thing a plant might need. *water*
What else might plants need to live? *sunlight*

LIFE · 11

Lesson 1

Introduction

National Standards
Focus: C1

Related: A1, A2, C3

Category
Life Science

Focus
Basic Needs

Objective
To explore some basic needs of plants and animals

Overview
Read the overview aloud to your students. The goal is to create an atmosphere of curiosity and inquiry.

Say: *"Plants and animals need certain things in order to 'survive and thrive.' Some of the most important needs are food, water, air, and sunlight."*

Additional Notes

To introduce this lesson, have students pretend they will be taken to a deserted island and left for one week. The island is mostly sand and a few trees. They can only take what will fit in a small backpack.

Now divide students into teams, and have them discuss what kinds of things they would need to survive. After discussion, have each student make a list of what they would put in their own backpack.

Discuss lists with the class. Point out the difference between "needs" (food, water, etc.) and "wants" (video games, candy, etc.).

Say, *"In this lesson, we'll discover some of the basic needs of plants and animals."*

Engage - Day 1

What To Do

Once students are seated in "research teams" with materials in front of them, read the first section (OBSERVE) aloud.

Say, *"To start this lesson, we're going to **observe** two different plants. Good scientists always carefully examine the things they will be working with before beginning. First, I will read the instructions to you. Then you can follow the instructions as you **observe** the items in front of you."*

Monitor teams closely as they follow instructions. When teams are finished with this section, repeat the process with the DESCRIBE section. Conclude with the DISCUSS section.

Options

Expand the DISCUSS section by having students trace dotted "key words" using crayons or markers. Trace the word **food** in green, the word **water** in blue, and the word **sunlight** in yellow.

FOCUS	Basic Needs
OBJECTIVE	To explore some basic needs of plants and animals
OVERVIEW	Plants and animals need certain things in order to "survive and thrive." Some of the most important needs are food, water, air, and sunlight.

Basic Needs — Lesson 1

WHAT TO DO

With your team, carefully follow each step below.

Observe

Look at the two plants your teacher gives you. **Look** at the soil they are planted in. **Look** at their leaves. **Think** about what these plants might need to live.

Describe

Describe the two plants. What **color** are they? What **shape** are the leaves? In what ways are the two plants the same? In what ways are they different?

Discuss

Name one thing a plant might need to live. food

Name another thing a plant might need. water

What else might plants need to live? sunlight

LIFE · 11

Teacher to Teacher

Plants are little "factories" that trap solar energy and convert it into food and oxygen. Everyone knows that!

But most people don't realize that plants also use oxygen themselves. Plants require oxygen to release the energy needed to make everything from timber to strawberries. However, plants make a lot more oxygen than they actually use.

And that's a good thing for the rest of the creatures on this planet since we all need oxygen to survive!

READ THE STORY
Plants and animals need certain things to survive. Some of these include **food, water, air,** and **sunlight.** Read the story below to find out more.

Basic Needs

Plants and animals have needs.
Plants and animals need certain things in order to survive. Some of these needs are food, water, air, and sunlight. If its needs are not met, a plant or animal could die.

Food and water are needs.

Plants and animals need water.
All plants need water. Without it, they dry up and die. Animals need water, too. Most can only live a few days without water.

Plants and animals need food.
Plants get food (nutrients) from the soil. They also make food from sunlight (photosynthesis). Animals get food from plants and sometimes other animals.

Air and sunlight are needs.

Plants and animals need air.
Plants use air in a different way than animals, but both need air to survive. Without air, an animal would die in minutes.

Plants and animals need sunlight.
When animals "soak up sun," it builds Vitamin D in their bodies. When plants use sunlight, they use it to make food.

Needs can be different.

Every kind of plant has special needs.
A cactus needs lots of sun, but little water. A fern needs lots of water, but little sun. Different places support different plants.

Every kind of animal has special needs.
A beaver can't live in a desert. A camel can't live in a swamp. Like plants, animals only survive where their needs can be met.

Extended Teaching

1. A variation on this activity is to let each team test a different variable. For instance, Team 1 might test "food" by removing the soil from the roots, but still giving the plant plenty of sunshine, air, and water; Team 2 might test "temperature" by putting their plant in a refrigerator; and so on.

2. To demonstrate plants' need for sunlight, place a shoe box on a grassy area. (Put a rock in the box so it stays put.) After one week, lift up the box and observe the grass. Remove the box and see how long it takes for the grass to turn green again.

3. Invite a sociologist or social studies teacher to visit your class. Ask him/ her to talk about places in the world where people are suffering because their basic needs are not being met. Talk about what some of these basic needs are, and about reasons these things are not readily available (drought, famine, politics, etc.). If possible, have him/her bring pictures or films showing such places.

Read The Story
Read the story aloud with your students. (See READING LEVELS on page 12.) After reading, monitor teams as they discuss what was read. Once you feel students have mastered the basic concepts, have them answer the comprehension questions (**What I Learned** - part 1) on the next page.

To introduce the story, say:

"The title of this story is 'Basic Needs.' Look at your story and follow along as we read it together."

If you wish, encourage Emergent readers to point to words and pictures as you read.

What I Learned (part 1)
These are basic fact-based comprehension questions. Student answers will vary, but suggested responses include:

① food, water, air, sunlight

② a) both need food, water, air, and sunlight b) fern needs a lot less sunlight and more water; cactus needs more sunlight and less water

③ a) it might die b) its needs could not be met; tree frogs need trees and more water than is in the desert

Field Trip
Go on a hike in a nature park or nearby woods. Look for evidences of plants struggling to survive because some basic need is not being met (too much sunlight, too dry, too wet, too shaded, etc.).

Guest Speaker
Invite a farmer or gardener to visit your class. Ask him/her to talk about the things that are needed to produce a healthy crop.

Materials Needed*
sealable plastic bag
water   paper towels
small plants (like tomato seedlings)

Safety Concerns
4. Slipping
There is a potential for spilled liquids. Remind students to exercise caution.

Do the Activity
Read the activity in advance so you understand it thoroughly. (If time allows, try it yourself.) Before students begin, carefully go over the **Safety Concerns** together.

Pass out materials, then have your students follow along as you read the instructions for **Step 1**. Monitor teams closely as they complete this step.

Once teams have completed **Step 1**, read instructions for **Step 2**. Monitor teams as before. Repeat for **Step 3** and **Step 4**.

After the activity, allow time for each team to share their observations. To encourage higher-level thinking, encourage teams to not only share their observations with each other, but also with other teams.

Special Instructions

Step 1 - Show students how to correctly water a plant. Remind them that using either too much or too little water does not meet a plant's needs.

Step 2 - Spread paper towels to make clean-up easier. Caution students not to tear roots or leaves while removing soil. A large cardboard box works well for storing the plants. Be sure to seal it well with masking tape. (The idea is that you're depriving these plants of food, water, air, and sunlight.)

Step 3 - Mark a class calendar to indicate the passing days, or keep a running record on the board.

* Bold-faced items supplied in kit.

DO THE ACTIVITY Working with your research team, carefully follow each step below. Before you start, be sure you know the **safety rules** for this activity.

STEP 1 Place Plant 1 in a sunny location. Water it as your teacher directs. (This plant is the "control" for the experiment. A control is a standard for comparing things.)

STEP 2 Take Plant 2 out of its container. Remove the soil from the roots. Seal Plant 2 in a plastic bag, then watch as your teacher seals all the bags in a box.

STEP 3 Wait three days. Remove Plant 2 from the box and compare it with Plant 1 (the control). Talk about differences between the two plants.

STEP 4 Review each step. Discuss what needs Plant 2 had that were not being met. Compare your observations with those of other research teams.

14 · LIFE

What Happened?

Immediately following the activity, help your students understand what they observed.

Say: *"In this activity, we were able to explore some of the basic needs of plants.*

First, you established a 'control' with Plant 1 — it had all of its basic needs met.

Second, you removed some needs from Plant 2. It's basic needs were no longer being met.

After waiting for three days, you compared the two plants. You discovered that when an organism's needs are not being met, it does not survive.

Finally, you confirmed your observations by comparing your results with the findings of other research teams."

NAME _____

SHOW WHAT YOU KNOW - 1
Plants and animals need certain things to survive. Some of these include **food, water, air,** and **sunlight.** Circle the pictures below that show basic needs.

The basic needs of plants and animals include what four things?

food, water, air, sunlight

To the Parent . . .   Scripture Connection: Philippians 4:19

Lesson Focus:
Basic Needs

Lesson Objective:
To explore some basic needs of plants and animals

National Science Education Standards:
Standard C1 — *"All students should develop an understanding of the characteristics of organisms . . . Organisms have basic needs. . . Organisms can survive only in environments in which their needs can be met . . ."*

Follow-up Questions:
Ask your child to describe some basic needs of plants and animals (food, water, air, sunlight, etc.).
Ask your child to explain what happens when needs are not being met (the plant or animal may die).
Ask your child to explain how needs may differ (a cactus needs lots of sun, but little water — a fern is the opposite; etc.).

16 · LIFE

Food For Thought

A related "Scripture Object Lesson" you can share with your students.

Philippians 4:19

Have you ever asked your parents for something you really wanted, but you didn't get it? Maybe you even begged, "Please, I neeeeeeed it!"

Perhaps your parents knew that although you *wanted* it, you really didn't *need* it.

Since we don't always know what's best for us, family members can help us make wise decisions.

God's help is even more important! God always knows what we *really* need, and this Scripture reminds us of His promise to meet those needs.

We may not always get what we want. In fact, that probably wouldn't be good for us! But if we ask God, He will always be there to supply our basic needs.

Expand - Day 4

Begin **Day 4** with a review of **Day 3**, then have students answer "part 2" questions.

What I Learned (part 2)
These are higher-level cognitive questions (explain, compare, predict). Student answers will vary but suggested responses may include:

1 food, air, water, sunlight

2 Plant 1 was healthy and growing; Plant 2 was dead and drying up

3 a) it might die b) its needs (sunlight, perhaps food and water) are not being met

Assess - Day 5

Suggestions for modifying assessments to reflect reading levels can be found under ASSESSMENT METHODS on page 12.

Show What You Know 1
(general assessment in Student Worktext)

The sun, corn, and water should be circled; the fill-in words should be food, water, air, and sunlight

Show What You Know 2
(optional test master in Teacher Guide)

1) yes 2) no 3) no 4) yes 5) no

To The Parent
Included at the bottom of all assessment tests, "To The Parent" provides a great way to solicit parent involvement. It not only gives parents an overview of the lesson, but also provides follow-up questions for home use.

NAME _____

Show What You Know 2

Read the sentences below. If the sentence describes a **basic need**, then circle "yes." If the sentence does not describe a basic need, then circle "no."

yes   no   **1.** My teacher drank a large glass of cold, clear water.

yes   no   **2.** My friend can play action video games for hours.

yes   no   **3.** My neighbor drove his new truck down to the barn.

yes   no   **4.** My mother moved the plant into a spot with more sun.

yes   no   **5.** My dog loves to dig holes in the back yard.

To the Parent . . .   **Scripture Connection:** Philippians 4:19

Lesson Focus:
Basic Needs

Lesson Objective:
To explore some basic needs of plants and animals

National Science Education Standards:
Standard C1 — *"All students should develop an understanding of the characteristics of organisms . . . Organisms have basic needs. . . Organisms can survive only in environments in which their needs can be met . . ."*

Follow-up Questions:
Ask your child to describe some basic needs of plants and animals (food, water, air, sunlight, etc.).
Ask your child to explain what happens when needs are not being met (the plant or animal may die).
Ask your child to explain how needs may differ (a cactus needs lots of sun, but little water — a fern is the opposite; etc.).

FOCUS Plant Structure and Function

OBJECTIVE To explore structure and function by studying the parts of plants

OVERVIEW Every part of a plant is made in a certain way (structure) so that it can do a certain kind of job (function). All the parts must work together to keep the plant healthy and alive.

WHAT TO DO
With your team, carefully follow each step below.

Observe

Look at your plant. Look at its leaves. Look at its stem. Move some dirt away and look at the plant's roots.

Describe

Describe the leaves, the stem, and the roots. What do they look like? What do they smell like? What do they feel like?

Discuss

What part of a plant is usually at the top? leaves
What part is usually in the middle? stems
What part usually grows underground? roots

LIFE · 17

Lesson 2

Introduction

National Standards
Focus: C1

Related: A1, A2, C3

Category
Life Science

Focus
Plant Structure/Function

Objective
To explore structure and function by studying the parts of plants

Overview
Read the overview aloud to your students. The goal is to create an atmosphere of curiosity and inquiry.

Say: *"Every part of a plant is made in a certain way (structure) so that it can do a certain kind of job (function). All the parts must work together to keep the plant healthy and alive."*

Additional Notes

As you introduce this lesson, focus on helping students see the relationship between an object's **structure** and its **function**.

For example, have students compare the bones in their legs to the bones in their hands.

Leg bones are large and strong to help support our bodies.

Hand bones are small and flexible to allow us to grasp and manipulate objects.

Have students imagine how life might change if their leg bones were tiny and flexible and their hand bones were large and long.

Materials

One small plant per team. (Small ivy, pepperomia, and philodendron plants are often available for just over a dollar . . . or a local nursery may be happy to donate some plants.)

What To Do

Once students are seated in "research teams" with materials in front of them, read the first section (OBSERVE) aloud.

Say, *"To start this lesson, we're going to **observe** some things. Observe is a word good scientists use often. It means 'to look at closely.' First, I will read the instructions to you. Then you can follow the instructions as you **observe** the items in front of you."*

Monitor teams closely as they follow instructions. When teams are finished with this section, repeat the process with the DESCRIBE section. Conclude with the DISCUSS section.

Options

Expand the DISCUSS section by having students trace dotted "key words" using crayons or markers. Trace the word **leaves** in yellow, the word **stems** in green, and the word **roots** in brown.

FOCUS   Plant Structure and Function

OBJECTIVE   To explore structure and function by studying the parts of plants

OVERVIEW   Every part of a plant is made in a certain way (structure) so that it can do a certain kind of job (function). All the parts must work together to keep the plant healthy and alive.

Plant Parts
Lesson 2

WHAT TO DO

With your team, carefully follow each step below.

Observe

Look at your plant. **Look** at its leaves. **Look** at its stem. **Move** some dirt away and **look** at the plant's roots.

Describe

Describe the leaves, the stem, and the roots. What do they **look** like? What do they **smell** like? What do they **feel** like?

Discuss

What part of a plant is usually at the top? leaves
What part is usually in the middle? stems
What part usually grows underground? roots

LIFE · 17

Teacher to Teacher

Plants are the only living things on Earth that can make their own food. Scientists call this process **photosynthesis**.

Here's how it works: Green leaves contain **chlorophyll** which captures solar energy. This energy helps the plant build food from carbon dioxide and water.

Oxygen is a by-product of photosythesis. It exits the plant through tiny holes in the leaves, called **stomata**. Stomata also allow plants to give up excess water drawn up through their roots. This is called **transpiration**.

It's a simple process, but all life depends on this constant change.

READ THE STORY
The three main parts of a plant are the **roots**, the **stem**, and the **leaves**. Read the story below to find out how they work together to keep the plant alive.

Plant Parts

Plants have many parts. All the parts help the plant.
Every part of a plant is made in a certain way (structure) so that it can do a certain kind of job (function). All the parts work together to keep the plant alive.

These are roots.
Plants have roots.
A plant's roots grow underground. They spread in all directions. The larger the plant, the farther the root system spreads.

The roots help feed the plant.
Roots keep the plant in place and hold the soil around it. Roots also absorb water and nutrients from the soil.

These are stems.
Plants have stems.
A plant's stem connects the roots to the leaves. A tree trunk is a very large plant stem.

The stem helps support the plant.
The stem supports the plant. It also carries water and nutrients from the roots to other parts of the plant.

These are leaves.
Plants have leaves.
Leaves come in many sizes and shapes. Leaves direct water to the roots and help keep rain from washing the soil away.

The leaves help protect the plant.
Leaves also absorb sunshine, turning it into food for the plant. Plants are the only living things that make their own food.

18 · LIFE

Extended Teaching

1. To extend vocabulary, discuss simple scientific language. In this story, "absorb" is another word for "soak up," and "food" refers to nutrients. When leaves absorb sunshine (turning it into food for the plant), the process is called "photosynthesis."

2. Many plants have flowers that produce seeds. Even though plant reproduction is another lesson, you may want to touch on it briefly at this time.

Read The Story
Read the story aloud with your students. (See READING LEVELS on page 12.)

After reading, monitor teams as they discuss what was read. Once you feel students have mastered the basic concepts, have them answer the comprehension questions (**What I Learned** - part 1) on the next page.

To introduce the story, say:

"The title of this story is 'Plant Parts.' Look at your story and follow along as we read it together."

If you wish, encourage Emergent readers to point to words and pictures as you read.

What I Learned (part 1)
These are basic fact-based comprehension questions. Student answers will vary, but suggested responses include:

(1) Roots keep the plant in place; hold soil around the plant; soak up food and water

(2) The stem helps support the plant; carries water from the roots to other parts of the plant

(3) Leaves keep rain from washing away soil; absorb sunshine to make food

Field Trip
Visit a local nursery or truck farm.

Guest Speaker
Invite an avid gardener or horticulturalist to visit your class. Ask him/her to talk about the basic needs of plants.

Materials Needed*
paper cup
food coloring - blue
scissors
water
paper towels

Safety Concerns

4. Sharp Objects
Remind students to exercise caution when using scissors.

4. Slipping
There is a potential for spilled liquids. Remind students to exercise caution.

Do the Activity
Read the activity in advance so you understand it thoroughly. (If time allows, try it yourself.) Before students begin, carefully go over the **Safety Concerns** together.

Pass out materials, then have your students follow along as you read the instructions for **Step 1**. Monitor teams closely as they complete this step.

Once teams have completed **Step 1**, read instructions for **Step 2**. Monitor teams as before. Repeat for **Step 3** and **Step 4**.

After the activity, allow time for each team to share their observations. To encourage higher-level thinking, encourage teams to not only share their observations with each other, but also with other teams.

Special Instructions

Step 2 - Make certain that students push *gently*! Remind teams that good scientists don't engage in horseplay.

Step 4 - Differences in motor skills development may cause some teams difficulty. If you see students having problems, join the group and demonstrate. This will shift the focus from the skill to the observation process.

* Bold-faced items supplied in kit.

DO THE ACTIVITY
Working with your research team, carefully follow each step below. Before you start, be sure you know the **safety rules** for this activity.

STEP 1 Sit on a chair with your hands in your lap. **Ask** a team member to **push** you sideways gently. How hard is it to stay on the chair? Trade places and **repeat** until everyone has had a turn.

STEP 2 Sit on the chair again. **Hold** it with your hands and feet. **Ask** a team member to gently **push** you sideways. How hard is it to stay on the chair? Why? **Repeat** until everyone has had a turn.

STEP 3 Fill a cup half full of water. **Watch** as your teacher adds food coloring. (This represents the food that a plant needs.) Now **cut** a paper towel into strips an inch wide.

STEP 4 Carefully **dip** the strip in the water. **Observe** what happens. Now **discuss** each step, then **compare** your observations with other research teams.

What Happened?

Immediately following the activity, help your students understand what they observed.

Say: *"The first part of this activity showed how roots help hold a plant in place. In **Step 2**, your fingers were like roots.*

They held you tightly to the chair.

*The second part of this activity showed how roots and stems soak up food and water. In **Step 4** the food coloring came up the strip toward the top of the cup!"*

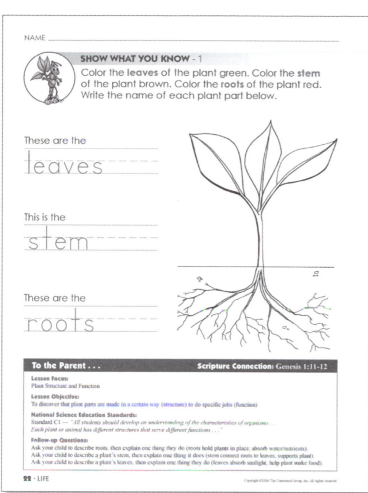

NAME _____

SHOW WHAT YOU KNOW - 1
Color the **leaves** of the plant green. Color the **stem** of the plant brown. Color the **roots** of the plant red. Write the name of each plant part below.

These are the

leaves

This is the

stem

These are the

roots

To the Parent . . .   **Scripture Connection:** Genesis 1:11-12

Lesson Focus:
Plant Structure and Function

Lesson Objective:
To discover that plant parts are made in a certain way (structure) to do specific jobs (function)

National Science Education Standards:
Standard C1 — "All students should develop an understanding of the characteristics of organisms . . . Each plant or animal has different structures that serve different functions . . ."

Follow-up Questions:
Ask your child to describe roots, then explain one thing they do (roots hold plants in place; absorb water/nutrients).
Ask your child to describe a plant's stem, then explain one thing it does (stem connect roots to leaves; supports plant).
Ask your child to describe a plant's leaves, then explain one thing they do (leaves absorb sunlight; help plant make food).

Food For Thought

A related "Scripture Object Lesson" you can share with your students.

Genesis 1:11-12

Have your friends ever told you they missed you when you were absent from school? It probably felt good to know they cared. You knew that you were an important part of their lives.

God has given each of us an important part in life. Everything we do can have an impact on the lives of others.

Your part may be to act like a root . . . to nurture and nourish those around you. Or you may be like a stem, strong and supportive. You may even be like a leaf . . . providing shelter and protection.

Ask God to help you discover the plan he has for your life. Whichever part you are, God can use it for good.

Expand - Day 4

Begin **Day 4** with a review of **Day 3**, then have students answer "part 2" questions.

What I Learned (part 2)
These are higher-level cognitive questions (explain, compare, predict). Student answers will vary but suggested responses may include:

1 a) roots b) because they keep the plant in place, because they soak up food and water

2 a) both move water and food around b) roots are below ground, stems are above ground

3 a) it might die b) it would probably fall over, it couldn't soak up water or food, etc.

Assess - Day 5

Suggestions for modifying assessments to reflect reading levels can be found under ASSESSMENT METHODS on page 12.

Show What You Know 1
(general assessment in Student Worktext)

Blanks: 1) leaves 2) stem 3) roots
Also, the leaves should be colored green, the stem should be colored brown, and the roots should be colored red.

Show What You Know 2
(optional test master in Teacher Guide)

1) R 2) S 3) L 4) R 5) L

To The Parent
Included at the bottom of all assessment tests, "To The Parent" provides a great way to solicit parent involvement. It not only gives parents an overview of the lesson, but also provides follow-up questions for home use.

Show What You Know 2

Read each sentence below. If it describes a plant's leaves, then circle **L**. If it describes a plant's stem, then circle **S**. If it describes a plant's roots, then circle **R**.

L S R 1. I am the strong anchor of the plant. I hold the plant in place.

L S R 2. I carry water from the roots to all the other parts of the plant.

L S R 3. I can help slow raindrops down so soil is not washed away.

L S R 4. I work a lot like a sponge. I soak up water from the soil.

L S R 5. I can soak up sunshine so the plant can make food.

To the Parent . . .   Scripture Connection: Genesis 1:11-12

Lesson Focus:
Plant Structure and Function

Lesson Objective:
To discover that plant parts are made in a certain way (structure) to do specific jobs (function)

National Science Education Standards:
Standard C1 — *"All students should develop an understanding of the characteristics of organisms . . .
Each plant or animal has different structures that serve different functions . . ."*

Follow-up Questions:
Ask your child to describe roots, then explain one thing they do (roots hold plants in place, and absorb water/nutrients).
Ask your child to describe a plant's stem, then explain one thing it does (stem connect roots to leaves; supports plant).
Ask your child to describe a plant's leaves, then explain one thing they do (leaves absorb sunlight; help plant make food).

FOCUS Animal Structure and Function

OBJECTIVE To explore structure and function by studying what animals "wear"

OVERVIEW Different creatures have different kinds of coverings (structure). These different coverings do different jobs (function). A creature's covering helps keep it healthy and alive.

WHAT TO DO
With your team, carefully follow each step below.

Observe

Look carefully at the three animal coverings.

Look at the fur. Look at the feathers.

Look at the scales.

Describe

Describe the fur, the feathers, and the scales.

What do they look like? What do they smell like?

What do they feel like?

Discuss

What covering might a bear have? fur

What covering might a bird have? feathers

What covering might a fish have? scales

LIFE · 23

Lesson 3

Introduction

National Standards
Focus: C1

Related: A1, A2, C3

Category
Life Science

Focus
Animal Structure/Function

Objective
To explore structure and function by studying what animals "wear"

Overview
Read the overview aloud to your students. The goal is to create an atmosphere of curiosity and inquiry.

Say: *"Different creatures have different kinds of coverings (structure). These different coverings do different jobs (function). A creature's covering helps keep it healthy and alive."*

Additional Notes

To help students better understand the relationship between **structure** and **function**, ask them to think about the equipment that a firefighter wears.

Have students list all the parts they can remember (hard hat with face shield, overcoat, boots, gloves, oxygen tank and mask, etc.).

Now emphasize the relationship between the way each piece is made (structure) and what it is designed to do (function).

Encourage students to talk about what each item is designed to do, and how the item helps keep the firefighter safe and protected.

What To Do

Once students are seated in "research teams" with materials in front of them, read the first section (OBSERVE) aloud.

Say, *"To start this lesson, we're going to **observe** some things. Observe is a word good scientists use often. It means 'to look at closely.' First, I will read the instructions to you. Then you can follow the instructions as you **observe** the items in front of you."*

Monitor teams closely as they follow instructions. When teams are finished with this section, repeat the process with the DESCRIBE section. Conclude with the DISCUSS section.

Options

Expand the DISCUSS section by having students trace dotted "key words" using crayons or markers. Trace the word **fur** in brown, the word **feathers** in red, and the word **scales** in blue.

FOCUS	Animal Structure and Function
OBJECTIVE	To explore structure and function by studying what animals "wear"
OVERVIEW	Different creatures have different kinds of coverings (structure). These different coverings do different jobs (function). A creature's covering helps keep it healthy and alive.

WHAT TO DO

With your team, carefully follow each step below.

Observe

Look carefully at the three animal coverings.

Look at the **fur**. **Look** at the **feathers**.

Look at the **scales**.

Describe

Describe the fur, the **feathers**, and the **scales**.

What do they **look** like? What do they **smell** like?

What do they **feel** like?

Discuss

What covering might a bear have? fur

What covering might a bird have? feathers

What covering might a fish have? scales

LIFE · 23

Teacher to Teacher

Vertebrates, which are creatures with backbones, can be covered with wet scales (fish), dry scales (reptiles), feathers (birds), fur or hair (animals).

These special coverings can help conserve body heat, prevent dehydration, provide camouflage, form a barrier to disease, lower friction (flying or swimming), protect against ultraviolet rays, and increase sensitivity to surroundings.

And while coverings are often very attractive (some are even used to attract mates), their primary purpose is to provide protection.

READ THE STORY

Some animals have **fur**. Some have **feathers**. Some have **scales**. Read the story below to find out how different coverings help different animals.

Animal Parts

Different kinds of animals have different coverings.
Every covering is made in a certain way (structure) so that it can do a certain kind of job (function). An animal's covering helps keep it healthy and alive.

This is fur.
Some animals have fur.
Fur is a thick layer of hair. Mammals have fur. There are many kinds of mammals — from tiny mice to huge bears.
Fur keeps mammals warm.
Fur helps keep mammals warm in very cold places. Without its warm layer of fur, a mammal would die.

This is a feather.
Some animals have feathers.
Birds have feathers. There are many different kinds of birds — from the tiny hummingbird to the huge ostrich.
Feathers keep birds dry.
Feathers are covered with a special oil that helps them shed water. Without its feathers, a bird would die.

This is a scale.
Some animals have scales.
Fish have scales. There are many different kinds of fish — from tiny goldfish to huge sailfish.
Scales help fish swim.
Scales make the body of the fish very smooth. This helps the fish swim very fast. Without its scales, a fish would die.

24 · LIFE

Extended Teaching

1. To extend vocabulary, discuss other words that indicate animal coverings — "wool," "fleece," "hide," etc. Ask students what kind of natural coverings *they* have (skin, hair, nails, etc.).

2. Discuss the artificial coverings people wear in different climates. Make a list on the board under labels like "Cold," "Hot," "Rainy," "Snowy," etc.

3. To emphasize structure and function, exam-ine an umbrella. Have students discuss its struc-ture and why it was made that way. Then discuss its function (protection from sun and rain).

4. Show students that many fruits and veg-etables have "coverings" too. Point out that some coverings are edible and some are not. Encourage them to compare edible coverings (apple peels, grape skins, etc.) with inedible ones (banana peels, pecan shells, etc.).

Read The Story
Read the story aloud with your students. (See READING LEVELS on page 12.) After read-ing, monitor teams as they discuss what was read. Once you feel students have mastered the basic concepts, have them answer the comprehension questions (**What I Learned - part 1**) on the next page.

To introduce the story, say:

"The title of this story is 'Animal Parts.' Look at your story and follow along as we read it together."

If you wish, encourage Emergent readers to point to words and pictures as you read.

What I Learned (part 1)
These are basic fact-based comprehension questions. Student answers will vary, but sug-gested responses include:

① 1) mouse, bear, etc. 2) helps keep the animal warm

② 1) hummingbird, ostrich, etc. 2) helps keep the bird dry

③ 1) goldfish, sailfish, etc. 2) helps the fish swim very fast

Field Trip
Arrange a trip to a pet store with live animals. Have students make a list of at least three creatures with fur, three with feathers, and three with scales. If possible, allow students to touch the creatures and describe what they feel.

Guest Speaker
Invite a taxidermist (or someone from a natu-ral history museum) to visit your class. Ask them to bring samples of animal skins as well as stuffed birds and fish for students to view.

Materials Needed*

fur	feather
cotton ball	fish scale
paper cup	water

Safety Concerns

4. Slipping

There is a potential for spilled water. Remind students to exercise caution.

Do the Activity

Read the activity in advance so you understand it thoroughly. (If time allows, try it yourself.) Before students begin, carefully go over the **Safety Concerns** together.

Pass out materials, then have your students follow along as you read the instructions for **Step 1**. Monitor teams closely as they complete this step.

Once teams have completed **Step 1**, read instructions for **Step 2**. Monitor teams as before. Repeat for **Step 3** and **Step 4**.

After the activity, allow time for each team to share their observations. To encourage higher-level thinking, encourage teams to not only share their observations with each other, but also with other teams.

Special Instructions

Step 2 - Keep paper towels handy so that students can quickly wipe up any spills.

DO THE ACTIVITY

Working with your research team, carefully follow each step below. Before you start, be sure you know the **safety rules** for this activity.

STEP 1

Blow on your hand. **Describe** how cool it feels. **Place** the fur on your hand, then **blow** on it. How does this feel? **Discuss** how fur might keep an animal warm.

STEP 2

Dip a cotton ball in water, then try to **blow** it dry. **Repeat** using a feather. **Compare** the results. **Discuss** how feathers might help keep a bird dry.

STEP 3

Rub your hands together rapidly. **Feel** the warmth. **Wet** your palms and **repeat**. How does this feel? Scales reduce friction. **Discuss** how this helps a fish.

STEP 4

Now **review** each step in this activity. **Discuss** how each kind of covering helps the creature. **Compare** your observations with other research teams.

26 · LIFE

What Happened?

Immediately following the activity, help your students understand what they observed.

Say: *"In Step 1 of this activity, you saw how a protective layer of fur can help keep an animal warm in cold winds.*

In Step 2, you saw how feathers repel water. This helps them dry much faster than other types of coverings.

Then in Step 3, you rubbed your hands together to create friction. Rubbing your hands together fast made them very warm. You also learned that a fish's scales help reduce this kind of friction, which can help the fish move through the water much easier."

---

* *Bold-faced items supplied in kit.*

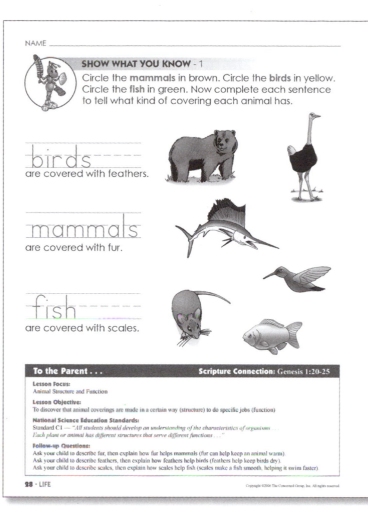

NAME _____

SHOW WHAT YOU KNOW - 1
Circle the **mammals** in brown. Circle the **birds** in yellow. Circle the **fish** in green. Now complete each sentence to tell what kind of covering each animal has.

birds
are covered with feathers.

mammals
are covered with fur.

fish
are covered with scales.

Food For Thought

A related "Scripture Object Lesson" you can share with your students.

Genesis 1:20-25

When God was creating Earth, why did He create oceans before He created fish? Why did He create land before He created deer, bears, and lions? Why did God create trees before He created birds?

God knows the perfect time for everything (see Ecclesiastes 3:1-8). Before there is even a need, God has already put in place the things needed to meet that need.

Remember God knows exactly what your future holds and what you need to meet it. He is always ready to provide just what you need — even before you ask Him!

Learn to trust in God, and He will provide all your needs.

Expand - Day 4

Begin **Day 4** with a review of **Day 3**, then have students answer "part 2" questions.

What I Learned (part 2)
These are higher-level cognitive questions (explain, compare, predict). Student answers will vary but suggested responses may include:

1. a) they live in the water and feathers help keep them dry b) fur would soak up water and not keep them dry

2. a) all are coverings b) accept answers that describe differences in feel, look, or purpose

3. a) it might die b) it needs fur to keep it warm

Assess - Day 5

Suggestions for modifying assessments to reflect reading levels can be found under ASSESSMENT METHODS on page 12.

Show What You Know 1
(general assessment in Student Worktext)

Blanks: 1) birds 2) mammals 3) fish
Also, the bear and mouse should be circled in brown; the ostrich and hummingbird in yellow; and the swordfish and goldfish in green.

Show What You Know 2
(optional test master in Teacher Guide)

1) T   2) T   3) F   4) T   5) F

To The Parent
Included at the bottom of all assessment tests, "To The Parent" provides a great way to solicit parent involvement. It not only gives parents an overview of the lesson, but also provides follow-up questions for home use.

NAME _____

Show What You Know 2

Read each sentence below. If the sentence is true, then circle **T**. If any part of the sentence is false, then circle **F**.

T F 1. Fur is a thick layer of hair.

T F 2. Many mammals are covered with fur.

T F 3. A layer of fur helps fish swim very fast.

T F 4. A creature covered with feathers is probably a bird.

T F 5. Scales can help keep birds warm in the winter.

To the Parent . . .   **Scripture Connection:** Genesis 1:20-25

Lesson Focus:
Animal Structure & Function

Lesson Objective:
To discover that animal coverings are made in a certain way (structure) to do specific jobs (function).

National Science Education Standards:
Standard C1 — *"All students should develop an understanding of the characteristics of organisms . . .*
Each plant or animal has different structures that serve different functions . . ."

Follow-up Questions:
Ask your child to describe fur, then explain how fur helps mammals (fur can help keep an animal warm).
Ask your child to describe feathers, then explain how feathers help birds (feathers help keep birds dry).
Ask your child to describe scales, then explain how scales help fish (scales make a fish smooth, helping it swim faster).

FOCUS Life Cycles (larva)

OBJECTIVE To explore the larva stage of a moth's life cycle

OVERVIEW Moth eggs (stage 1) hatch into larva (stage 2) that are called caterpillars. Caterpillars eat almost constantly to get energy for the pupa (stage 3) part of their life cycle.

WHAT TO DO

With your team, carefully follow each step below.

Observe

Think about a caterpillar you have seen (in nature, books, or on TV). How did it move around? How was it like other caterpillars? How was it different?

Describe

Describe another caterpillar you have seen. What did it look like? What color was it? What shape was it? What do you think it would feel like?

Discuss

How do you think caterpillars get around? crawl
What do caterpillars do most of the time? eat
What do you think caterpillars like to eat? leaves

LIFE · 29

Lesson 4

Introduction

National Standards
Focus: C2

Related: A1, A2, B3, C1, F2, F4

Category
Life Science

Focus
Life Cycles (larva)

Objective
To explore the larva stage of a moth's life cycle

Overview
Read the overview aloud to your students. The goal is to create an atmosphere of curiosity and inquiry.

Say: *"Moth eggs (stage 1) hatch into larva (stage 2) that are called caterpillars. These caterpillars eat almost constantly to get energy for the pupa (stage 3) part of their life cycle."*

Additional Notes

Introduce this lesson by helping your students understand how life cycles relate to growth and development.

Discuss the stages of growth that students have experienced so far. Start with birth, and have them list some developmental stages of infants (such as lifting their head, rolling over, crawling, etc.).

Compare this to the advanced skills they have now (walking, talking, reading, etc.), as well as physical changes. Continue by discussing adulthood and aging.

Be sure to use the phrase "life cycles" in your discussions.

What To Do

Once students are seated in "research teams" with materials in front of them, read the first section (OBSERVE) aloud.

Say, *"To start this lesson, we're going to* **think** *about what we know about caterpillars. Good scientists spend part of each day thinking about what they already know. Then they* **observe** *what they're studying, and add to or modify their ideas. First, I will read the questions to you. Then you can follow with group discussion."*

Monitor teams closely as they follow instructions. When teams are finished with this section, repeat the process with the DESCRIBE section. Conclude with the DISCUSS section.

Options

Expand the DISCUSS section by having students trace the dotted "key words" using crayons or markers. Trace the word **crawl** in dark blue, **eat** in brown, and **leaves** in light green.

FOCUS — Life Cycles (larva)

OBJECTIVE — To explore the larva stage of a moth's life cycle

OVERVIEW — Moth eggs (stage 1) hatch into larva (stage 2) that are called caterpillars. Caterpillars eat almost constantly to get energy for the pupa (stage 3) part of their life cycle.

WHAT TO DO
With your team, carefully follow each step below.

Observe

Think about a caterpillar you have seen (in nature, books, or on TV). How did it move around? How was it like other caterpillars? How was it different?

Describe

Describe another caterpillar you have seen. What did it **look** like? What color was it? What shape was it? What do you think it would **feel** like?

Discuss

How do you think caterpillars get around? c r a w l

What do caterpillars do most of the time? e a t

What do you think caterpillars like to eat? l e a v e s

LIFE · **29**

Teacher to Teacher

Metamorphosis is the scientific term for the way insects change forms as they grow. There are two basic types of metamorphosis — **incomplete** and **complete**.

Around ten percent of insect species have incomplete metamorphosis. An *egg* hatches into a *nymph* (small adult) that molts several times before becoming an *adult*.

Most insects, however, go through complete metamorphosis. This has four stages. An *egg* hatches into a *larva* (grub, caterpillar, maggot, etc.) that doesn't look a bit like the adult. The larva turns into a *pupa* (a non-mobile stage where huge changes take place inside some form of enclosure). Finally the pupa emerges as an *adult,* which begins the life cycle anew.

READ THE STORY
A **caterpillar** is actually just one step in the life cycle of a **moth**. Read the story below to find out more about this stage of the moth's life.

Caterpillars

A caterpillar is one stage in a moth's life.
Insects often change into different forms as they grow. Scientists call this a life cycle. Moths go through four stages: egg, larva, pupa, and adult. Then the cycle repeats.

Caterpillars start as eggs.

Moths lay tiny eggs.
Many moths attach their eggs to the bottom of leaves. This helps keep the eggs safe. Eggs are the first stage in a moth's life.

Moth eggs hatch into caterpillars.
A caterpillar is the second stage in a moth's life. Scientists call this stage "larva." Many other insect eggs hatch into larva, too.

Eating helps caterpillars.

Caterpillars eat a lot!
Caterpillars need lots of energy to grow for the third stage of their life cycle. To get this energy, they eat almost all the time.

Caterpillars eat leaves.
A caterpillar's favorite food is leaves. But if there are too many caterpillars eating a plant's leaves, the plant can die.

Color helps caterpillars.

Color can hide caterpillars.
Many caterpillars are the color of the plants they eat. They blend in so they are hard to see. This helps keep them safe.

Color can warn predators.
Other caterpillars are easy to see. Their colors warn birds and other predators that they taste bad. This helps keep them safe.

Extended Teaching

1. To extend vocabulary, discuss other words for "cycle." In this story, "cycle" can be described as a "circle," "sequence," or "pattern." The physical change of a moth from egg to adult is called "metamorphosis."

2. Explore some other "cycle" words such as bicycle, motorcycle, recycle, etc. Draw pictures and discuss what part or aspect of each one suggests "cycle."

3. The life cycles of moths are similar to butterflies. Using pictures from magazines and cal-endars, make a bulletin board displaying moths and butterflies. (In North America there are about 8,000 types of moths and about 700 kinds of butterflies.)

4. To emphasize how caterpillars eat constantly, bring several bags of bite-size snacks (raisins, crackers, M&Ms, pretzels, etc.). Give every student three pieces of each. Have them line up their snacks in a row. Now have them eat their way down the row, chewing each item thoroughly. Caterpillers eat a lot!

Read The Story

Read the story aloud with your students. (See READING LEVELS on page 12 of this Teacher Guidebook.) After reading, monitor teams as they discuss what was read. Once you feel students have mastered the basic concepts, have them answer the comprehension questions (**What I Learned** - part 1) on the next page.

To introduce the story, say:

"The title of this story is 'Caterpillars.' Look at your story and follow along as we read it together."

If you wish, encourage Emergent readers to point to words and pictures as you read.

What I Learned (part 1)

These are basic fact-based comprehension questions. Student answers will vary, but suggested responses include:

① a) egg b) larva or caterpillar

② a) eat b) they need to store energy for the third stage in their life cycle

③ a) helps them blend in so they can't be seen b) are a color that warns predators that they taste bad

Field Trip

See if your local museum or university has a botany department. Ask about viewing displays of moths and butterflies. In the spring, visit an arboretum or flower garden. Have students spot and identify various types of flying insects. Talk about their life cycles.

Guest Speaker

Invite a biology teacher to visit your class. Have him/her bring a display or slides of the various types of moths that can be found in your region.

Materials Needed*
balloon   yarn
construction paper
scissors   tape

Safety Concerns

3. Poison Hazard
Children can choke trying to blow up balloons! Depending on developmental readiness, you may wish to blow up the balloons in advance.

4. Sharp Objects
Remind students to exercise caution when using scissors.

Do the Activity
Read the activity in advance so you understand it thoroughly. (If time allows, try it yourself.) Before students begin, carefully go over the **Safety Concerns** together.

Pass out materials, then have your students follow along as you read the instructions for **Step 1**. Monitor teams closely as they complete this step.

Once teams have completed **Step 1**, read instructions for **Step 2**. Monitor teams as before. Repeat for **Step 3** and **Step 4**.

After the activity, allow time for each team to share their observations. To encourage higher-level thinking, encourage teams to not only share their observations with each other, but also with other teams.

Special Instructions
SAVE the caterpillars students create in this project for the "Cocoon Cover" lesson!

Step 1 - Some students may have difficulty tying the yarn. Encourage them to help each other. Assist as needed.

Step 3 - To prevent students from cutting *through* the fold, have them draw a line along it, then cut to this line. Legs can be attached with either tape or rubber bands.

Step 4 - Use only dull points (i.e. - markers, not pencils) to decorate the balloon.

* *Bold-faced items supplied in kit.*

DO THE ACTIVITY
Working with your research team, carefully follow each step below. Before you start, be sure you know the **safety rules** for this activity.

STEP 1
Inflate the balloon and **tie** the end. **Wrap** a piece of yarn around its center. **Pull** gently on the ends of the yarn until it begins to dent the balloon slightly. **Tie** the yarn and **cut** the ends.

STEP 2
Use more yarn (**repeat** Step 1) to **divide** each of the balloon's two halves in half. Now **cut** a strip of construction paper four inches wide and the same length as your balloon.

STEP 3
Fold the paper down the middle lengthwise. Now **cut** slits about a quarter inch apart up to the fold line. (Don't cut through the fold!) **Open** the paper and **attach** it to the balloon to make legs.

STEP 4
Decorate your balloon to look like caterpillars you have seen (in nature, books, or on TV). **Compare** your caterpillar with the ones that were created by other research teams.

What Happened?

Immediately following the Activity, help your students understand what they observed.

Say: *"This activity helped demonstrate the unique structure of a caterpillar — the second stage of a moth's life.*

*In **Step 1** and **2**, you showed the caterpillar's long and round shapes, as well as its fatness from eating so much.*

*In **Step 3**, you added the many little legs that help caterpillars move around.*

*In **Step 4**, you compared your team's caterpillar with those made by other teams. This showed that even when creatures are almost identical, every individual one is unique. Just like people, there are no two caterpillars in this world that are exactly alike."*

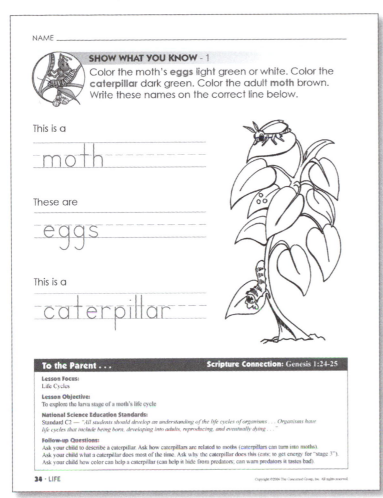

NAME _____

SHOW WHAT YOU KNOW - 1

Color the moth's **eggs** light green or white. Color the **caterpillar** dark green. Color the adult **moth** brown. Write these names on the correct line below.

This is a

moth

These are

eggs

This is a

caterpillar

To the Parent . . .   Scripture Connection: Genesis 1:24-25

Lesson Focus:
Life Cycles

Lesson Objective:
To explore the larva stage of a moth's life cycle

National Science Education Standards:
Standard C2 — "All students should develop an understanding of the life cycles of organisms . . . Organisms have life cycles that include being born, developing into adults, reproducing, and eventually dying . . ."

Follow-up Questions:
Ask your child to describe a caterpillar. Ask how caterpillars are related to moths (caterpillars can turn into moths). Ask your child what a caterpillar does most of the time. Ask why the caterpillar does this (eats; to get energy for "stage 3"). Ask your child how color can help a caterpillar (can help it hide from predators; can warn predators it tastes bad).

34 · LIFE

Food For Thought

A related "Scripture Object Lesson" you can share with your students.

Genesis 1:24-25

Have you ever seen a small crawling creature and yelled, "Yuck! a bug!"?

Sometimes when we see something different or unusual, we become critical. We may not see any use for it, and may even wish it didn't exist. But God says everything He created is good, and that everything has a purpose according to its kind.

You have a purpose, too! Even when you feel like no one likes you, or no one really cares if you're around, God is always there.

Just as God has a purpose even for a silly-looking bug, He has a "master plan" for your life. God has even given us a special promise about this very thing — just read Jeremiah 29:11.

Expand - Day 4

Begin **Day 4** with a review of **Day 3**, then have students answer "part 2" questions.

What I Learned (part 2)

These are higher-level cognitive questions (explain, compare, predict). Student answers will vary but suggested responses may include:

1 same materials, same basic shape, all have legs, etc.

2 real caterpillars are alive; they are also much smaller

3 add wings (may also include comments like "make smaller," "change color," etc.

Assess - Day 5

Suggestions for modifying assessment options to reflect student reading levels are shown under ASSESSMENT METHODS on page 12.

Show What You Know 1
(general assessment in Student Worktext)

Blanks: 1) moth 2) eggs 3) caterpillar
Also, the moth eggs should be colored light green or white, the caterpillar dark green, and the moth brown.

Show What You Know 2
(optional test master in Teacher Guide)

1) second 2) bottom 3) four
4) color   5) leaves

To The Parent

This box is included at the bottom of all assessment tests and provides a great way to solicit parent involvement. It not only gives parents an overview of the lesson, but also provides simple follow-up questions for home use.

NAME _____

Show What You Know 2

Read each sentence below. Circle the word in the parenthesis that best completes the sentence.

1. A caterpillar is the (first second) stage in a moth's life.

2. Many moths attach their eggs to the (top bottom) of leaves.

3. Moths go through (four eight) stages in their life cycle.

4. (Smell Color) can warn birds not to eat caterpillars.

5. A caterpillar's favorite food is usually (seeds leaves).

To the Parent . . .   **Scripture Connection:** Genesis 1:24-25

Lesson Focus:
Life Cycles (larva)

Lesson Objective:
To explore the larva stage of a moth's life cycle

National Science Education Standards:
Standard C2 — *"All students should develop an understanding of the life cycles of organisms . . . Organisms have life cycles that include being born, developing into adults, reproducing, and eventually dying . . ."*

Follow-up Questions:
Ask your child to describe a caterpillar. Ask how caterpillers are related to moths (caterpillars can turn into moths).
Ask your child what a caterpillar does most of the time. Ask why the caterpillar does this (eats; to get energy for "stage 3").
Ask your child how color can help a caterpillar (can help it hide from predators; can warn predators it tastes bad).

FOCUS   Life Cycles (pupa)

OBJECTIVE   To explore the pupa stage of a moth's life cycle

OVERVIEW   When caterpillars have stored enough energy, they enter the third stage of the moth life cycle. In the "pupa" stage, they create and live in a special place called a "cocoon."

WHAT TO DO

With your team, carefully follow each step below.

Observe

Look closely at the cocoon your teacher is holding.

Look at its color. Look at its shape. How is it different from a caterpillar? How is it different from a moth?

Describe

Describe the cocoon. What does it look like?

What color is the cocoon? What shape is it?

What do you think the cocoon might feel like?

Discuss

What might be inside the cocoon? caterpillar

How does its color help the caterpillar? hides

What do you think is happening inside? changes

LIFE · 35

Lesson 5

Introduction

National Standards
Focus: C2

Related: A1, A2, B3, C1, F2, F4

Category
Life Science

Focus
Life Cycles (pupa)

Objective
To explore the pupa stage of a moth's life cycle

Overview
Read the overview aloud to your students. The goal is to create an atmosphere of curiosity and inquiry.

Say: *"When caterpillars have stored enough energy, they enter the third stage of the moth life cycle. In the "pupa" stage, they create and live in a special place called a cocoon."*

Additional Notes

Introduce this lesson by helping your students understand the importance of sleep.

Start by asking them why they think most parents give children a "bedtime." Ask them why they think a regular time to sleep each night might be important.

Explain that it is mostly during sleep that a person's body gets the chance to "recharge." Tired muscles, organs, and tissues can rest and be restored.

Sleep is especially important during childhood since it releases a special hormone that promotes healthy growth. Encourage your students to compare how they feel with and without adequate sleep.

What To Do

Once students are seated in "research teams" with materials in front of them, read the first section (OBSERVE) aloud.

Say, *"To start this lesson, we're going to **observe** some things. Good scientists always carefully examine the things they will be working with before beginning. First, I will read the instructions to you. Then you can follow the instructions as you **observe** the items in front of you."*

Monitor teams closely as they follow instructions. When teams are finished with this section, repeat the process with the DESCRIBE section. Conclude with the DISCUSS section.

Options

Expand the DISCUSS section by having students trace dotted "key words" using crayons or markers. Trace the word **caterpillar** in light green, the word **hides** in dark green, and the word **changes** in orange.

FOCUS   Life Cycles (pupa)

OBJECTIVE   To explore the pupa stage of a moth's life cycle

OVERVIEW   When caterpillars have stored enough energy, they enter the third stage of the moth life cycle. In the "pupa" stage, they create and live in a special place called a "cocoon."

Cocoon Cover
Lesson 5

WHAT TO DO

With your team, carefully follow each step below.

Observe

Look closely at the cocoon your teacher is holding.

Look at its color. **Look** at its shape. How is it different from a caterpillar? How is it different from a moth?

Describe

Describe the cocoon. What does it **look** like?

What color is the cocoon? What shape is it?

What do you think the cocoon might **feel** like?

Discuss

What might be inside the cocoon? *caterpillar*

How does its color help the caterpillar? *hides*

What do you think is happening inside? *changes*

   LIFE · 35

Teacher to Teacher

Only insect species that experience complete metamorphosis have pupae. Examples include moths and butterflies (Lepidoptera), beetles (Coleoptera), and bees, wasps, and ants (Hymenoptera).

The pupa stage requires an enclosure. Within this protected area, the insect changes into an adult. Moths usually pupate in cocoons, although some species make cavities in loose soil. Many beetles pupate underground. Butterflies form chrysalides, similar to cocoons but often quite beautiful. Wasps and bees use enclosures like honeycombs or paper-like nests.

Regardless of the type of enclosure, the purpose is always the same — to protect the insect while it is undergoing tremendous changes in form.

READ THE STORY
A **cocoon** is only one part of the life cycle of a **moth**. Read the story below to find out more about this stage in the moth's life.

Cocoons

A cocoon starts one stage in a moth's life.
Insects often change into different forms as they grow. Scientists call this a life cycle. Moths go through four stages: egg, larva, pupa, adult. Then the cycle repeats itself.

Caterpillars make cocoons.

Caterpillars start as eggs.
To begin the life cycle, moths lay tiny eggs (stage 1). These eggs hatch into larva called caterpillars (stage 2).

Caterpillars make cocoons.
To start the pupa stage (stage 3), the caterpillar makes itself a cocoon. A cocoon is a kind of sleeping bag for caterpillars.

Cocoons help caterpillars.

Cocoons help caterpillars hide.
Cocoons blend in with their surroundings. This helps keep the caterpillar from being eaten while it hides inside.

Cocoons help caterpillars rest.
In the cocoon, the caterpillar does not eat. It moves very little and lives on energy it has stored up (during stage 2).

Cocoons change caterpillars.

Cocoons help caterpillars change.
The caterpillar is called a pupa now. The cocoon gives the pupa a safe place to live while it makes big changes.

Caterpillars change a lot!
Imagine getting into a sleeping bag, then coming out weeks later as an adult! A caterpillar's change is a lot like that.

36 · LIFE

Copyright ©2006 The Concerned Group, Inc. All rights reserved.

Extended Teaching

1. To expand your students' vocabulary, discuss the term "energy." Use words like "fuel," "power," or "food" to help them understand how caterpillars "fill their tanks" with enough energy to survive without eating while living in the cocoon.

2. Bring a sample of pure silk for your students to feel. Explain that silk is produced by the fine webs spun by certain caterpillars to make their cocoons. These caterpillars (called silkworms) were discovered by the Chinese thousands of years ago. Today they are raised in China, Japan, India, France, Spain, and Italy. Silk is appreciated for its beauty, richness, and softness.

3. For a fun snack, make "Caterpillars in Cocoons" — a variation of "Pigs in a Blanket." Cover half a hot dog (caterpillar) with a roll from a refrigerated tube (cocoon). Bake according to the directions. When finished, have students bite into the "cocoon" to discover the "caterpillar"!

Read The Story

Read the story aloud with your students. (See READING LEVELS on page 12.) After reading, monitor teams as they discuss what was read. Once you feel students have mastered the basic concepts, have them answer the comprehension questions (**What I Learned** - part 1) on the next page.

To introduce the story, say:

"The title of this story is 'Cocoons.' Look at your story and follow along as we read it together."

If you wish, encourage Emergent readers to point to words and pictures as you read.

What I Learned (part 1)

These are basic fact-based comprehension questions. Student answers will vary, but suggested responses include:

1 a) pupa   b) with a cocoon

2 rests, hides, changes forms

3 it might be found and eaten

Field Trip

Visit a fabric store. Explore the wide varieties of fabrics, embroideries, and thread. Ask the manager to show your students some samples of various silks.

Guest Speaker

Invite some salespeople from a clothing store to your class. Ask them to bring samples of clothing and accessories made from silk. Have them demonstrate various ways to wear and tie silk scarves.

Materials Needed*

tissue paper	flour
yarn	spoon
bowl	paper towels
caterpillar (from Lesson 4)	water

Safety Concerns

4. Sharp Objects

Remind students to exercise caution when using scissors.

4. Slipping

There is a potential for spilled liquids. Remind students to exercise caution.

Do the Activity

Read the activity in advance so you understand it thoroughly. (If time allows, try it yourself.) Before students begin, carefully go over the **Safety Concerns** together.

Pass out materials, then have your students follow along as you read the instructions for **Step 1**. Monitor teams closely as they complete this step.

Once teams have completed **Step 1**, read instructions for **Step 2**. Monitor teams as before. Repeat for **Step 3** and **Step 4**.

After the activity, allow time for each team to share their observations. To encourage higher-level thinking, encourage teams to not only share their observations with each other, but also with other teams.

Special Instructions

Step 1 - Differences in motor skills development may make it difficult for some teams to tie the yarn. If you see problems, join the group and demonstrate. This will shift the focus from the skill to the observation process.

Step 2 - You may wish to prepare the paste for the students in advance. Making good paste may be difficult for some.

Step 3 - Keep paper towels handy for immediate cleanup of any mess.

* Bold-faced items supplied in kit.

DO THE ACTIVITY
Working with your research team, carefully follow each step below. Before you start, be sure you know the **safety rules** for this activity.

STEP 1 Cut tissue paper into strips about 1 inch wide. Now **tie** a piece of yarn to the end of your balloon caterpillar (created in Lesson 4). Make sure the yarn is secure.

STEP 2 Mix flour and water together to make a thin paste. **Dip** a strip of tissue paper in the paste. Carefully **lay** the wet paper on your caterpillar and **smooth** it down.

STEP 3 **Add** more strips of paper until your caterpillar is completely covered. (Keep the yarn free.) **Ask** your teacher to help you hang your new cocoon to dry.

STEP 4 **Compare** your cocoon with the ones that were created by the other research teams. **Discuss** how it is like a real cocoon, and how it is not.

What Happened?

Immediately following the activity, help your students understand what they observed.

Say: *"In this activity you actually worked with two stages in the moth's life cycle. The caterpillar was one stage. The cocoon was another.*

In Steps 1, 2, and 3, you imitated the process by which a caterpillar creates a cocoon.

In Step 4, you had the chance to compare the cocoon created by your team with the ones that were created by other research teams."

SHOW WHAT YOU KNOW - 1
Color the **plant** a pretty green. Color the **cocoon** the same color green. Draw an arrow to where the **pupa** is hiding. Write these names on the correct line below.

The cocoon is attached to the

plant

Here is the

cocoon

Hiding inside is a

pupa

To the Parent . . .   **Scripture Connection:** Isaiah 32:2

Lesson Focus:
Life Cycles (pupa)

Lesson Objective:
To explore the pupa stage of a moth's life cycle.

National Science Education Standards:
Standard C2 — "All students should develop an understanding of the life cycles of organisms . . . Organisms have life cycles that include being born, developing into adults, reproducing, and eventually dying . . ."

Follow-up Questions:
Ask your child to describe a cocoon. Ask why cocoons are important to moths (help them hide, help them rest).
Ask your child what a pupa does inside the cocoon (changes from a caterpillar into a moth).
Ask your child how color can keep a cocoon hidden. Ask how this keeps the pupa safe (predators can't find it).

40 · LIFE

Food For Thought

A related "Scripture Object Lesson" you can share with your students.

Isaiah 32:2

Have you ever played a game of "Hide and Seek" with your friends?

It's really fun to find good places to hide so that it takes a long time for others to find you.

Of course, it also can be fun when you're found . . . so you can start the game all over again!

Were you hiding because you were afraid? No, it was only a game.

But there are times in life when we may be afraid. This text reminds us that God can keep those that love Him hidden and safe from harm.

Put your trust in God, and He will guide you and protect you with His abundant wisdom and strength.

Expand - Day 4

Begin **Day 4** with a review of **Day 3**, then have students answer "part 2" questions.

What I Learned (part 2)
These are higher-level cognitive questions (explain, compare, predict). Student answers will vary but suggested responses may include:

(1) same materials, same process, same general shape

(2) not real; much bigger; made by students, not caterpillars

(3) Answers will vary. The most common might be: "It would change into a really big moth!"

Assess - Day 5

Suggestions for modifying assessments to reflect reading levels can be found under ASSESSMENT METHODS on page 12.

Show What You Know 1
(general assessment in Student Worktext)

Blanks: 1) plant 2) cocoon 3) pupa or caterpillar Also, plant and cocoon should be colored the same green. An arrow should be pointing to the cocoon.

Show What You Know 2
(optional test master in Teacher Guide)

Circled words: hide, rest, change, survive (one should be written in each sentence)

To The Parent
Included at the bottom of all assessment tests, "To The Parent" provides a great way to solicit parent involvement. It not only gives parents an overview of the lesson, but also provides follow-up questions for home use.

NAME _____

Show What You Know 2

Circle four words from the list below that best describe how a cocoon can help a caterpillar. Then complete the sentences by writing one word in each blank.

hide   rest   fly   change

eat   play   crawl   survive

1. A cocoon can help a caterpillar _____ .

2. A cocoon can help a caterpillar _____ .

3. A cocoon can help a caterpillar _____ .

4. A cocoon can help a caterpillar _____ .

To the Parent . . .   **Scripture Connection:** Isaiah 32:2

Lesson Focus:
Life Cycles (pupa)

Lesson Objective:
To explore the pupa stage of a moth's life cycle

National Science Education Standards:
Standard C2 — *"All students should develop an understanding of the life cycles of organisms . . . Organisms have life cycles that include being born, developing into adults, reproducing, and eventually dying . . ."*

Follow-up Questions:
Ask your child to describe a cocoon. Ask why cocoons are important to moths (help them hide, help them rest).
Ask your child what a pupa does inside the cocoon (changes from a caterpillar into a moth).
Ask your child how color can keep a cocoon hidden. Ask how this keeps the pupa safe (predators can't find it).

FOCUS Life Cycles (adult)

OBJECTIVE To explore the adult stage of a moth's life cycle

OVERVIEW When the pupa emerges from the cocoon, it begins stage 4 of the moth life cycle (adult). The adult looks very different from the larva that entered the cocoon. Now it can even fly!

WHAT TO DO

With your team, carefully follow each step below.

Observe

Look at pictures of moths, or think about a moth you have seen (in nature, books, or on TV). How are moths and caterpillars different?

Describe

Describe a moth. What does it look like? What color is it? What shape is it? What do you think a moth might feel like if it crawled on your hand?

Discuss

What did a moth used to look like? caterpillar
Name something moths do that caterpillars can't. fly
Where does a pupa change into a moth? cocoon

LIFE · 41

Lesson 6

Introduction

National Standards
Focus: C2

Related: A1, A2, B3, C1, F2, F4

Category
Life Science

Focus
Life Cycles (adult)

Objective
To explore the adult stage of a moth's life cycle

Overview
Read the overview aloud to your students. The goal is to create an atmosphere of curiosity and inquiry.

Say: *"When the pupa emerges from the cocoon, it begins stage four of the moth life cycle (adult). The adult looks very different from the larva that entered the cocoon. Now it can even fly!"*

Additional Notes

Introduce this lesson by asking your students if they've ever seen pictures of what their parents looked like when their parents were babies.

Encourage them to think about, then describe, how different their parents looked when they were babies as opposed to the way they look now.

To help make a vocabulary connection, be sure to use the word "adult" whenever you talk about the parents' grown up stage.

What To Do

Once students are seated in "research teams" with materials in front of them, read the first section (OBSERVE) aloud.

Say, *"To start this lesson, let's **look** at some pictures of moths.* (Note: If you do not have moth pictures, say: *"To start this lesson, let's talk about moths we have seen."*) *Good scientists always carefully examine the things they will be working with and **observe** details closely. First, I will read the instructions to you. Then you can follow the instructions as you do the activity."*

Monitor teams closely as they follow instructions. When teams are finished with this section, repeat the process with the DESCRIBE section. Conclude with the DISCUSS section.

Options

Expand the DISCUSS section by having students trace dotted "key words" using crayons or markers. Trace the word **caterpillar** in dark green, the word **fly** in blue, and the word **cocoon** in brown.

FOCUS	Life Cycles (adult)
OBJECTIVE	To explore the adult stage of a moth's life cycle
OVERVIEW	When the pupa emerges from the cocoon, it begins stage 4 of the moth life cycle (adult). The adult looks very different from the larva that entered the cocoon. Now it can even fly!

WHAT TO DO

With your team, carefully follow each step below.

Observe

Look at pictures of moths, or **think** about a moth you have seen (in nature, books, or on TV). How are moths and caterpillars different?

Describe

Describe a moth. What does it **look** like? What color is it? What shape is it? What do you think a moth might **feel** like if it crawled on your hand?

Discuss

What did a moth used to look like? caterpillar

Name something moths do that caterpillars can't. fly

Where does a pupa change into a moth? cocoon

LIFE ·41

Teacher to Teacher

Here's a question you're sure to get! What's the difference between a **moth** and a **butterfly**?

Both are insects. Both have a larva called a caterpillar. And both experience complete metamorphosis.

However, most moths fly at night, while butterflies prefer daylight. Moth antennae are feathery, while butterfly antennae are more like a stalk with a knob on the end. Moths rest with their wings in a horizontal position, while butterflies rest with their wings in a vertical position. During the pupa stage, a butterfly forms a chrysalid, but a moth forms a cocoon.

In addition, moths are much more common! Some scientists estimate there are up to six times more species of moths than butterflies.

READ THE STORY

An adult **moth** is only one part of a complete insect life cycle. Read the story below to find out more about this stage of a moth's life.

Moths

An adult moth is one stage in a complete insect life cycle.
Insects often change into different forms as they grow. Scientists call this a life cycle. Moths go through four stages: egg, larva, pupa, and adult. Then the cycle repeats.

This moth is changing.

Big changes happen in the cocoon.
Inside the cocoon, the larva completely changes its form and turns into an adult. Scientists call this process "metamorphosis."

Changes are part of the life cycle.
A moth makes many changes in its life — from a moth egg, to a caterpillar (larva), to a pupa (in a cocoon), to an adult moth.

These are adult moths.

There are many kinds of moths.
Some moths live in the forest. Some live in vegetable fields. Some even live around piles of old clothes!

Moths are different from butterflies.
Moths have stout, hairy bodies. Their antennae look feathery. They fly mostly at night. When they rest, their wings lie flat.

The life cycle goes on.

Moths eventually die.
The life of a moth is short compared to human life. Soon it will die. But before they die, some moths will lay eggs.

Moths' eggs continue the life cycle.
When moths lay eggs, the moth life cycle starts all over again. Soon there is a new generation growing and changing.

42 · LIFE

Copyright ©2006 The Concerned Group, Inc. All rights reserved.

Extended Teaching

1. To extend vocabulary, discuss the word "adult" with your students. Use words like "full-grown" or "mature." Think of animal names that differentiate between the adult stage and earlier stages. Examples include horse/colt, dog/puppy, cow/calf, kangaroo/joey, etc.

2. Examine the wing designs of adult moths. Emphasize the symmetric patterns that are there. Have your students create their own symmetric designs by folding construction paper in half,

dabbing different colors of paint on one inside fold, then pressing the paper together to transfer paint to the other half of the fold. Let dry, then have students cut the paper into wing shapes.

3. (Note: this activity requires advance planning.) Order a butterfly garden kit from a school supply store. Set it up in your classroom. This will allow students to watch caterpillars eat and grow, spin a cocoon, emerge as moths, and lay eggs to start the life cycle all over again.

Inform - Day 2

Read The Story

Read the story aloud with your students. (See READING LEVELS on page 12.) After reading, monitor teams as they discuss what was read. Once you feel students have mastered the basic concepts, have them answer the comprehension questions (**What I Learned** - part 1) on the next page.

To introduce the story, say:

"The title of this story is 'Moths.' Look at your story and follow along as we read it together."

If you wish, encourage Emergent readers to point to words and pictures as you read.

What I Learned (part 1)

These are basic fact-based comprehension questions. Student answers will vary, but suggested responses include:

① egg, larva, pupa, adult

② a) similar looks, similar life cycle
b) moths have stout hairy bodies; feathery antennae; they fly at night; their wings lie flat when they are resting

③ The life cycle would stop. There would be no more moths.

Field Trip

Visit the entomology department at a university or your local zoo. Check their calendar of events for the best times to view when adult moths and butterflies emerge.

Guest Speaker

Contact the director of a local butterfly garden or a related auxiliary club. Invite someone to visit your class. Have them bring and display their collection of moths and butterflies, and talk about similarities and differences.

Materials Needed*

pipe cleaners - 4   moth pictures
moth wings (master)   scissors
polystyrene tube   round pencil
crayons/colored pencils   glue

Safety Concerns

4. Sharp Objects
Remind students to exercise caution when using scissors and pipe cleaners.

Do the Activity

Read the activity in advance so you understand it thoroughly. (If time allows, try it yourself.) Before students begin, carefully go over the **Safety Concerns** together.

Pass out materials, then have your students follow along as you read the instructions for **Step 1**. Monitor teams closely as they complete this step.

Once teams have completed **Step 1**, read instructions for **Step 2**. Monitor teams as before. Repeat for **Step 3** and **Step 4**.

After the activity, allow time for each team to share their observations. To encourage higher-level thinking, encourage teams to not only share their observations with each other, but also with other teams.

Special Instructions

Step 1 - The moth wings master is on page 239. Make one copy for each team. (It's a good idea to run a few extra copies in case of accidents!) Remind students to color wings in mirror image designs.

Step 2 - Teach students this trick: To cut something in equal halves, fold it in half, then cut on the fold. This trick works quite well, even for pipe cleaners!

Option: Instead of using glue to attach the wings, you may wish to cut two slots in each polystyrene tube in advance, then have students insert the wings in these slots.

* Bold-faced items supplied in kit.

DO THE ACTIVITY
Working with your research team, carefully follow each step below. Before you start, be sure you know the **safety rules** for this activity.

STEP 1 **Look** at the different moths on page 42, or think about a moth you have seen. Working with your team, **color** the wings and body of your moth to look like one of these moths.

STEP 2 Carefully **cut** the wings out of the sheet of paper. **Color** any areas that still need it. Now **glue** the wings to the body of your moth. Make sure they are straight while they dry.

STEP 3 **Cut** three pipe cleaners in half. **Push** the pieces into the body to make six legs. **Wind** a pipe cleaner around a pencil. **Remove**, then **cut** in half. **Push** the curled pieces in (one for each antenna).

STEP 4 **Compare** your moth model with those created by other research teams. **Discuss** what the models have in common. How are the models like real moths? How are they different?

44 · LIFE

What Happened?

Immediately following the activity, help your students understand what they observed.

Say: *"In this activity you explored the structure of a moth in its adult stage.*

In Steps 1, 2, and 3, you constructed a "moth model" that showed the structure of the moth's body, wings, legs, and antennae.

In Step 4, you compared your model to those of other research teams and talked about what your moth models had in common. You also compared the features of the models the teams created with the features of real moths you have seen."

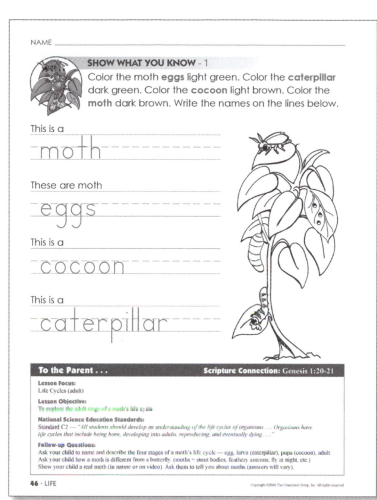

NAME _____

SHOW WHAT YOU KNOW - 1
Color the moth **eggs** light green. Color the **caterpillar** dark green. Color the **cocoon** light brown. Color the **moth** dark brown. Write the names on the lines below.

This is a
moth

These are moth
eggs

This is a
cocoon

This is a
caterpillar

To the Parent . . .   **Scripture Connection:** Genesis 1:20-21

Lesson Focus:
Life Cycles (adult)

Lesson Objective:
To explore the adult stage of a moth's life cycle

National Science Education Standards:
Standard C2 — *"All students should develop an understanding of the life cycles of organisms . . . Organisms have life cycles that include being born, developing into adults, reproducing, and eventually dying . . ."*

Follow-up Questions:
Ask your child to name and describe the four stages of a moth's life cycle — egg, larva (caterpillar), pupa (cocoon), adult. Ask your child how a moth is different from a butterfly. (moths = stout bodies, feathery antenna, fly at night, etc.) Show your child a real moth (in nature or on video). Ask them to tell you about moths (answers will vary).

Food For Thought

A related "Scripture Object Lesson" you can share with your students.

Genesis 1: 20-21

There's an old riddle that goes, "Which came first, the egg or the chicken?"

You could argue all day about the right answer, but it doesn't really matter. Whichever came first, there have been chickens and eggs ever since!

As far back as creation, God ordained that nature would function in an orderly and predict-able fashion. Life cycles continue in the same patterns. A moth egg will always become a moth, not a bluebird! A chicken egg will always become a chicken, not a pig!

The laws of God's world are consistent and stable because God is always the same. It's the same with God's love — it never changes! We can always put our trust in Him.

Expand - Day 4

Begin **Day 4** with a review of **Day 3**, then have students answer "part 2" questions.

What I Learned (part 2)
These are higher-level cognitive questions (explain, compare, predict). Student answers will vary but suggested responses may include:

1 all made with same instruction; all made with same materials

2 model is much larger and made with man-made materials; model is not alive

3 different wings, antennae not "fuzzy", body not as thick, etc.

Assess - Day 5

Suggestions for modifying assessments to reflect reading levels can be found under ASSESSMENT METHODS on page 12.

Show What You Know 1
(general assessment in Student Worktext)

Blanks: 1) moth 2) eggs 3) cocoon 4) caterpillar Also, eggs should be colored light green, caterpillar dark green, cocoon light brown, and moth dark brown.

Show What You Know 2
(optional test master in Teacher Guide)

1) 2   2) 1   3) 4   4) 3   5) 4

To The Parent
Included at the bottom of all assessment tests, "To The Parent" provides a great way to solicit parent involvement. It not only gives parents an overview of the lesson, but also provides follow-up questions for home use.

NAME _____

Show What You Know 2

Read each sentence below. Circle the number that best describes that stage in the moth's **life cycle**.
(**1** = egg, **2** = larva, **3** = cocoon, **4** = adult)

1 2 3 4   1. A caterpillar is eating leaves in your garden.

1 2 3 4   2. You find tiny moth eggs on the underside of a leaf.

1 2 3 4   3. A moth has just emerged from a cocoon.

1 2 3 4   4. There is a caterpillar changing inside its cocoon.

1 2 3 4   5. A moth is flying around your porch light.

To the Parent . . .   **Scripture Connection:** Genesis 1:20-21

Lesson Focus:
Life cycles (adult)

Lesson Objective:
To explore the adult stage of a moth's life cycle

National Science Education Standards:
Standard C2 — *"All students should develop an understanding of the life cycles of organisms . . . Organisms have life cycles that include being born, developing into adults, reproducing, and eventually dying . . ."*

Follow-up Questions:
Ask your child to name and describe the four stages of a moth's life cycle — egg, larva (caterpillar), pupa (cocoon), adult. Ask your child how a moth is different from a butterfly (moths = stout bodies, feathery antenna, fly at night, etc.). Show your child a real moth (in nature or on video). Ask them to tell you about moths (answers will vary).

FOCUS   Camouflage

OBJECTIVE   To explore how blending in with the environment protects a creature

OVERVIEW   Many creatures need protection from predators that might eat them. If they blend in with their surroundings, they are much harder to see. This helps keep them hidden and safe.

WHAT TO DO

With your team, carefully follow each step below.

Observe

Look at the fish on page 48. Look at the bug on page 48. Look at the rabbit on page 48. Think about how each creature is like its surroundings.

Describe

Describe a fish you have seen (in nature, a book, or on TV). What did it look like? What color was it? What do you think a fish would feel like?

Discuss

What is one way a creature can blend in?   color
What does blending in help a creature do?   hide
What might a creature hide from?   predator

LIFE · 47

National Standards
Focus: C3

Related: A1, A2, B1, B2

Category
Life Science

Focus
Camouflage

Objective
To explore how blending in with the environment protects a creature

Overview
Read the overview aloud to your students. The goal is to create an atmosphere of curiosity and inquiry.

Say: *"Many creatures need protection from predators that might eat them. If they blend in with their surroundings, they are much harder to see. This helps keep them hidden and safe."*

Additional Notes

To introduce this lesson, show students a white bowl with one goldfish cracker in it. Talk about how easy it is to see the goldfish because the bright orange color stands out clearly against the white bowl.

Show students a second bowl half full of goldfish crackers. Drop the first goldfish into this bowl and stir the crackers around.

Now challenge students to find the original goldfish. Talk about how difficult it is to find when it is surrounded by the same colors and shapes.

Say, *"In this lesson, we'll look at some ways creatures blend into their surroundings, and find out how this helps keep them safe."*

What To Do

Once students are seated in "research teams" with materials in front of them, read the first section (OBSERVE) aloud.

Say, *"To start this lesson, we're going to **observe** some pictures. Good scientists always spend time thinking carefully about what they see. First, I will read the instructions to you. Then you can follow the instructions as you **observe** the creatures in the pictures."*

Monitor teams closely as they follow instructions. When teams are finished with this section, repeat the process with the DESCRIBE section. Conclude with the DISCUSS section.

Options

Expand the DISCUSS section by having students trace dotted "key words" using crayons or markers. Trace the words **color**, **hide**, and **predator** using a thick black line. Point out how the dots that form the letters seem to disappear!

Find-a-Fish
Lesson 7

FOCUS	Camouflage
OBJECTIVE	To explore how blending in with the environment protects a creature
OVERVIEW	Many creatures need protection from predators that might eat them. If they blend in with their surroundings, they are much harder to see. This helps keep them hidden and safe.

WHAT TO DO

With your team, carefully follow each step below.

Observe

Look at the fish on page 48. **Look** at the bug on page 48. **Look** at the rabbit on page 48. **Think** about how each creature is like its surroundings.

Describe

Describe a fish you have seen (in nature, a book, or on TV). What did it **look** like? What **color** was it? What do you think a fish would **feel** like?

Discuss

What is one way a creature can blend in? color

What does blending in help a creature do? hide

What might a creature hide from? predator

LIFE · 47

Teacher to Teacher

The chameleon has a special ability when it comes to camouflage. It can shift colors as it moves through different surroundings.

The chameleon's outer skin is transparent. Beneath this skin are layers of cells containing red, yellow, blue, and white coloring. As these cells contract or expand, the chameleon's color shifts.

Changes in these cells are often triggered by light, temperature, or mood. If a chameleon is cold, for example, it might turn a darker color to absorb more heat from the rays of the sun.

These special cells give the chameleon the ability to change its color according to its needs and its varied environment.

READ THE STORY

Many creatures need protection from predators. Read the story below to find out how blending in with their surroundings helps keep creatures safe.

Hidden Creatures

Color helps many creatures hide.
Many creatures use color to help them hide from predators. They blend in with their surroundings so they are hard to see. Scientists call this coloring "camouflage."

A fish can hide.
A fish can be tan like the sand.
The halibut is a fish that lives in the ocean where it is very sandy. A halibut is speckled tan. This helps it blend in with the sand.

Many fish use color to hide.
A scorpion fish looks like a rock. A flounder can change from dark colors to light. Some fish even match seaweed colors.

A bug can hide.
A bug can be green like a leaf.
Green leaf bugs live on green plants. Since they are the same color as the plant, they are very hard to see.

Leaf bugs are different colors.
Red leaf bugs live on red plants. Brown leaf bugs live on brown plants. Every leaf bug is the same color as the plant it lives on.

A rabbit can hide.
A rabbit can be brown like old grass.
Most rabbits live where there is lots of grass. Their fur is brown with dots and streaks so they blend in with old, brown grass.

Some rabbits can change color.
Some rabbits live where there is lots of snow. In the winter, their fur turns white. This helps them blend in with the snow.

48 · LIFE

Copyright ©2006 The Concerned Group, Inc. All rights reserved.

Extended Teaching

1. To expand vocabulary, discuss words related to "camouflage" like cover, disguise, conceal, or even trick. Point out that soldiers and hunters wear clothing that blends into their environment so they are harder to see. Even warships and fighter planes have special paint that serves as a kind of camouflage.

2. Challenge students to think of other animals that can blend into their environment (a polar bear in the snow, a field mouse in the grass, a squirrel against the bark of a tree, etc.).

3. Have each team choose an "environment" from the school grounds (field, woods, parking lot, flower bed, etc.), then create a "camouflage creature" that fits that environment. Start by giving each team a toilet tissue tube, then have them glue on things that help it blend into its environment. After creating their creature, let them hide it in the environment they chose and take snapshots to display on a bulletin board.

Copyright ©2006 The Concerned Group, Inc. All rights reserved.

Inform - Day 2

Read The Story
Read the story aloud with your students. (See READING LEVELS on page 12.) After reading, monitor teams as they discuss what was read. Once you feel students have mastered the basic concepts, have them answer the comprehension questions (**What I Learned** - part 1) on the next page.

To introduce the story, say:

"The title of this story is 'Hidden Creatures.' Look at your story and follow along as we read it together."

If you wish, encourage Emergent readers to point to words and pictures as you read.

What I Learned (part 1)
These are basic fact-based comprehension questions. Student answers will vary, but suggested responses include:

(1) answers will vary, but should include examples from the story

(2) a) they all hide by looking like leaves b) they are different colors depending on the kinds of leaves they live on

(3) it would easily be seen because it is tan and the rock is black; it might be eaten by a predator

Field Trip
Visit a local university and view their insect collection. Ask your guide to show students how insects blend into their environment for protection from predators.

Guest Speaker
Invite an army reservist to visit your class. Ask him/her to bring samples of clothing and equipment designed to help soldiers blend into their environment.

Copyright ©2006 The Concerned Group, Inc. All rights reserved.

FIND A FISH · 59

Materials Needed*

paper fish (4 red, 4 blue)
scissors   newspapers

Safety Concerns

4. **Sharp Objects**
Remind students to exercise caution when using scissors.

Do the Activity

Read the activity in advance so you understand it thoroughly. (If time allows, try it yourself.) Before students begin, carefully go over the **Safety Concerns** together.

Pass out materials, then have your students follow along as you read the instructions for **Step 1**. Monitor teams closely as they complete this step.

Once teams have completed **Step 1**, read instructions for **Step 2**. Monitor teams as before. Repeat for **Step 3** and **Step 4**.

After the activity, allow time for each team to share their observations. To encourage higher-level thinking, encourage teams to not only share their observations with each other, but also with other teams.

Special Instructions

Step 1 - Depending on the developmental readiness of the group, you may need to demonstrate the process of using one of the colored fish as a stencil. They should end up with 12 fish — four red, four blue, four newsprint.

Step 2 - To ensure students take a "glance" instead of a long stare, you may want to make up a command like, "Back, glance, back!" ("Back" means student's back is to the fish, "glance" means turn quickly and look at the fish, and "back" again means turn away from the fish.)

Step 3 - As an option, you may wish to record the guesses on the board and see if there is a pattern or common number.

DO THE ACTIVITY

Working with your research team, carefully follow each step below. Before you start, be sure you know the **safety rules** for this activity.

STEP 1
Cut out four red fish and four blue fish. **Place** one of these fish on a piece of newspaper. **Trace** around it to make an outline, then **cut out** the fish. **Repeat** to make three more "news" fish.

STEP 2
Lay a large sheet of newspaper on the floor. Ask your team to turn around. **Scatter** several fish on the newspaper. Now have everyone **glance** at the newspaper, then look away.

STEP 3
When everyone has had a turn, have them **guess** how many fish were there. If time permits, **repeat** Step 2 using a different number of fish each time.

STEP 4
Discuss why some fish were hard to see. Why might its surroundings be important to a creature? **Compare** your observations with other teams.

50 · LIFE

What Happened?

Immediately following the activity, help your students understand what they observed.

Say: *"In this activity you discovered how camouflage works, and how it helps creatures blend into their environment.*

*In **Step 1**, you cut out and created fish of various colors and patterns.*

*In **Steps 2** and **3**, you used a large sheet of newspaper to create an environment. You scattered different kinds of fish on this background, then had team members guess how many there were.*

*Finally in **Step 4**, you shared and compared your observations about camouflage with those of other research teams."*

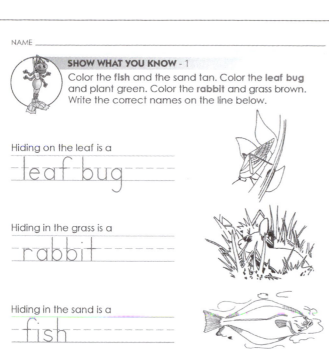

NAME _____

SHOW WHAT YOU KNOW - 1
Color the **fish** and the sand tan. Color the **leaf bug** and plant green. Color the **rabbit** and grass brown. Write the correct names on the line below.

Hiding on the leaf is a
leaf bug

Hiding in the grass is a
rabbit

Hiding in the sand is a
fish

To the Parent . . .   Scripture Connection: Psalms 17:8

Lesson Focus:
Camouflage

Lesson Objective:
To explore how blending with the environment helps protect a creature

National Science Education Standards:
Standard C3 — "All students should develop an understanding of organisms and environments . . . patterns of behavior are related to the nature of the organism's environment . . . all organisms cause changes in the environment where they live . . ."

Follow-up Questions:
Ask your child how color can help creatures hide (it helps them blend into their surroundings).
Ask your child why hiding is important to some creatures. What are they hiding from? (keeps them safe; predators).
Ask your child to name a creature they have studied, then describe how it hides (examples were fish, bugs, and rabbits).

Food For Thought

A related "Scripture Object Lesson" you can share with your students.

Psalms 17:8

We've seen how blending with their environment helps protect many creatures. For some, hiding is the only way they can defend themselves.

But humans have many ways to defend themselves. God has given us the ability to think, to reason, and to communicate. Usually we can solve our problems just by talking to the people involved.

Sometimes, though, our problems are much too big for us and we need more. Isn't it nice to know that no problem is too big for God?

In this Scripture verse, God promises us that we can hide in Him and that He will protect us. Do you have a need today? Learn to trust in God and He will keep you hidden and safe from harm.

Expand - Day 4

Begin **Day 4** with a review of **Day 3**, then have students answer "part 2" questions.

What I Learned (part 2)

These are higher-level cognitive questions (explain, compare, predict). Student answers will vary but suggested responses may include:

1 If the surroundings match the creature's colors, it can hide better, keeping it safe from predators.

2 a) all the same shape and size
b) different colors and patterns

3 the blue fish and the newspaper fish would be easier to see; the red fish would be harder to see

Assess - Day 5

Suggestions for modifying assessments to reflect reading levels can be found under ASSESSMENT METHODS on page 12.

Show What You Know 1
(general assessment in Student Worktext)

Blanks: 1) leaf bug 2) rabbit 3) fish
Also, the leaf bug and plant should be colored green; the rabbit and grass brown; and the fish and sand tan

Show What You Know 2
(optional test master in Teacher Guide)

1) no   2) yes   3) no   4) yes   5) no

To The Parent

Included at the bottom of all assessment tests, "To The Parent" provides a great way to solicit parent involvement. It not only gives parents an overview of the lesson, but also provides follow-up questions for home use.

NAME _____

Show What You Know 2

Read each sentence below. If the creature blends well with this environment, then circle **yes**. If the creature does not blend well with this environment, then circle **no**.

yes   no   1. A bright red bird is sitting on a snow-covered bush.

yes   no   2. A speckled halibut is lying on the sandy ocean floor.

yes   no   3. A leaf bug is climbing up the side of a white house.

yes   no   4. A brown rabbit is lying in a field of old, dead grass.

yes   no   5. A grasshopper is crawling on a sheet of newspaper.

To the Parent . . .   **Scripture Connection:** Psalms 17:8

Lesson Focus:
Camouflage

Lesson Objective:
To explore how blending with the environment helps protect a creature

National Science Education Standards:
Standard C3 — *"All students should develop an understanding of organisms and environments . . . patterns of behavior are related to the nature of the organism's environment . . . all organisms cause changes in the environment where they live . . ."*

Follow-up Questions:
Ask your child how color can help creatures hide (it helps them blend into their surroundings).
Ask your child why hiding is important to some creatures. What are they hiding from? (keeps them safe; predators)
Ask your child to name a creature they have studied, then describe how it hides (examples were fish, bugs, and rabbits).

Habitat-Home
Lesson 8

FOCUS Habitats

OBJECTIVE To understand how creatures interact with their environment

OVERVIEW Every creature has a special type of home (habitat). A creature's habitat must meet its unique needs. Different types of birds build different nests to help create their special habitats.

WHAT TO DO

With your team, carefully follow each step below.

Observe

Look at your home. Think about how it was made.

Now look at the birds' nests on page 54. Think about how each of these nests was made.

Describe

Describe a bird's nest that you have seen. What did it look like? What color was it? What was it made from? What do you think it would feel like?

Discuss

What word means an animal's home? habitat

What kind of home do most birds build? nest

What might be in a bird nest in the spring? eggs

LIFE · 53

National Standards
Focus: C3

Related: A1, A2, C1, C2

Category
Life Science

Focus
Habitats

Objective
To understand how creatures interact with their environment

Overview
Read the overview aloud to your students. The goal is to create an atmosphere of curiosity and inquiry.

Say: *"Every creature has a special type of home called a habitat. A creature's habitat must meet its unique needs. For instance, different types of birds build different kinds of nests to help create their special habitats."*

Additional Notes

To help students see the unique relationship between a creature and its environment, discuss the different kinds of "homes" that creatures live in.

Make two columns on the board. Label column one "Creature" and column two "Home".

Write the name of a creature in column one, then ask students what kind of home should be written in column two.

Examples include: human/house, bear/den, rabbit/hole, bee/hive, cow/barn, ant/anthill, etc. Use the word "habitat" often.

Engage - Day 1

What To Do

Once students are seated in "research teams" with materials in front of them, read the first section (OB-SERVE) aloud.

Say, *"To start this lesson, we're going to observe some things. Good scientists always carefully examine the things they will be working with before beginning. First, I will read the instructions to you. Then you can follow the instructions as you observe the pictures of birds' nests on page 54."*

Monitor teams closely as they follow instructions. When teams are finished with this section, repeat the process with the DE-SCRIBE section. Conclude with the DISCUSS section.

Options

Expand the DISCUSS section by having students trace dotted "key words" using crayons or markers. Trace the word **habitat** in green, the word **nest** in brown, and the word **eggs** in light blue.

FOCUS   Habitats

OBJECTIVE   To understand how creatures interact with their environment

OVERVIEW   Every creature has a special type of home (habitat). A creature's habitat must meet its unique needs. Different types of birds build different nests to help create their special habitats.

Habitat Home
Lesson 8

WHAT TO DO

With your team, carefully follow each step below.

Observe

Look at your home. **Think** about how it was made. Now **look** at the birds' nests on page 54. **Think** about how each of these nests was made.

Describe

Describe a bird's nest that you have seen. What did it **look** like? What **color** was it? What was it made from? What do you think it would **feel** like?

Discuss

What word means an animal's home? habitat
What kind of home do most birds build? nest
What might be in a bird nest in the spring? eggs

LIFE · 53

Teacher to Teacher

Every organism relies on its habitat to survive. Destruction of their unique habitat is the primary reason that many forms of life have become extinct.

Deforestation (removing all the trees) and habitat fragmentation (splitting wild areas into separate "islands") are two common forms of land usage that cause significant damage to animal, bird, and plant populations.

A healthy environment constantly maintains a balance. When a species becomes extinct, there is a negative impact on biodiversity (ecosystem variety). Over time, unplanned development that upsets this important balance can threaten our quality of life.

A **nest** is an important part of a bird's habitat. Read the story below to find out how different birds build different nests to meet their special needs.

Bird Nests

Different kinds of birds build different nests.
Different kinds of birds have different needs. Every kind of bird builds a different kind of nest that is specifically designed to meet that bird's needs.

This nest is in a tree.
Many birds build nests in trees.
A large area filled with trees is called a forest. Many kinds of birds live in the forest. Most forest birds build nests in trees.

Birds need the trees.
A nest built high in a tree helps keep birds safe from many kinds of predators. The leafy branches also help hide the nest.

This nest is in the prairie.
Many birds build nests in the prairie.
A prairie is a huge area with few trees. Many kinds of birds live in the prairie. Most prairie birds build nests in tall grass.

Birds need the prairie.
The prairie provides lots of food for birds. The tall grass helps hide the birds. It also gives them material to build their nests.

This nest is in a marsh.
Many birds build nests in a marsh.
A marsh is a large area covered with shallow water. Many kinds of birds live in the marsh. Most build nests in the reeds.

Birds need the marsh.
The marsh gives birds food and shelter. Sometimes a marsh is set aside just for birds. This is called a conservation area.

54 · LIFE

Extended Teaching

1. To expand vocabulary, use other habitat words such as "home," "surroundings," or "environment." Explain how animals depend on warm, safe homes for survival. Ask them to think of ways we can help ensure the safety of animals by respecting their environment.

2. Ask students why most birds lay their eggs in bowl-shaped nests. Discuss how a flat nest might affect an egg. To illustrate, let them try to balance three plastic eggs on a paper plate, then repeat the activity with a styrofoam bowl. Now ask which shape provides better protection.

3. For a special SNACK, make edible nests! Melt a bag of butterscotch chips in a pan. Add Chinese noodles. Mix thoroughly and spoon onto waxed paper. While the mixture is still warm, press down in the center with a large spoon to make a bowl-shaped depression. Now add white yogurt-covered raisins for eggs — and let the feast begin!

Read The Story

Read the story aloud with your students. (See READING LEVELS on page 12.) After reading, monitor teams as they discuss what was read. Once you feel students have mastered the basic concepts, have them answer the comprehension questions (**What I Learned** - part 1) on the next page.

To introduce the story, say:

"The title of this story is 'Bird Nests.' Look at your story and follow along as we read it together."

If you wish, encourage Emergent readers to point to words and pictures as you read.

What I Learned (part 1)

These are basic fact-based comprehension questions. Student answers will vary, but suggested responses include:

1 different birds have different needs

2 a) both are designed to keep birds safe
b) forest nests are high in trees; prairie nests are hidden in the grass

3 they would lose their food and shelter; they probably would die

Field Trip

Visit a large tree! Have students sit near the tree, close their eyes, and sit silently for 60 seconds. Ask them to listen for different sounds coming from the tree or its residents. When they open their eyes, challenge them to spot signs of birds or insects that live in or near the tree.

Guest Speaker

Invite an avid bird watcher to your class. Ask him/her to bring displays or personal pictures of various types of nests.

Materials Needed*

wax paper - 3	toothpicks
yarn (brown)	feathers
bowl	flour
plastic eggs - 2	spoon

Safety Concerns

4. Sharp Objects

Remind students to exercise caution when usiing toothpicks.

4. Slipping

There is a potential for spilled liquids. Remind students to exercise caution.

Do the Activity

Read the activity in advance so you understand it thoroughly. (If time allows, try it yourself.) Before students begin, carefully go over the **Safety Concerns** together.

Pass out materials, then have your students follow along as you read the instructions for **Step 1**. Monitor teams closely as they complete this step.

Once teams have completed **Step 1**, read instructions for **Step 2**. Monitor teams as before. Repeat for **Step 3** and **Step 4**.

After the activity, allow time for each team to share their observations. To encourage higher-level thinking, encourage teams to not only share their observations with each other, but also with other teams.

Special Instructions

Steps 1 and **2** - Differences in motor skills development may make it difficult for some teams to build these nests. If you see problems, join the group and demonstrate. This will shift the focus from the skill to the observation process.

Step 3 - If the "mud" is too sticky, sprinkle some flour onto the students' fingers. Keep paper towels on hand for immediate cleanup of any mess.

* Bold-faced items supplied in kit.

DO THE ACTIVITY

Working with your research team, carefully follow each step below. Before you start, be sure you know the **safety rules** for this activity.

STEP 1 — Place a piece of wax paper on your work table. Carefully **stack** toothpicks on it in a small circle to make a nest. When finished, gently **move** this nest aside.

STEP 2 — Repeat Step 1, only this time try to **weave** yarn and feathers into the nest to help hold the toothpicks together. When finished, gently **move** this nest aside.

STEP 3 — In a bowl, **mix** flour and water to make a thick "mud." **Dump** the mud on the paper, then **mold** it into the shape of a nest. **Add** a lining of feathers.

STEP 4 — **Observe** your three nests. **Place** the eggs in each nest to see how they look. **Compare** the nests you made with those created by other research teams.

What Happened?

Immediately following the activity, help your students understand what they observed.

Say: *"In **Steps 1**, **2**, and **3**, you learned about different kinds of bird nests by building models.*

Every type of bird builds its own unique kind of nest that is designed to meet the special needs of that kind of bird.

*In **Step 4**, you compared the nests you built with those built by other research teams. You discovered that even though many nests were very similar, each individual nest was unique."*

SHOW WHAT YOU KNOW - 1

Color the **forest** nest gray. Color the **prairie** nest brown. Color the **marsh** nest green. Write the names of each habitat on the correct line below.

This nest is in the

marsh

This nest is in the

prairie

This nest is in the

forest

To the Parent . . .   Scripture Connection: Psalms 84:3

Lesson Focus:
Habitats

Lesson Objective:
To understand how creatures interact with their environment

National Science Education Standards:
Standard C3 — "All students should develop an understanding of organisms and environments . . . patterns of behavior are related to the nature of the organism's environment . . . all organisms cause changes in the environment where they live . . ."

Follow-up Questions:
Ask your child to describe one type of bird's nest (see lesson . . . answers will vary).
Ask your child why different kinds of birds make different kinds of nests (to meet their different needs).
Ask your child why nests are an important part of a bird's habitat (hide eggs, keep eggs safe, give birds shelter, etc.).

Food For Thought

A related "Scripture Object Lesson" you can share with your students.

Psalms 84:3

Have you ever wondered how a bird knows how to build its nest? Why do some birds build nests in trees and some birds build nests on the ground?

God gave creatures "instincts" which help them function effectively. An instinct is an inborn, natural way to behave that doesn't require thought or choice.

God gave creatures instincts because He loves them and wants to take care of them. If God loves creatures that cannot think about Him, or choose to love Him — how much more do you think He loves a boy or girl like *you*?

Why not say a prayer right now to tell God how much you love Him?

Expand - Day 4

Begin **Day 4** with a review of **Day 3**, then have students answer "part 2" questions.

What I Learned (part 2)

These are higher-level cognitive questions (explain, compare, predict). Student answers will vary, but suggested responses may include:

1 Nest 1: sticks only. Nest 2: sticks, yarn, feathers. Nest 3: mud, feathers

2 a) same basic shape b) made from different materials

3 a) they might break or won't hatch b) eggs need protection to hatch

Assess - Day 5

Suggestions for modifying assessments to reflect reading levels can be found under ASSESSMENT METHODS on page 12.

Show What You Know 1

(general assessment in Student Worktext)

Blanks: 1) marsh 2) prairie 3) forest
The top nest should be green; the middle nest should be brown; the bottom nest should be gray.

Show What You Know 2

(optional test master in Teacher Guide)

1) M   2) F   3) P   4) M   5) P

To The Parent

Included at the bottom of all assessment tests, "To The Parent" provides a great way to solicit parent involvement. It not only gives parents an overview of the lesson, but also provides follow-up questions for home use.

NAME _____

Show What You Know 2

Read each sentence below. If it describes a forest, then circle **F**. If it describes a prairie, then circle **P**. If it describes a marsh, then circle **M**.

F P M   1. A nest built in an area covered with shallow water.

F P M   2. A nest built in an area filled with trees.

F P M   3. A nest built in a huge area that has very few trees.

F P M   4. A wet conservation area set aside just for birds.

F P M   5. An area where tall grass helps to hide birds.

To the Parent . . .   Scripture Connection: Psalms 84:3

Lesson Focus:
Habitats

Lesson Objective:
To understand how creatures interact with their environment

National Science Education Standards:
Standard C3 — *"All students should develop an understanding of organisms and environments . . . patterns of behavior are related to the nature of the organism's environment . . . all organisms cause changes in the environment where they live . . ."*

Follow-up Questions:
Ask your child to describe one type of bird's nest (see lesson ... answers will vary).
Ask your child why different kinds of birds make different kinds of nests (to meet their different needs).
Ask your child why nests are an important part of a bird's habitat (hide eggs, keep eggs safe, give birds shelter, etc.).

68 · HABITAT HOME   Copyright ©2006 The Concerned Group, Inc. Permission to photocopy is granted to the purchaser only. All rights reserved.

FOCUS Pollutants

OBJECTIVE To explore how pollutants impact the environment and living creatures

OVERVIEW Oil is an important resource. It provides fuel for cars, heat for homes, and many other good things. But oil in the wrong place is very harmful to living creatures. In this activity we'll explore what happens to birds in an oil spill.

WHAT TO DO

With your team, carefully follow each step below.

Observe

Look at the oil. Look at the water. Look at the feather.

Think about how oil and water are alike. Think about how oil and water are different.

Describe

Describe the oil. What does it look like? What does it smell like? What does it feel like? How is the feel of oil different from the feel of water?

Discuss

Which item works best for taking a bath? water

Which item would be helpful in cooking? oil

Which item is from a living creature? feather

LIFE · 59

Lesson 9

Introduction

National Standards
Focus: C3

Related: A1, A2, C1, C2 F3, F4, F5

Category
Life Science

Focus
Pollutants

Objective
To explore how pollutants can impact the environment and living creatures

Overview
Read the overview aloud to your students. The goal is to create an atmosphere of curiosity and inquiry.

Say: *"Oil is an important resource. It provides fuel for cars, heat for homes, and many other good things. But oil in the wrong place is very harmful to living creatures. In this activity, we'll explore what happens to birds in an oil spill."*

Additional Notes

To introduce this lesson, squirt a small amount of hand lotion on each student's right hand. When you give them the signal, have students rub the lotion into their hands until it disappears.

Now ask them how their hands feel . . . does their skin feel a little slick and oily?

Talk about the fact that hand lotion absorbs quickly, leaving softer skin. But other kinds of oil are not good for us! Have students discuss what this activity would have been like with used motor oil instead of hand lotion. (Yuck!) This will give them a better picture of the problems birds and other wildlife experience during a major oil spill.

What To Do

Once students are seated in "research teams" with materials in front of them, read the first section (OBSERVE) aloud.

Say, *"To start this lesson, we're going to **observe** some familiar objects. Look for details you may never have noticed before. Good scientists always carefully examine the things they will be working with before beginning. First, I will read the instructions to you. Then you can follow the instructions as you **observe** the items in front of you."*

Monitor teams closely as they follow instructions. When teams are finished with this section, repeat the process with the DESCRIBE section. Conclude with the DISCUSS section.

Options

Expand the DISCUSS section by having students trace dotted "key words" using crayons or markers. Trace the word **water** in blue, the word **oil** in black, and the word **feather** in brown.

FOCUS   Pollutants

OBJECTIVE   To explore how pollutants impact the environment and living creatures

OVERVIEW   Oil is an important resource. It provides fuel for cars, heat for homes, and many other good things. But oil in the wrong place is very harmful to living creatures. In this activity we'll explore what happens to birds in an oil spill.

WHAT TO DO

With your team, carefully follow each step below.

Observe

Look at the oil. **Look** at the water. **Look** at the feather.

Think about how oil and water are alike. **Think** about how oil and water are different.

Describe

Describe the oil. What does it **look** like? What does it **smell** like? What does it **feel** like? How is the feel of oil **different** from the feel of water?

Discuss

Which item works best for taking a bath? *water*

Which item would be helpful in cooking? *oil*

Which item is from a living creature? *feather*

LIFE · **59**

Teacher to Teacher

Our modern world is dependent on petroleum (crude oil). We not only use it for powering motor vehicles and producing heat, but it's also an important source of hydrocarbons (substances containing hydrogen and carbon). Hydrocarbons are used to create a wide variety of products including medicines, lubricants, plastics, fertilizers, pesticides, and solvents.

However, transporting oil is a major task and oil spills can be deadly. Although one can happen on land, oil spills usually happen in the ocean. Birds, fish, shellfish, plants, mammals, and even microorganisms are affected by these spills. And when life forms are killed, food chains are disrupted, damaging the environment and negatively impacting human life.

READ THE STORY
Oil is an important resource. But oil in the wrong place can be very harmful to many living creatures. Read the story below to find out how.

Oil Spill

An oil spill can be very harmful.
When a big ship (tanker) that carries oil has an accident, oil can get into the ocean. This is called an "oil spill." Loose oil in the ocean can be very harmful.

Oil can hurt birds.
Oil can cover a bird's feathers.
In an oil spill, seabirds get oil on their feathers as they swim. The oil makes their feathers heavy so they cannot fly.

Oil can make a bird very sick.
When a seabird tries to clean oil off its feathers, it may eat some of the oil. The bird can become sick or even die.

Oil can hurt animals.
Oil can cover an animal's fur.
When there is an oil spill, animals that swim in the ocean can get oil on their fur. Oily fur cannot keep the animal warm.

Oil can make an animal very sick.
Oil can also get in the animal's lungs or stomach. This poisons the animal. It can become sick or even die.

Oil can hurt plants.
Oil can cover a plant's surface.
When there is an oil spill, oil can wash up on the shore. It can cover the shoreline grasses. It also can damage seaweed.

The fewer oil spills, the better!
The effects of an oil spill last a long time. New laws and new kinds of ships may lead to fewer oil spills in the future.

60 · LIFE

Extended Teaching

1. To extend vocabulary, explain that the word "oil" refers to many different things. (Cooking oil comes from vegetable sources and is quite different from motor oil!) The "oil" we refer to in this lesson is also known as "petroleum." It is found underground, and is used to make heating oil and gasoline.

2. Explain that a big problem with oil spills is that oil and water don't mix. The oil is lighter and floats on top of the water. The action of wind and waves causes it to spread over a much larger area than the original spill.

3. To help your students better understand how difficult it is to clean up an oil spill, pour half a cup of vegetable oil into a large clear glass salad bowl full of water. Now have two volunteers try to "clean up" the oil using paper towels. Once the students have removed all the oil they can from the surface, have everyone examine the water and the edge of the bowl, then discuss the results.

Read The Story

Read the story aloud with your students. (See READING LEVELS on page 12.) After reading, monitor teams as they discuss what was read. Once you feel students have mastered the basic concepts, have them answer the comprehension questions (**What I Learned** - part 1) on the next page.

To introduce the story, say:

"The title of this story is 'Oil Spill.' Look at your story and follow along as we read it together."

If you wish, encourage Emergent readers to point to words and pictures as you read.

What I Learned (part 1)

These are basic fact-based comprehension questions. Student answers will vary, but suggested responses include:

① can hurt birds, animals, and plants

② birds can't fly; animals can't keep warm

③ answers will vary, but should include oily feathers making it hard to fly, or references to possible poisoning

Field Trip

Visit an oil refinery or a local petroleum recycler. (Check the Yellow Pages for "waste oil service.") Have them describe the environmental precautions they take. (Most oil companies have videos available on this topic as well.)

Guest Speaker

Invite a geologist to visit your class. Ask him/her to bring samples of the rock stratum where petroleum can be found, and talk about the search for new sources.

Materials Needed*

paper cups - 2   vegetable oil
feather   **spoon**
water   marker

Safety Concerns

4. Slipping

There is a potential for spilled liquids. Remind students to exercise caution.

4. Other

Have students wash their hands thoroughly when finished.

Do the Activity

Read the activity in advance so you understand it thoroughly. (If time allows, try it yourself.) Before students begin, carefully go over the **Safety Concerns** together.

Pass out materials, then have your students follow along as you read the instructions for **Step 1**. Monitor teams closely as they complete this step.

Once teams have completed **Step 1**, read instructions for **Step 2**. Monitor teams as before. Repeat for **Step 3** and **Step 4**.

After the activity, allow time for each team to share their observations. To encourage higher-level thinking, encourage teams to not only share their observations with each other, but also with other teams.

Special Instructions

Step 1 - Don't let students get cups too full! (You may wish to make a "water level" mark on each cup before students begin.) Labeling (A, B) can be done directly on the cup with a permanent marker or with a regular pen on a piece of masking tape.

Step 2 and **3** - Remind your students to blow *gently* on the feather, and never to blow toward anyone. Keep paper towels on hand for immediate cleanup of spills.

* Bold-faced items supplied in kit.

DO THE ACTIVITY

Working with your research team, carefully follow each step below. Before you start, be sure you know the **safety rules** for this activity.

STEP 1 — **Label** two cups "A" and "B." **Fill** both cups with water. (The cups represent two tiny oceans.) Now carefully **pour** three spoons of oil into Cup B. (This represents an oil spill.) **Compare** the cups.

STEP 2 — **Dip** one feather in Cup A. (This represents a bird swimming in clean water.) **Remove** the feather and blow on it softly. **Make notes** about what you see.

STEP 3 — **Dip** the other feather in Cup B. (This represents a bird swimming in an oil spill.) **Remove** the feather and blow on it softly. **Make notes** about what you see.

STEP 4 — **Discuss** what you saw in Step 2 and Step 3 with your research team. Now **compare** your findings with those of other teams. How were the results similar?

What Happened?

Immediately following the activity, help your students understand what they observed.

Say: *"In **Step 1**, you quickly discovered that oil and water do not mix.*

*In **Step 2**, you saw that water runs off a bird's feathers, and that wet feathers dry quickly.*

*In **Step 3**, you observed the damage that oil can cause to feathers. It does not come off feathers easily and does not dry up or disappear. Birds covered with oil from an oil spill often die.*

Remember, oil is a valuable resource, but it must be carefully controlled to protect the environment."

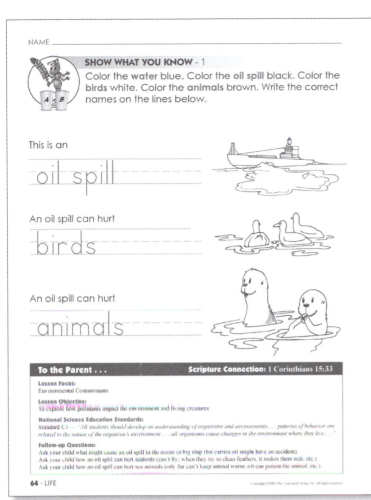

NAME _____

SHOW WHAT YOU KNOW - 1
Color the **water** blue. Color the **oil spill** black. Color the **birds** white. Color the **animals** brown. Write the correct names on the lines below.

This is an

oil spill

An oil spill can hurt

birds

An oil spill can hurt

animals

Food For Thought

A related "Scripture Object Lesson" you can share with your students.

I Corinthians 15:33

You've probably heard the expression "oil and water don't mix." Some things just aren't supposed to be together.

Scripture reminds us that this also applies to the people we spend time with. Being around some people helps us stay close to God. They are the kind of people who love God and try to honor Him in everything they do.

But there are other people who draw us away from God. They do not value the things God values, and they may cause us to forget the importance of staying close to Him.

Always remember to "look for the right mix." Stay close to family and friends whose hearts reflect God's love, and whose lives help bring you closer to Him.

Expand - Day 4

Begin **Day 4** with a review of **Day 3**, then have students answer "part 2" questions.

What I Learned (part 2)
These are higher-level cognitive questions (explain, compare, predict). Student answers will vary but suggested responses may include:

1 answers will vary, but should include the idea that oil stuck to the feather and damaged it

2 answers should include the fact that the cups and their contents were identical except that Cup B also contained oil

3 a) no b) oil does not evaporate like water; oil will leave feather permanently damaged

Assess - Day 5

Suggestions for modifying assessments to reflect reading levels can be found under ASSESSMENT METHODS on page 12.

Show What You Know 1
(general assessment in Student Worktext)

1) oil spill 2) birds 3) animals
Also, the water should be colored blue, the oil spill black, the birds white, and the animals brown.

Show What You Know 2
(optional test master in Teacher Guide)

1) F 2) F 3) T 4) T 5) T

To The Parent
Included at the bottom of all assessment tests, "To The Parent" provides a great way to solicit parent involvement. It not only gives parents an overview of the lesson, but also provides follow-up questions for home use.

Show What You Know 2

Read each sentence below. If the sentence is true, then circle the letter **T**. If the sentence is false, then circle the letter **F**.

T   F   1. Oil is not an important resource. We don't really need it.

T   F   2. Oil spills can hurt animals, but seldom harm plants.

T   F   3. New kinds of ships may lead to fewer oil spills.

T   F   4. A bird may be poisoned when it cleans its oily feathers.

T   F   5. Loose oil floating in the ocean can be very harmful.

To the Parent . . .   **Scripture Connection:** 1 Corinthians 15:33

Lesson Focus:
Pollutants

Lesson Objective:
To explore how pollutants impact the environment and living creatures

National Science Education Standards:
Standard C3 — *"All students should develop an understanding of organisms and environments . . . patterns of behavior are related to the nature of the organism's environment . . . all organisms cause change in the environment where they live . . ."*

Follow-up Questions:
Ask your child what might cause an oil spill in the ocean (a big ship that carries oil might have an accident).
Ask your child how an oil spill can hurt seabirds (can't fly; when they try to clean feathers, it makes them sick; etc.).
Ask your child how an oil spill can hurt sea animals (oily fur can't keep animal warm; oil can poison the animal, etc.).

Natural or Not?
Lesson 10

FOCUS Earth Materials

OBJECTIVE To explore differences between natural and manufactured materials

OVERVIEW Some materials like sand or soil occur naturally on Earth. Others like plastic, paper, or glass are manufactured. The manufacturing process changes natural materials in some way.

WHAT TO DO
With your team, carefully follow each step below.

Observe

Look at each material carefully. Think about where it came from. How are these materials similar to each other? How are they different?

Describe

Describe each material. What does it look like? What does it feel like? What color is it? What shape is it? What might it be used for?

Discuss

What is one common natural material? sand
What is one manufactured material? plastic
Name another manufactured material. paper

Introduction

National Standards
Focus: D1

Related: A1, A2, B1, E2, E3, F2, F3

Category
Earth Science

Focus
Earth Materials

Objective
To explore differences between natural and manufactured materials

Overview
Read the overview aloud to your students. The goal is to create an atmosphere of curiosity and inquiry.

Say: *"Some materials like sand or soil occur naturally on Earth. Others like plastic, paper, or glass are manufactured. The manufacturing process changes natural materials in some way."*

Additional Notes

To introduce this lesson, ask your students to look around the room for things that have been "manufactured." Explain that this word means *"to make or process a raw material into a finished product."*

Make a list on the board of items the students point out (desks, shelves, carpet, books, lights, etc). Now ask students what kinds of materials they think were used to make each item. Where do these materials come from? When you are finished, repeat this activity looking for "natural" materials (plants, water, sand or soil, etc.).

Say, *"In this lesson, we will learn to tell the difference between Earth materials that are natural and those that are not."*

What To Do

Once students are seated in "research teams" with materials in front of them, read the first section (OBSERVE) aloud.

Say, *"To start this lesson, we're going to observe some things. Good scientists always carefully examine the things they will be working with before beginning. First, I will read the instructions to you. Then you can follow the instructions as you observe the items in front of you."*

Monitor teams closely as they follow instructions. When teams are finished with this section, repeat the process with the DESCRIBE section. Conclude with the DISCUSS section.

Options

Expand the DISCUSS section by having students trace dotted "key words" using crayons or markers. Trace the word **sand** in brown, the word **plastic** in red, and the word **paper** in yellow.

Special Note

Don't forget that *recycling* is an important part of using materials wisely! There are ways to recycle many manufactured materials (and to minimize the use of those that can't be recycled). Emphasize this throughout the lesson.

Natural or Not?
Lesson 10

FOCUS	Earth Materials
OBJECTIVE	To explore differences between natural and manufactured materials
OVERVIEW	Some materials like sand or soil occur naturally on Earth. Others like plastic, paper, or glass are manufactured. The manufacturing process changes natural materials in some way.

WHAT TO DO
With your team, carefully follow each step below.

Observe

Look at each material carefully. **Think** about where it came from. How are these materials similar to each other? How are they different?

Describe

Describe each material. What does it **look** like? What does it **feel** like? What **color** is it? What **shape** is it? What might it be used for?

Discuss

What is one common natural material? *sand*

What is one manufactured material? *plastic*

Name another manufactured material. *paper*

EARTH · 67

Teacher to Teacher

How important are basic natural materials to everyday life? Very!

In an average year, we use about 40,000 lbs. of Earth materials per American. That breaks down to about 18,000 lbs. of stone, sand, and gravel, 700 lbs. of limestone for cement, 350 lbs. of table salt, 350 lbs. of clay, and 1700 lbs. of other **non-metals**.

We also use about 1200 lbs. of iron, 40 lbs. of aluminum, 20 lbs. of copper, 10 lbs. each of lead and zinc, 7 lbs. of manganese, and 25 lbs. of other **metals**.

Of course, we also use about 17,000 lbs. of **fossil fuels** for every American per year. And we rely on natural materials to make our manufactured materials as well!

READ THE STORY
There are many kinds of materials on Earth. Some are natural; some are manufactured. Read the story below to learn how they are different.

Earth Materials

There are many kinds of materials on Earth.
Some materials (sand, soil, etc.) occur naturally on Earth. Other materials (glass, paper, plastic, etc.) are manufactured by changing natural materials in some way.

These are natural materials.

There are many natural materials.
A natural material is one that has not been changed by man. These resources are sometimes called "raw materials."

Sand is a natural material.
Sand is an example of a natural material. It is commonly found on the banks of some rivers or along the ocean shore.

These are manufactured materials.

There are many manufactured materials.
A product is "manufactured" when natural materials and other ingredients are processed to make something different.

Paper is a manufactured material.
Paper is an example of a manufactured material. Although wood occurs naturally, it must be processed to make paper.

Earth materials are resources.

Some resources are renewable.
Some materials can be used over and over (recycled). For example, a managed forest is a renewable source of wood.

Some resources are not renewable.
When some natural materials are gone, they will be gone forever. Oil is an example of a non-renewable resource.

68 · EARTH

Extended Teaching

1. To expand vocabulary, describe Earth's natural resources as "assets" (valuable or useful things). Remind students that protecting assets helps ensure our future. Also discuss the word "processed" (a change through steps). Processed foods provide products with longer shelf life or more consumer appeal. However, such foods are often not as nutritious as the natural forms.

2. Compare a variety of manufactured products to natural materials by bringing samples to class (fresh oranges vs. powdered orange drink; cotton fabric vs. polyester fabric, fresh milk vs. dried milk; natural flowers vs. silk flowers; etc.) Compare and discuss the advantages and disadvantages of each.

3. For "Natural or Not" snacks, bring one tray of natural foods (nuts, fresh fruits, etc.), and one of manufactured foods (processed cheese slices, crackers, etc.). Discuss the advantages and disadvantages of each.

Read The Story

Read the story aloud with your students. (See READING LEVELS on page 12.) After reading, monitor teams as they discuss what was read. Once you feel students have mastered the basic concepts, have them answer the comprehension questions (**What I Learned** - part 1) on the next page.

To introduce the story, say:

"The title of this story is 'Earth Materials.' Look at your story and follow along as we read it together."

If you wish, encourage Emergent readers to point to words and pictures as you read.

What I Learned (part 1)

These are basic fact-based comprehension questions. Student answers will vary, but suggested responses include:

1 a) natural, manufactured   b) natural = sand, soil, rocks, trees, etc.; manufactured = glass, paper, plastic, etc.

2 natural materials occur naturally; manufactured materials are processed

3 Answers will vary, but should reflect problems with transporation, heating, access to food, etc.

Field Trip

Visit a local factory. Ask your guide to show students what raw materials are used, and how they are made into a finished product.

Guest Speaker

Invite an avid conservationist to visit your class. Ask him/her to talk about how we can become more responsible and involved in preserving Earth's natural resources.

Materials Needed*

twig   craft stick
pea gravel   beads
potting soil   card stock - small
rock salt   balloon

Safety Concerns

4. Slipping

There is a potential for small items (especially beads) to fall on the floor. Remind students to exercise caution.

4. Choking Hazard

Students must keep all these materials out of their mouths.

Do the Activity

Read the activity in advance so you understand it thoroughly. (If time allows, try it yourself.) Before students begin, carefully go over the **Safety Concerns** together.

Pass out materials, then have your students follow along as you read the instructions for **Step 1**. Monitor teams closely as they complete this step.

Once teams have completed **Step 1**, read instructions for **Step 2**. Monitor teams as before. Repeat for **Step 3** and **Step 4**.

After the activity, allow time for each team to share their observations. To encourage higher-level thinking, encourage teams to not only share their observations with each other, but also with other teams.

Special Instructions

Step 1 - Make sure students keep materials in separate piles! Mixing materials will make it impossible to use them again.

Step 2 - Encourage students to choose one member of their team to be the "recorder" (list maker) for this activity.

Step 3 - If students have trouble thinking of other materials, a supply of picture-filled magazines may be useful for ideas.

* *Bold-faced items supplied in kit.*

DO THE ACTIVITY
Working with your research team, carefully follow each step below. Before you start, be sure you know the **safety rules** for this activity.

STEP 1 — Place all the materials on your work surface. Examine each material closely. Discuss which might be natural and which might be manufactured.

STEP 2 — Now separate the materials into two groups — one for natural materials; one for manufactured materials. Make a list of the items in each group.

STEP 3 — Make a second list of natural and manufactured materials that are not in your kit. Discuss other items that might be difficult to classify this way.

STEP 4 — Review each step in this activity. Discuss how the materials were alike and different. Now compare your lists with those of the other research teams.

70 · EARTH

What Happened?

Immediately following the activity, help your students understand what they observed.

Say: *"In this activity you explored the differences between natural and manufactured materials.*

*In **Steps 1** and **2**, you carefully examined the various materials and sorted them into groups.*

*In **Step 3**, you discussed other materials you have seen, classifying them as natural or manufactured. You also realized that some materials are hard to group this way.*

*Finally, in **Step 4**, you acted like good scientists, by sharing and comparing your lists with the lists compiled by other research teams."*

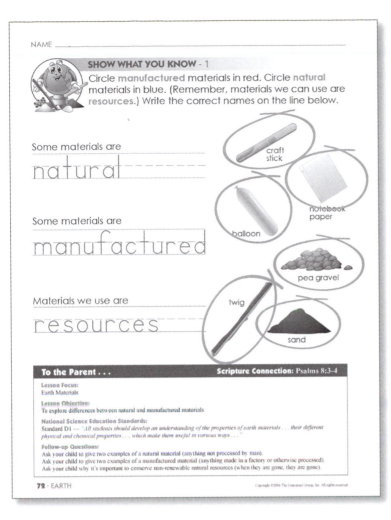

NAME _____

SHOW WHAT YOU KNOW - 1

Circle manufactured materials in red. Circle natural materials in blue. (Remember, materials we can use are resources.) Write the correct names on the line below.

Some materials are

natural

Some materials are

manufactured

Materials we use are

resources

craft stick

notebook paper

balloon

pea gravel

twig

sand

To the Parent . . .   Scripture Connection: Psalms 8:3-4

Lesson Focus:
Earth Materials

Lesson Objective:
To explore differences between natural and manufactured materials

National Science Education Standards:
Standard D1 — "All students should develop an understanding of the properties of earth materials . . . their different physical and chemical properties . . . which make them useful in various ways . . ."

Follow-up Questions:
Ask your child to give two examples of a natural material (anything not processed by man).
Ask your child to give two examples of a manufactured material (anything made in a factory or otherwise processed).
Ask your child why it's important to conserve non-renewable natural resources (when they are gone, they are gone).

Food For Thought

A related "Scripture Object Lesson" you can share with your students.

Psalms 8:3-4

Man has made many beautiful things. Museums are filled with the works of very talented people. The world is full of wonderful paintings and sculptures, creative designs, and impressive architecture.

But Scripture reminds us of the infinite source for all this talent, the source of the very materials that artists and architects use to create their wonder-ful works. God is the ultimate "resource" — the Creator of all good things! Nothing made by man could ever compare to the wonders of God's incredible universe.

Be proud of the things you make or do, but always remember to give credit to the source of your creative power — our loving heavenly Father.

Expand - Day 4

Begin **Day 4** with a review of **Day 3**, then have students answer "part 2" questions.

What I Learned (part 2)

These are higher-level cognitive questions (explain, compare, predict). Student answers will vary but suggested responses may include:

① Answers will vary (three of each). Examples from materials kit could include: natural = twig, pea gravel, potting soil, and rock salt; manufactured = craft stick, beads, heavy paper, and the balloon

② a) both are made of wood b) the craft stick had to be processed

③ answers will vary, but should refer to loss of comfort or convenience ... depending on your emphasis, some may focus on less pollution and conserving resources

Assess - Day 5

Suggestions for modifying assessments to reflect reading levels can be found under ASSESSMENT METHODS on page 12.

Show What You Know 1
(general assessment in Student Worktext)

Blanks: 1) natural 2) manufactured 3) resources (first two blanks are interchangable). Also, the twig, sand, and pea gravel should be circled in blue; the craft stick, balloon, and notebook paper in red.

Show What You Know 2
(optional test master in Teacher Guide)

1) natural 2) manufactured 3) natural 4) manufactured 5) manufactured

To The Parent

Included at the bottom of all assessment tests, "To The Parent" provides a great way to solicit parent involvement. It not only gives parents an overview of the lesson, but also provides follow-up questions for home use.

NAME _____

Show What You Know 2

Read each sentence below. If it describes a kind of manufactured material, fill in the word **manufactured**. If it describes a natural material, fill in the word **natural**.

1. Sand is a very common _____ material.

2. Paper is a very common _____ material.

3. Oil is a _____ material that is non-renewable.

4. Glass is a very useful _____ material.

5. Plastic is a common _____ material.

To the Parent . . .   **Scripture Connection:** Psalms 8:3-4

Lesson Focus:
Earth Materials

Lesson Objective:
To explore differences between natural and manufactured materials

National Science Education Standards:
Standard D1 — *"All students should develop an understanding of the properties of earth materials . . . their different physical and chemical properties . . . which make them useful in various ways . . ."*

Follow-up Questions:
Ask your child to give two examples of a natural material (anything not processed by man).
Ask your child to give two examples of a manufactured material (anything made in a factory or otherwise processed).
Ask your child why it's important to conserve non-renewable natural resources (when they are gone, they are gone).

Wonderful Rocks
Lesson 11

FOCUS: Geology

OBJECTIVE: To understand that different rocks have different characteristics

OVERVIEW: There are many kinds of "rocks," but not all rocks are alike. Rocks can be smooth or rough, dull or full of beautiful colors. In this activity, we'll look at three very different and unusual rocks.

WHAT TO DO

With your team, carefully follow each step below.

Observe

Look at Rock 1 (pyrite). Look at Rock 2 (wonderstone). Look at Rock 3 (pumice). Think about how these rocks are the same. Think about how they are different.

Describe

Describe each rock. What does it look like? What color is it? What does it feel like? What shape is it? Is it heavier or lighter than the other rocks?

Discuss

Which rock has layers of color? wonderstone
Which rock is the lightest rock? pumice
Which rock looks a lot like gold? pyrite

EARTH · 73

Lesson 11

Introduction

National Standards
Focus: D1

Related: A1, A2, B1, F3

Category
Earth Science

Focus
Geology

Objective
To understand that different rocks have different characteristics

Overview
Read the overview aloud to your students. The goal is to create an atmosphere of curiosity and inquiry.

Say: *"There are many kinds of 'rocks,' but not all rocks are alike. Rocks can be smooth or rough, dull or full of beautiful colors. In this activity, we'll look at three very different and unusual rocks."*

Additional Notes

To introduce this lesson, help your students better understand the characteristics of objects by having them describe something they cannot see.

Place a classroom item in a fabric bag or sack. Allow a student volunteer to feel the item in the bag (no peeking!).

Now ask him to describe what he feels. Encourage him to use various descriptive words, such as rough, smooth, rounded, straight, cornered, soft, heavy, etc.

As the item is described, allow students to guess what it is. Once the item is guessed, repeat with a different item and volunteer.

What To Do

Once students are seated in "research teams" with materials in front of them, read the first section (OBSERVE) aloud.

Say, *"To start this lesson, we're going to carefully **observe** some different kinds of rocks. Scientists are good observers. A good observer always examines and inspects things very carefully. First, I will read the instructions to you. Then you can follow the instructions as you **observe** the different rocks in front of you."*

Monitor teams closely as they follow instructions. When teams are finished with this section, repeat the process with the DESCRIBE section. Conclude with the DISCUSS section.

Options

Expand the DISCUSS section by having students trace the dotted "key words" using crayons or markers. Trace each letter of the word **wonderstone** in a different shade of red, orange or brown. Trace the word **pumice** in gray, and the word **pyrite** in yellow or gold.

Wonderful Rocks
Lesson 11

FOCUS	Geology
OBJECTIVE	To understand that different rocks have different characteristics
OVERVIEW	There are many kinds of "rocks," but not all rocks are alike. Rocks can be smooth or rough, dull or full of beautiful colors. In this activity, we'll look at three very different and unusual rocks.

WHAT TO DO

With your team, carefully follow each step below.

Observe

Look at Rock 1 (pyrite). Look at Rock 2 (wonderstone). Look at Rock 3 (pumice). Think about how these rocks are the same. Think about how they are different.

Describe

Describe each rock. What does it **look** like? What **color** is it? What does it **feel** like? What **shape** is it? Is it heavier or lighter than the other rocks?

Discuss

Which rock has layers of color? *wonderstone*
Which rock is the lightest rock? *pumice*
Which rock looks a lot like gold? *pyrite*

EARTH · 73

Teacher to Teacher

"Wonderstone" is a term that is often applied to banded sandstones sold under names like "Thirstystone," "Kanab Wonderstone," "Picture Sandstone," and so forth.

Technically, however, the term refers to banded rhyolite — which is an igneous rock used to make gems! Since rhyolite is nothing like sandstone, this has caused a lot of confusion.

Many geologists believe the best solution would be to abandon the term "wonderstone" entirely. But this is unlikely since the average person now equates "wonderstone" with one of the beautiful forms of banded sandstone.

READ THE STORY
There are many kinds of rocks on Earth, but rocks can be very different. Read the story below to learn about three very different rocks.

Wonderful Rocks

Rocks can be very different.
There are many kinds of rocks. They can be hard or soft, light or heavy, smooth or rough. They come in many colors. Different rocks can be used in different ways.

This is pyrite.
Pyrite is a common mineral.
Iron pyrite is very hard. Because of its rich golden color, iron pyrite is sometimes called "fool's gold."

Pyrite has many uses.
Pyrite is an important source of the chemical sulphur. It is also prized by rock collectors, and is even used in jewelry.

This is pumice.
Pumice comes from volcanoes.
Some lava is filled with gases. When it spews from a volcano, it creates rocks full of holes from trapped gas bubbles.

Pumice has many uses.
Pumice is an ingredient in concrete blocks. It's also used for agriculture, cleaning abrasives, and even aging blue jeans.

This is wonderstone.
Wonderstone comes from sand.
Wonderstone is a type of sandstone that has beautiful colors. Sandstone is sand turned to rock. It is formed in many layers.

Wonderstone can be decorative.
Since it is relatively soft, wonderstone is often shaped and carved to make bookends, drink coasters, and more.

74 · EARTH

Extended Teaching

1. To extend vocabulary, define the word "molten." Molten means "melted by heat." The farther you go below Earth's crust, the hotter it becomes. About 20 miles down, it's hot enough to melt most rock. This "molten rock" is rarely seen except in volcanic eruptions.

2. Ask each student to bring a rock from home. In their research teams, allow students time to examine these samples. Instruct them to compare different rocks to find out which ones are similar. Now as a class, group the rocks according to their characteristics.

Read The Story
Read the story aloud with your students. (See READING LEVELS on page 12 of this Teacher Guidebook.) After reading, monitor teams as they discuss what was read. Once you feel students have mastered the basic concepts, have them answer the comprehension questions (**What I Learned** - part 1) on the next page.

To introduce the story, say:

"The title of this story is 'Wonderful Rocks.' Look at your story and follow along as we read it together."

If you wish, encourage Emergent readers to point to words and pictures as you read.

What I Learned (part 1)
These are basic fact-based comprehension questions. Student answers will vary, but suggested responses include:

1 pyrite = chemicals, jewelry, etc.
pumice = concrete block, agriculture, cleaning, fading jeans, etc.
wonderstone = decorative items

2 a) both have many uses b) pumice full of holes, pyrite used for jewelry, etc.

3 a) it might break b) it's relatively soft

Field Trip
Arrange a hike at a park with steep hills and scattered rocks where digging is allowed. Bring small digging utensils (metal spoons, tongue depressors, small brushes, etc.) and buckets. Encourage students to dig and collect various kinds of rocks.

Guest Speaker
Invite a geologist or nursery "hardscaper" to visit your class. Have him/her bring samples of various kinds of rocks.

Materials Needed*

pyrite   pumice
wonderstone (sandstone)
bowl   water

Safety Concerns

4. Slipping

There is a potential for spilled water. Remind students to exercise caution.

4. Sharp Objects

Some of the rocks can be sharp! Remind students to exercise caution.

Do the Activity

Read the activity in advance so you understand it thoroughly. (If time allows, try it yourself.) Before students begin, carefully go over the **Safety Concerns** together.

Pass out materials, then have your students follow along as you read the instructions for **Step 1**. Monitor teams closely as they complete this step.

Once teams have completed **Step 1**, read instructions for **Step 2**. Monitor teams as before. Repeat for **Step 3** and **Step 4**.

After the activity, allow time for each team to share their observations. To encourage higher-level thinking, encourage teams to not only share their observations with each other, but also with other teams.

Special Instructions

Step 1 - Remind students to take their time examining fine details that may not be immediately noticeable. Offer assistance as needed. Encourage teams to use scientific and descriptive words.

Step 3 - Remind students to place the rocks in the bowl gently.

Bold-faced items supplied in kit.

DO THE ACTIVITY
Working with your research team, carefully follow each step below. Before you start, be sure you know the **safety rules** for this activity.

STEP 1 Look closely at the pyrite. Make notes about what you see (its color, shape, size, etc.). Repeat this process with the pumice, then the wonderstone.

STEP 2 Rub the pyrite between your fingers and thumb. Make notes about what you feel (texture). Repeat this process with the pumice, then the wonderstone.

STEP 3 Fill a bowl with water. Place the pyrite in the water. Record the results. Remove and dry the pyrite, then repeat this step with the pumice, then the wonderstone.

STEP 4 Review each step in this activity. Discuss your observations with team members. Now compare your findings with those of other research teams.

What Happened?

Immediately following the Activity, help your students understand what they observed.

Say: *"In **Step 1**, you closely examined three very different and very unusual rocks. You looked at each rock, then you compared it to the others as you thought about how they were similar or different.*

*In **Step 2**, you compared the rocks' textures. Each rock felt different from the others.*

*In **Step 3**, you tested how the rocks behaved in water. You discovered that pyrite and wonderstone sink, but pumice floats. (This is because the air trapped in pumice is less dense than water.)*

*Finally, in **Step 4**, you did like all good scientists, and compared your observations with those of other research teams."*

NAME _____

SHOW WHAT YOU KNOW - 1
Color the **pyrite** gold. Color the **pumice** light grey.
Color the **wonderstone** with reds or browns. Write the
correct names on the line below.

This light, porous rock is

pumice

This colorful, layered rock is

wonderstone

This hard, golden rock is

pyrite

To the Parent . . .	**Scripture Connection:** Matthew 7:24-27

Lesson Focus:
Geology

Lesson Objective:
To understand that different rocks have different characteristics

National Science Education Standards:
Standard D1 — *"All students should develop an understanding of the properties of Earth materials . . . their different physical and chemical properties . . . which make them useful in various ways . . ."*

Follow-up Questions:
Ask your child to describe pyrite. Ask what other name it is sometimes called (fool's gold).
Ask your child to describe pumice. Ask what is unusual about this rock (it floats).
Ask your child to describe wonderstone. Ask what it is often used for (to make decorative items).

Food For Thought

A related "Scripture Object Lesson" you can share with your students.

Matthew 7:24-27

Have you ever wondered what it might be like to be a jellyfish? A jellyfish spends its life just floating around in the ocean. It goes wherever the currents take it.

You've probably been to a lake or pool. While it's fun to float around for a little while, would you want to spend the rest of your life just floating? No way!

Humans need support — something that is stable and unmoving, something "solid as a rock." Jesus told this parable to show that a relationship with God provides that kind of foundation.

The choice is yours — to build your life on "shifting sands" with no support, or to ground it firmly on the rock of a loving relationship with God.

Expand - Day 4

Begin **Day 4** with a review of **Day 3**, then have students answer "part 2" questions.

What I Learned (part 2)
These are higher-level cognitive questions (explain, compare, predict). Student answers will vary but suggested responses may include:

① shape, size, color, texture, weight or density, hardness, uses, how they're formed, etc.

② a) both rocks, both decorative, etc.
b) pyrite is hard, wonderstone is soft, etc.

③ a) yes b) still full of trapped air which is less dense than water

Assess - Day 5

Suggestions for modifying assessment options to reflect student reading levels are shown under ASSESSMENT METHODS on page 12.

Show What You Know 1
(general assessment in Student Worktext)

Blanks: 1) pumice 2) wonderstone 3) pyrite
Also, the top rock should be colored light gray, the middle rock red or brown, the bottom rock gold.

Show What You Know 2
(optional test master in Teacher Guide)

1) F   2) T   3) T   4) F   5) T

To The Parent
Included at the bottom of all assessment tests, "To The Parent" provides a great way to solicit parent involvement. It not only gives parents an overview of the lesson, but also provides follow-up questions for home use.

Show What You Know 2

Read each sentence below. If the sentence is true, then circle the letter **T**. If the sentence is false, then circle the letter **F**.

T F 1. All rocks are the same.

T F 2. Wonderstone is formed in many layers.

T F 3. Pyrite is sometimes called "fool's gold."

T F 4. Pumice will not float in water.

T F 5. Sandstone is sand turned to rock.

To the Parent . . .   **Scripture Connection:** Matthew 7: 24-27

Lesson Focus:
Geology

Lesson Objective:
To understand that different rocks have different characteristics

National Science Education Standards:
Standard D1 — *"All students should develop an understanding of the properties of earth materials . . . their different physical and chemical properties . . . which make them useful in various ways . . ."*

Follow-up Questions:
Ask your child to describe pyrite. Ask what other name it is sometimes called (fool's gold).
Ask your child to describe pumice. Ask what is unusual about this rock (it floats).
Ask your child to describe wonderstone. Ask what it is often used for (to make decorative items).

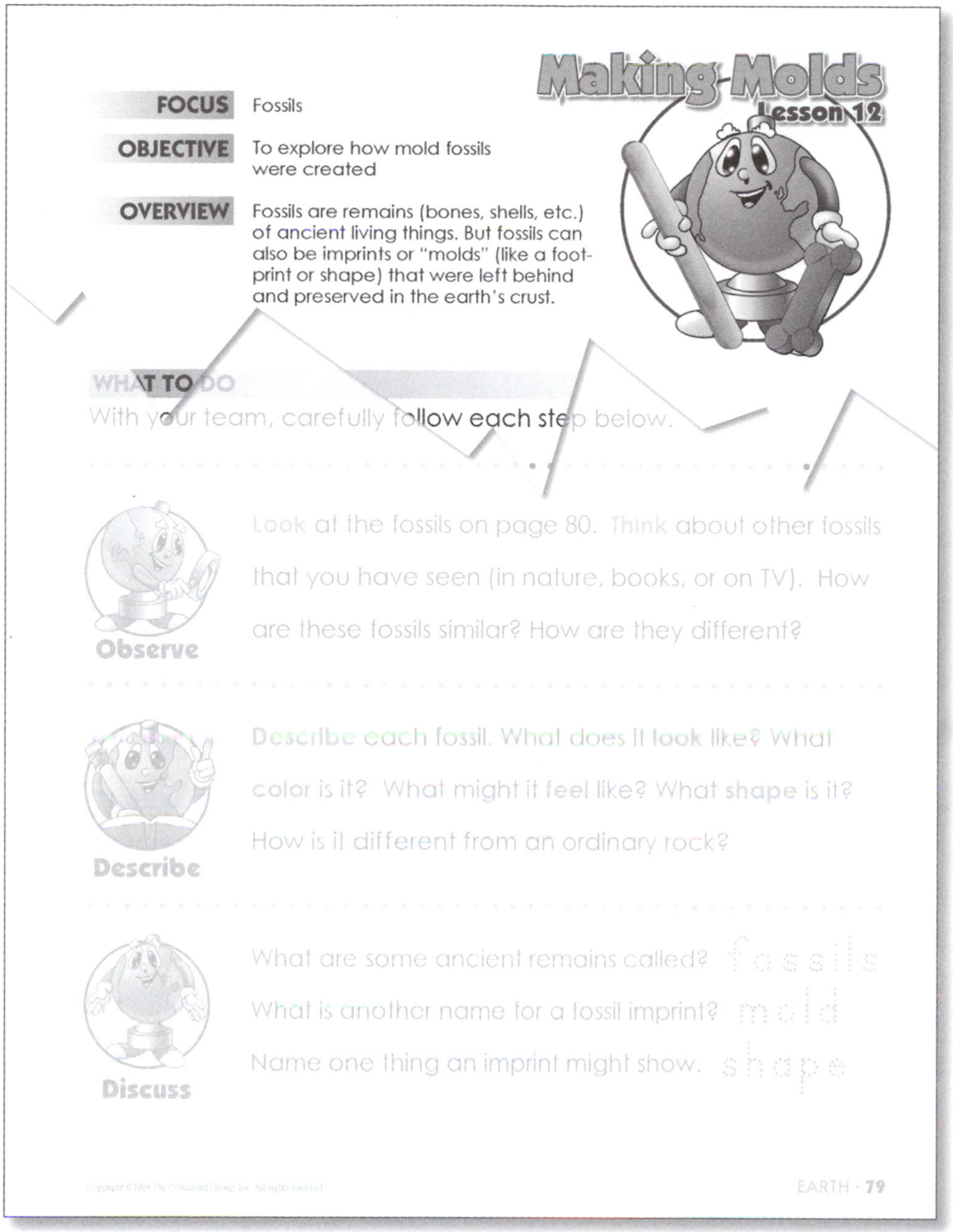

Lesson 12

Introduction

National Standards
Focus: D1

Related: A1, A2, B1, C1, C2, C3, F3, F4

Category
Earth Science

Focus
Fossils

Objective
To explore how mold fossils were created

Overview
Read the overview aloud to your students. The goal is to create an atmosphere of curiosity and inquiry.

Say: *"Fossils are remains (like bones or shells) of ancient living things. But fossils can also be imprints or "molds" (like a footprint or shape) that were left behind and preserved in the earth's crust."*

Worksheet reproduced at left:

FOCUS Fossils

OBJECTIVE To explore how mold fossils were created

OVERVIEW Fossils are remains (bones, shells, etc.) of ancient living things. But fossils can also be imprints or "molds" (like a footprint or shape) that were left behind and preserved in the earth's crust.

WHAT TO DO
With your team, carefully follow each step below.

Observe
Look at the fossils on page 80. Think about other fossils that you have seen (in nature, books, or on TV). How are these fossils similar? How are they different?

Describe
Describe each fossil. What does it look like? What color is it? What might it feel like? What shape is it? How is it different from an ordinary rock?

Discuss
What are some ancient remains called? fossils
What is another name for a fossil imprint? mold
Name one thing an imprint might show. shape

EARTH · 79

Additional Notes

To introduce this lesson, ask your students if they have ever made footprints while walking in the snow, sand, or mud. What did the footprints look like? How were they similar to the shape of their feet or shoes?

Explain that soft surfaces like mud can be "molded" and take "im-prints" of the objects that press down on them. Changes in weather, wind, and water usually make these molds disappear quickly.

But sometimes things occur that cause these molds to be preserved. These become the ancient "mold fossils" that we can find in certain kinds of stone today.

What To Do

Once students are seated in "research teams" with materials in front of them, read the first section (OBSERVE) aloud.

Say, *"To start this lesson, we're going to* **observe** *some things. Good scientists always carefully examine the things they will be working with before beginning. First, I will read the instructions to you. Then you can follow the instructions as you* **observe** *the pictures of fossils on page 80."*

Monitor teams closely as they follow instructions. When teams are finished with this section, repeat the process with the DESCRIBE section. Conclude with the DISCUSS section.

Options

Expand the DISCUSS section by having students trace dotted "key words" using crayons or markers. Trace the word **fossils** in brown, the word **mold** in red, and the word **shape** in green.

FOCUS   Fossils

OBJECTIVE   To explore how mold fossils were created

OVERVIEW   Fossils are remains (bones, shells, etc.) of ancient living things. But fossils can also be imprints or "molds" (like a footprint or shape) that were left behind and preserved in the earth's crust.

WHAT TO DO

With your team, carefully follow each step below.

Observe

Look at the fossils on page 80. Think about other fossils that you have seen (in nature, books, or on TV). How are these fossils similar? How are they different?

Describe

Describe each fossil. What does it look like? What color is it? What might it feel like? What shape is it? How is it different from an ordinary rock?

Discuss

What are some ancient remains called? *fossils*

What is another name for a fossil imprint? *mold*

Name one thing an imprint might show. *shape*

EARTH · **79**

Teacher to Teacher

Paleontology is the study of fossils. The word "fossil" comes from the Latin word for "having been dug up" — so it fits well.

A fossil is any trace of a once living thing. This not only includes body parts, but also signs like tracks and imprints. Fossils can tell us a lot about the creature's structure, its environment, and sometimes even details like how it obtained food! They're like a detective story, giving us clues about what happened.

However, there's a lot of information that fossils don't contain. And large fossils are relatively rare, since the conditions favorable to their formation (quick covering of a body preventing decomposition) were not common.

There are many kinds of fossils on Earth. Fossils can be very different. Read the story below to learn about some different kinds of fossils.

Fossils

There are many kinds of fossils.
Fossils can be the petrified remains of ancient creatures or plants. But many fossils are an imprint (mold) of a creature's shape or a similar trace of their existence.

This is an animal fossil.

A fossil can be an animal part.
Since the soft parts of animals decompose quickly, animal fossils are usually just hard parts like shells, bones, or teeth.

An animal fossil can be stone.
Often an animal part is slowly replaced by minerals in the water around it. This makes an exact replica of the part in stone!

This is a plant fossil.

A fossil can be a plant part.
Some ancient plants were buried in sediment which became stone. Plant fossils include branches, seeds, and leaves.

A plant fossil can be stone.
Just like animal parts, plant parts can also be replaced by surrounding minerals, making an exact replica in stone.

This is a mold fossil.

Mold fossils are very common.
Many fossils are not actual animal or plant parts. They are imprints (molds), often made in ancient mud or sand.

One type of rock has many fossils.
Most fossils are found in "sedimentary" rock (mud or sand turned to stone). Limestone and sandstone are examples.

Extended Teaching

1. To extend vocabulary, use synonyms along with the word "petrified" ("harden," "turn to stone," etc.). The most popular petrified fossils are trees and dinosaurs. People love to look for dinosaur fossils!

2. Define "mold." Help students understand that this meaning is unrelated to fungi like bread mold.

3. Use synonyms along with the word "decompose" ("decay," "rot," "waste away," etc.)

Have students describe food that is decaying. What did it look like? What did it smell like? Remind them that all living things eventually decompose by breaking into their basic parts. These parts go back into the soil, giving it valuable nutrients so new life may continue.

4. Bring some samples of sedimentary rocks to class. (Limestone is common and especially good for this purpose.) Use a magnifying glass to look for tiny fossils.

Inform - Day 2

Read The Story

Read the story aloud with your students. (See READING LEVELS on page 12.) After reading, monitor teams as they discuss what was read. Once you feel students have mastered the basic concepts, have them answer the comprehension questions (**What I Learned** - part 1) on the next page.

To introduce the story, say:

"The title of this story is 'Fossils.' Look at your story and follow along as we read it together."

If you wish, encourage Emergent readers to point to words and pictures as you read.

What I Learned (part 1)

These are basic fact-based comprehension questions. Student answers will vary, but suggested responses include:

1 a) animal, plant, mold b) mold

2 a) all very old, hard, etc. b) animal and plant fossils are actual parts; mold fossils are only imprints

3 a) mold b) sedimentary rock was once mud or sand — both of which take imprints easily.

Field Trip

Visit a spot where a stream or road cuts through a hill, leaving rocky strata. You may wish to encourage local rock hounds to join you and assist your students as they search for common fossils.

Guest Speaker

Invite a paleontologist from a local university or museum to visit your class. Ask him/her to bring a collection of fossils to show your students. Be sure they include animal, plant, and mold fossils.

Materials Needed*

flour	**soybean meal**
salt	**bowl**
spoon	**wax paper**
dog biscuit	water
turtle	

Safety Concerns

3. Hygiene

Don't allow students to put anything in their mouths, or eat any ingredient.

4. Slipping

There is a potential for spilled liquids. Remind students to exercise caution.

Do the Activity

Read the activity in advance so you understand it thoroughly. (If time allows, try it yourself.) Before students begin, carefully go over the **Safety Concerns** together.

Pass out materials, then have your students follow along as you read the instructions for **Step 1**. Monitor teams closely as they complete this step.

Once teams have completed **Step 1**, read instructions for **Step 2**. Monitor teams as before. Repeat for **Step 3** and **Step 4**.

After the activity, allow time for each team to share their observations. To encourage higher-level thinking, encourage teams to not only share their observations with each other, but also with other teams.

Special Instructions

Step 1 - Have students add water slowly, stopping regularly to test the consistency. The resulting mixture must be firm — like stiff bread dough. Too much water will make it runny and unusable.

Step 2 - If dough is sticky to the touch, have students dust their hands with flour before they try to flatten the mix.

* Bold-faced items supplied in kit.

DO THE ACTIVITY

Working with your research team, carefully follow each step below. Before you start, be sure you know the **safety rules** for this activity.

STEP 1 — Stir the flour, soybean meal, and salt together in a bowl. Slowly **add** water to make a thick paste. (This represents sediment for your sedimentary rock.)

STEP 2 — Scoop your sediment onto the wax paper and **flatten**. Dip the dog biscuit in flour. Now **press** it into the sediment to make an imprint (mold), then **remove**.

STEP 3 — Set your "mold fossil" aside to dry overnight. If you wish, **repeat** step 1 and 2 of this activity using a toy creature (turtle, lizard, etc.) to see what kind of imprint it makes.

STEP 4 — Review each step in this activity. **Discuss** your observations with team members. Now **compare** your "fossils" with those of other research teams.

What Happened?

Immediately following the activity, help your students understand what they observed.

Say: *"In this activity you made a model to explore the way that mold fossils are created.*

In Step 1, you made a mixture to represent the patch of mud or sand that will become sedimentary rock.

In Steps 2 and 3, you made imprints in the mixture, resulting in the formation of a mold.

After your molds dry, you can compare the mold fossils your team made with those made by other research teams."

SHOW WHAT YOU KNOW - 1

Color the animal fossil in browns. Color the plant fossil in grays. Color the mold fossil light reds. Write the correct names on the line below.

This fossil is called a

mold

This fossil is from a

plant

This fossil is from an

animal

To the Parent . . .   Scripture Connection: Isaiah 64:8

Lesson Focus:
Fossils

Lesson Objective:
To understand how mold fossils were created

National Science Education Standards:
Standard D1 — "All students should develop an understanding of the properties of earth materials . . . their different physical and chemical properties . . . which make them useful in various ways . . ."

Follow-up Questions:
Ask your child to name three kinds of fossils (animal fossils, plant fossils, mold fossils).
Ask your child which fossil is the most common kind of fossil (the mold fossil).
Ask your child how a mold fossil is different from other fossils (a mold fossil is an imprint, not the thing itself).

84 · EARTH   Copyright ©2006 The Concerned Group, Inc. All rights reserved.

Food For Thought

A related "Scripture Object Lesson" you can share with your students.

Isaiah 64:8

Do you enjoy working with modeling clay? Most of us do.

At first the clay can be a little tough to work with. But the more you squeeze it back and forth in your hands, the more it warms up and the more pliable it becomes.

As you continue to work the clay, you can roll it, pull it apart, and squeeze it back together. Before long you can begin to shape the clay, eventually molding it into just the form it needs to be.

We are like clay in the hands of God. If we allow Him, He will constantly work to mold us into His perfection. Learn to trust God and place yourself in His life-changing hands!

Begin **Day 4** with a review of **Day 3**, then have students answer "part 2" questions.

What I Learned (part 2)

These are higher-level cognitive questions (explain, compare, predict). Student answers will vary but suggested responses may include:

1. a mold fossil

2. They are imprints, not actual animal or plant parts.

3. a) yes b) a footprint is an imprint

Assess - Day 5

Suggestions for modifying assessments to reflect reading levels can be found under ASSESSMENT METHODS on page 12.

Show What You Know 1
(general assessment in Student Worktext)

Blanks: 1) mold 2) plant 3) animal
Also, the top fossil should be colored light red, the middle fossil gray, and the bottom fossil brown.

Show What You Know 2
(optional test master in Teacher Guide)

1) T 2) F 3) T 4) T 5) F

To The Parent

Included at the bottom of all assessment tests, "To The Parent" provides a great way to solicit parent involvement. It not only gives parents an overview of the lesson, but also provides follow-up questions for home use.

Show What You Know 2

Read each sentence below. If the sentence is true, then circle **T**. If the sentence is false, then circle **F**.

T   F   1. There are many different types of fossils.

T   F   2. Animal fossils come mostly from the soft parts of animals.

T   F   3. Most fossils are found in sedimentary rock.

T   F   4. Minerals sometimes make replicas of plant and animal parts.

T   F   5. A "mold fossil" is a type of plant fossil.

To the Parent . . .   **Scripture Connection:** Isaiah 64:8

Lesson Focus:
Fossils

Lesson Objective:
To understand how mold fossils were created

National Science Education Standards:
Standard D1 — *"All students should develop an understanding of the properties of earth materials . . . their different physical and chemical properties . . . which make them useful in various ways . . ."*

Follow-up Questions:
Ask your child to name three kinds of fossils (animal fossils, plant fossils, mold fossils).
Ask your child which fossil is the most common kind of fossil (the mold fossil).
Ask your child how a mold fossil is different from other fossils (a mold fossil is an imprint, not the thing itself).

Solar System
Lesson 13

FOCUS Solar System

OBJECTIVE To explore the relationship between the Sun, planets, and moons

OVERVIEW Objects in our solar system (the Sun, moons, and planets) have locations and movements that can be seen and described.

WHAT TO DO

With your team, carefully follow each step below.

Observe

Look at each planet carefully. Think about how it is like other planets. Think about how it is different. Look at the solar system. Think about how planets move.

Describe

Describe each planet. What does it look like? What color is it? What shape is it? How big is it compared to the other planets?

Discuss

What is at the center of the solar system? Sun
What is the third planet from the sun? Earth
What object circles around the earth? Moon

EARTH · 85

Lesson 13

Introduction

National Standards
Focus: D2

Related: A1, A2, B2, D3

Category
Earth Science

Focus
The Solar System

Objective
To explore the relationship between the Sun, planets, and moons

Overview
Read the overview aloud to your students. The goal is to create an atmosphere of curiosity and inquiry.

Say: *"Objects in our solar system (the Sun, the planets and moons) have locations and movements that can be seen and described."*

Additional Notes

To introduce this lesson, ask your students if they have ever spent time looking at the sky after dark. Ask them what kinds of things they have seen (stars, the Moon, lights from passing planes, etc.).

Tell students that many stars are quite similar to our Sun. But stars appear to be small because they are very, very far away.

Encourage students to go outside on the next clear night and look carefully at the sky. Have them ask their parents to help them locate a bright star that is easy to find. Have them wait two days, then try to find that star again. Is it in the same spot? This activity should help students better understand the relationship between Earth's movement and star positions.

What To Do

Once students are seated in "research teams" with materials in front of them, read the first section (OBSERVE) aloud.

Each student should have a planet sheet (p. 233, Student Worktext) before you begin. Have them turn to the side with the pictures of the planets. Say, *"To start this lesson, we're going to **look** at illustrations of the planets in our solar system. Good scientists always carefully examine the things they will be studying before beginning. First, I will read the instructions to you. Then you can follow the instructions as you **look** at the different planets shown on your sheet."*

Monitor teams closely as they follow instructions. When teams are finished with this section, repeat the process with the DESCRIBE section. Conclude with the DISCUSS section.

Options

Expand the DISCUSS section by having students trace dotted "key words" using crayons or markers. Trace the word **Sun** in orange, the word **Earth** in blue, and the word **Moon** in yellow.

FOCUS	Solar System
OBJECTIVE	To explore the relationship between the Sun, planets, and moons
OVERVIEW	Objects in our solar system (the Sun, moons, and planets) have locations and movements that can be seen and described.

WHAT TO DO

With your team, carefully follow each step below.

Observe

Look at each planet carefully. **Think** about how it is like other planets. **Think** about how it is different. **Look** at the solar system. **Think** about how planets move.

Describe

Describe each planet. What does it **look** like? What **color** is it? What **shape** is it? How **big** is it compared to the other planets?

Discuss

What is at the center of the solar system? Sun

What is the third planet from the sun? Earth

What object circles around the earth? Moon

EARTH · 85

Teacher to Teacher

The inner planets (Mercury, Venus, and Mars) have structural similarities to Earth. By contrast, the outer planets (Jupiter, Saturn, Uranus, and Neptune) are "gas giants" with very unstable surfaces.

What about Pluto? It's mostly rock and ice, and it is so small that as recently as 1999 there was a move to declassify it as a planet!

Here's another interesting fact: Since most planets have elliptical orbits, the distance of each planet from the Sun is based on "average" distance over time. This can be very misleading — even to the extent of putting the planets in the wrong order! How is that possible? Pluto's orbit is so elliptical that some years it is actually *closer* to the Sun than Neptune!

Extended Teaching

1. To extend vocabulary, define "solar" (having to do with the Sun). Tell students that "sol" is the Latin word for "sun." Talk about things like solar energy, solar tea, and solariums. Expand further by discussing "lunar" (of or like the moon). "Luna" is the Latin word for moon.

2. To help the students remember planet order, write this sentence on the board: "My very excellent mother just sent us nine pizzas." Underline the first letter of each word to represent the first letter of each planet.

3. For a "Solar System Snack," have students wash their hands, then give them one round orange slice, four round crackers, four round slices of cheese, and one red cherry. Have them arrange the items on a paper towel. (Orange slice = sun; crackers = solid planets; cheese = gaseous planets; cherry = Pluto.) Once you've checked their work, see if they are really hungry enough to eat a solar system!

Read The Story

Read the story aloud with your students. (See READING LEVELS on page 12.) After reading, monitor teams as they discuss what was read. Once you feel students have mastered the basic concepts, have them answer the comprehension questions (**What I Learned** - part 1) on the next page.

To introduce the story, say:

"The title of this story is 'Solar System.' Look at your story and follow along as we read it together."

If you wish, encourage Emergent readers to point to words and pictures as you read.

What I Learned (part 1)

These are basic fact-based comprehension questions. Student answers will vary, but suggested responses include:

① a) solid, gas b) solid examples: Mercury, Mars, Earth, or Venus; gas examples: Jupiter, Saturn, Uranus, or Neptune

② a) like all moons, it orbits a planet b) compared to its planet, it is much larger than most moons

③ a) it would get much hotter b) because the closer a planet is to the Sun, the hotter it gets

Field Trip

Visit a planetarium to learn more about constellations and planet positions. Ask students to discover one new thing they didn't know before the trip.

Guest Speaker

Ask an amateur astronomer to visit your class. Ask him/her to bring pictures or slides to share. Find out if there are local "star gazing parties" your students and their parents can attend.

Materials Needed*

punch ball
5 inch balloons - 5
9 inch balloons - 4

Safety Concerns

3. Poison Hazard
Balloons can pose a choking hazard. Depending on developmental readiness, you may wish to blow up balloons in advance.

Do the Activity

Read the activity in advance so you understand it thoroughly. (If time allows, try it yourself.) Before students begin, carefully go over the **Safety Concerns** together.

Pass out materials, then have your students follow along as you read the instructions for **Step 1**. Monitor teams closely as they complete this step.

Once teams have completed **Step 1**, read instructions for **Step 2**. Monitor teams as before. Repeat for **Step 3** and **Step 4**.

After the activity, allow time for each team to share their observations. To encourage higher-level thinking, encourage teams to not only share their observations with each other, but also with other teams.

Special Instructions

Step 3 - You may want to make marks where each planet belongs in advance (see "Model Scale" at right). Since a football field is quite a large area, you may also need a megaphone to be heard.

To avoid confusion, instruct teams to line up in "planet order" before you begin. Remind students to not set their balloons down on the field — they will probably burst! (The balloons, not the students.)

Point out that this model uses a scale of 1 inch = 1 million miles. Tell students that at this scale, the Sun would actually be about the size of a marble, and Earth would be smaller than the head of a pin!

Bold-faced items supplied in kit.

DO THE ACTIVITY
Working with your research team, carefully follow each step below. Before you start, be sure you know the **safety rules** for this activity.

STEP 1 Using an encyclopedia or the Internet, **list** the nine planets in order. **Write** down how far each one is from the Sun. Now **discuss** which four planets are largest.

STEP 2 Your teacher will assign each team a planet, then give you a balloon. **Inflate** your balloon, then use construction paper to **make** a sign for your planet.

STEP 3 **Follow** your teacher to the football field. A punch ball on the goal line will represent the Sun. **Move** your "planet" to the spot your teacher indicates.

STEP 4 **Predict** how long it might take each team to walk in a circle around the Sun (staying at this distance). **Compare** your prediction with other teams'.

88 · EARTH

What Happened?

Immediately following the activity, help your students understand what they observed.

Say: "In **Step 1** of this activity, you began to get a clearer idea of the enormous distances that are between the Sun and the planets.

In **Step 3**, you helped make a huge model that showed those relationships even more clearly.

In **Step 4**, you predicted the orbital path of your planet, and compared it to those of other planets. Isn't our solar system an amazing place?"

Model Scale

Sun = goal line • **Mercury** = 1 yard • **Venus** = 1 yard, 31 inches • **Earth** = 2 yards, 22 inches • **Mars** = 4 yards **Jupiter** 13 yards, 14 inches • **Saturn** = 24 yards, 22 inches • **Uranus** = 49 yards, 23 inches • **Nepture** = 77 yards • **Pluto** 102 yards

SHOW WHAT YOU KNOW - 1

Circle the sun with red. Circle the planet with blue.
Circle the moon with brown. Write the correct names
on the lines below.

At the center of the solar system is the

Sun

Orbiting the Sun is a

planet

Orbiting the planet is a

moon

To the Parent . . .   Scripture Connection: Psalms 8:3-4

Lesson Focus:
Solar System

Lesson Objective:
To explore the relationship between the sun, the planets, and moons.

National Science Education Standards:
Standard D2 — "All students should develop an understanding of objects in the sky . . . the sun, moon, stars . . .
all have properties, locations, and movements that can be observed and described . . ."

Follow-up Questions:
Ask your child what object is at the center of the solar system (the sun).
Ask your child about the relationship between the planets and the sun (planets orbit the sun).
Ask your child about the relationship between a moon and a planet (moons orbit planets).

Food For Thought

*A related "Scripture Object Lesson"
you can share with your students.*

Psalms 8: 3-4

Have you ever heard the song: *"Twinkle, twinkle, little star, How I wonder what you are."*? There are many theories about where the stars came from and how the universe came to be. Many believe solar systems were created over billions of years from clouds of gas and dust being compressed by gravity. Others believe our universe began with an enormous explosion in space.

But Scripture says that "God created the Heavens and the Earth." And our powerful God not only created the stars, planets, and suns — He also created you and me!

So instead of wondering where the stars came from and how this Earth came to be, we can sing:

*"Twinkle, twinkle, little star, **God** has placed us where we are."*

Expand - Day 4

Day 4 with a review of **Day 3**, then have students answer "part 2" questions. You may also wish to discuss how long it would take to travel a million miles at 100 miles an hour, and compare this to the distances in yesterday's model.

What I Learned (part 2)

These are higher-level cognitive questions (explain, compare, predict). Student answers will vary but suggested responses may include:

(1)   a) Neptune, Pluto b) They are the farthest from the Sun.

(2)   a) both solid, both relatively small b) Mercury very hot; Pluto very cold

(3)   **a)** very, very hot b) It is the closest planet to the Sun

Assess - Day 5

Suggestions for modifying assessments to reflect reading levels can be found under ASSESSMENT OPTIONS on page 12.

Show What You Know 1

(general assessment in Student Worktext)

Blanks: 1) Sun 2) planet 3) moon
Also, the Sun should be circled in red, the planet in blue, the moon in brown

Show What You Know 2

(optional test master in Teacher Guide)

1) star   2) nine   3) solid
4) gas   5) moons

To The Parent

Included at the bottom of all assessment tests, "To The Parent" provides a great way to solicit parent involvement. It not only gives parents an overview of the lesson, but also provides follow-up questions for home use.

NAME _____

Show What You Know 2

Read each sentence below. Using the **word bank**, choose the best word to complete each sentence, then write it on the line. (Some words will not be used.)

1. The object that we call "the Sun" is really a _____ .

2. Our solar system has a total of _____ planets.

3. Mercury, Mars, Earth, and Venus are _____ planets.

4. Jupiter, Saturn, Uranus, and Neptune are _____ planets.

5. Some planets in our solar system are circled by _____.

WORD BANK:

star   moons   eight   solid   comets   balloons   gas   nine

---

To the Parent . . .   **Scripture Connection:** Psalms 8: 3-4

Lesson Focus:
Solar System

Lesson Objective:
To explore the relationship between the Sun, the planets, and moons

National Science Education Standards:
Standard D2 — "All students should develop an understanding of objects in the sky . . . the Sun, Moon, stars . . . all have properties, locations, and movements that can be observed and described . . ."

Follow-up Questions:
Ask your child what object is at the center of the solar system (the Sun).
Ask your child about the relationship between the planets and the Sun (planets orbit the Sun).
Ask your child about the relationship between a moon and a planet (moons orbit planets).

Lesson 14

FOCUS	Eclipses
OBJECTIVE	To explore how solar and lunar eclipses occur
OVERVIEW	The movement of objects in our solar system can sometimes create unusual sights. Solar and lunar eclipses have fascinated people since the beginning of time.

WHAT TO DO

With your team, carefully follow each step below.

Observe
Think about pictures you have seen of the Sun, Moon and Earth. Think about how they were alike. Think about how they were different.

Describe
Describe the Sun, Moon, and Earth. What does each one look like? What color is it? What shape is it? How big is it compared to the others?

Discuss
What do you think the Earth goes around? Sun
What do you think the Moon goes around? Earth
What can reflect the Sun's light at night? Moon

EARTH · 91

National Standards
Focus: D2

Related: A1, A2, B2, D3

Category
Earth Science

Focus
Eclipses

Objective
To explore how solar and lunar eclipses occur

Overview
Read the overview aloud to your students. The goal is to create an atmosphere of curiosity and inquiry.

Say: *"The movement of objects in our solar system can sometimes create unusual sights. Solar and lunar eclipses have fascinated people since the beginning of time."*

Additional Notes

To introduce this lesson, play a game of "Shadow Tag." (The student who is "it" tries to tag the other players by stepping on their shadows.)

After playing for a while, ask students what would happen if they tried to play this game on a dark, cloudy day. (They couldn't see the other players' shadows.)

Remind students that shadows appear when a solid object blocks a light source. Point out that the shadows in this game were never much bigger than a person. But in this lesson, they'll learn about shadows so huge they can darken the entire sky!

What To Do

Once students are seated in "research teams" with materials in front of them, read the first section (OB-SERVE) aloud.

Say, *"To start this lesson, we're going to **picture** some things in our minds. Good scientists often spend time thinking about things they will be working with before beginning a project. First, I will read the instructions to you. Then you can follow the instructions as you **picture** the objects in your mind."*

Monitor teams closely as they follow instructions. When teams are finished with this section, repeat the process with the DE-SCRIBE section. Conclude with the DISCUSS section.

Options

Expand the DISCUSS section by having students trace dotted "key words" using crayons or markers. Trace the word **Sun** in yellow, the word **Earth** in blue, and the word **Moon** in orange.

FOCUS	Eclipses
OBJECTIVE	To explore how solar and lunar eclipses occur
OVERVIEW	The movement of objects in our solar system can sometimes create unusual sights. Solar and lunar eclipses have fascinated people since the beginning of time.

WHAT TO DO

With your team, carefully follow each step below.

Observe

Think about pictures you have seen of the Sun, Moon, and Earth. **Think** about how they were alike. **Think** about how they were different.

Describe

Describe the Sun, Moon, and Earth. What does each one **look** like? What **color** is it? What **shape** is it? How **big** is it compared to the others?

Discuss

What do you think the Earth goes around? Sun
What do you think the Moon goes around? Earth
What can reflect the Sun's light at night? Moon

EARTH · 91

Teacher to Teacher

Some students may wonder why the Sun and Moon look about the same size.

Although the Sun is much larger, it's also much farther away. The Moon looks large because it's very close. The Moon's distance from Earth is vital in an eclipse. If the Moon were a little farther away (or its diameter was only 140 miles smaller), a TOTAL eclipse would be impossible!

It's also important to note that lunar and solar eclipses are equally frequent. Solar eclipses just seem "rare" because they only touch a small part of Earth. For many, it's a "once in a lifetime" experience.

READ THE STORY

An **eclipse** happens when the Sun, Moon, and Earth line up in a certain way. Read the story below to learn more about eclipses.

Eclipse

An eclipse is like a giant shadow.
In our solar system, all light comes from the Sun. But sometimes the Earth or the Moon gets in the way. The light is blocked, making a huge shadow called an eclipse.

This is a solar eclipse.
The Moon blocks the Sun's light.
When the Moon's orbit moves it between the Earth and the Sun, it causes a solar eclipse. The Moon's shadow falls on the Earth.

A solar eclipse makes the day dark.
A solar eclipse only lasts a short time, but it makes the daytime sky turn dark. Birds and animals often think night has come!

This is a lunar eclipse.
The Earth blocks the Sun's light.
When the Earth's orbit moves it between the Moon and the Sun, it causes a lunar eclipse. The Earth's shadow falls on the Moon.

A lunar eclipse makes the Moon dark.
Since the Moon only reflects the light from the Sun, the Earth's shadow makes it turn dark. A dark moon looks very strange.

Scientists study eclipses.
Eclipses can be predicted.
Scientists know that the positions of the Sun, Moon, and Earth cause a solar or lunar eclipse about once every six months.

Lunar eclipses are easier to see.
Each solar eclipse only covers a tiny area of Earth. But a lunar eclipse can be seen from anywhere on Earth's night side.

92 · EARTH

Extended Teaching

1. To expand vocabulary compare the word "eclipse" with "cover." In an eclipse, the Earth's shadow covers the Moon (or the Moon's shadow covers the Earth).

2. To demonstrate how shadows occur, hang a large white paper on the wall and shine a bright light on it. Point out that nothing is blocking the light. Now have a student place a hand between the light and the paper. A hand-shaped shadow forms. Trace around the shadow with crayon, then turn off the light. Discuss how an object's shape relates to the shadow it casts.

3. Make "eclipse sandwiches." Use a cookie cutter to cut round slices of cheese (Sun), white bread (Moon), and rye bread (Earth). After washing their hands, have students use slices to explain relationships in an eclipse. After they finish, stack and eat!

Inform - Day 2

Read The Story
Read the story aloud with your students. (See READING LEVELS on page 12.) After reading, monitor teams as they discuss what was read. Once you feel students have mastered the basic concepts, have them answer the comprehension questions (**What I Learned** - part 1) on the next page.

To introduce the story, say:

"The title of this story is 'Eclipse.' Look at your story and follow along as we read it together."

If you wish, encourage Emergent readers to point to words and pictures as you read.

What I Learned (part 1)
These are basic fact-based comprehension questions. Student answers will vary, but suggested responses include:

① The Moon blocks the Sun's light.

② a) both create huge shadows b) solar = moon blocks Sun's light; lunar = Earth blocks Sun's light

③ a) think night has come; go to sleep; etc. b) because it is dark outside like night

Field Trip
Go on a "shadow search" by exploring the school grounds on a sunny day! Have each student lay a sheet of paper in a shadow, then trace the shadow on the paper. Afterward go back to the classroom and see if students can guess the object from the tracing of its shadow.

Guest Speaker
Invite an astronomy teacher from a local college or high school to visit your class. Ask them to bring photos of eclipses and discuss how eclipses occur.

Materials Needed*

polystyrene ball (large)   flashlight
polystyrene ball (small)   dowel rods - 2
paint brush/tempera paints (optional)

Safety Concerns

4. Slipping

There is a potential for falls in a darkened room. Have students exercise caution.

4. Other

Warn students about the dangers of looking directly at a solar eclipse! (Note: lunar eclipses are safe to view.)

Do the Activity

Read the activity in advance so you understand it thoroughly. (If time allows, try it yourself.) Before students begin, carefully go over the **Safety Concerns** together.

Pass out materials, then have your students follow along as you read the instructions for **Step 1**. Monitor teams closely as they complete this step.

Once teams have completed **Step 1**, read instructions for **Step 2**. Monitor teams as before. Repeat for **Step 3** and **Step 4**.

After the activity, allow time for each team to share their observations. To encourage higher-level thinking, encourage teams to not only share their observations with each other, but also with other teams.

Special Instructions

Option - For a more realistic effect, let students use tempera paints to color the Earth before beginning this activity.

Step 1 - Some teams may need assistance pushing the rod into the balls. Emphasize that the balls are not to scale! (The Moon is about 1/4 the size of Earth.)

Step 2 and **3** - For best results, darken the room as much as possible. So students can better see what's happening, encourage them to take turns doing each function.

* Bold-faced items supplied in kit.

DO THE ACTIVITY
Working with your research team, carefully follow each step below. Before you start, be sure you know the **safety rules** for this activity.

STEP 1 **Push** a dowel rod into both balls (large for Earth; small for moon). **Ask** a team member to shine a flashlight directly at the "Earth" from about one foot away.

STEP 2 Slowly **move** the Moon behind the Earth. **Watch** as the Moon goes from light to dark as the shadow of the Earth covers it. (This models a lunar eclipse.)

STEP 3 Now **move** the Moon between the Earth and the Sun. **Watch** as the Moon's shadow moves across the Earth. (This models a solar eclipse.)

STEP 4 **Discuss** what an ant would have seen from your Earth during the simulated eclipses. **Compare** your observations with those of other research teams.

94 · EARTH

What Happened?

Immediately following the activity, help your students understand what they observed.

Say: *"In this activity you were able to explore how solar and lunar eclipses occur.*

In Step 1, you set up the alignment for an eclipse.

In Steps 2 and 3, you re-enacted the orbits of the Earth and the Moon, and modeled how both kinds of eclipses occur.

In Step 4, you discussed how an eclipse appears to us on Earth, and you compared your observations with those of other research teams.

Remember, never look directly at a real solar eclipse. The intense rays can damage your eyes!"

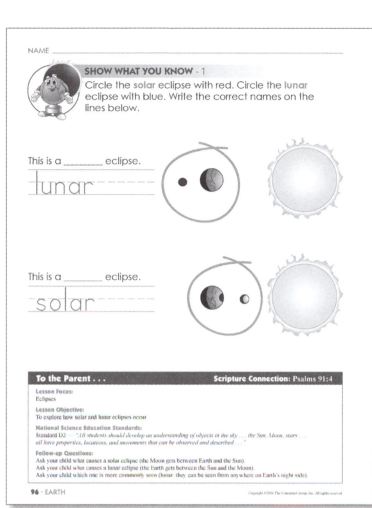

NAME _____

SHOW WHAT YOU KNOW - 1
Circle the **solar** eclipse with red. Circle the **lunar** eclipse with blue. Write the correct names on the lines below.

This is a _____ eclipse.
lunar

This is a _____ eclipse.
solar

To the Parent . . .   Scripture Connection: Psalms 91:4

Lesson Focus:
Eclipses

Lesson Objective:
To explore how solar and lunar eclipses occur

National Science Education Standards:
Standard D2 — "All students should develop an understanding of objects in the sky . . . the Sun, Moon, stars . . . all have properties, locations, and movements that can be observed and described . . ."

Follow-up Questions:
Ask your child what causes a solar eclipse (the Moon gets between Earth and the Sun).
Ask your child what causes a lunar eclipse (the Earth gets between the Sun and the Moon).
Ask your child which one is more commonly seen (lunar: they can be seen from anywhere on Earth's night side).

Food For Thought

A related "Scripture Object Lesson" you can share with your students.

Psalms 91:4

During a lunar eclipse, the Earth's shadow covers the Moon like a dark, cozy blanket.

Did you have a special blanket you loved when you were a toddler? If you did, you probably carried it everywhere! Why do children love a special blanket so much? It's because they feel snug and protected when they feel its closeness. It becomes their comforter and their friend.

Do you still carry your special blanket everywhere? Of course not!

But just like a blanket, Jesus can surround us with his love and protection. We can always feel safe and secure when we place our trust in Him.

Expand - Day 4

Begin **Day 4** with a review of **Day 3**, then have students answer "part 2" questions.

What I Learned (part 2)
These are higher-level cognitive questions (explain, compare, predict). Student answers will vary but suggested responses may include:

1 The Earth blocks the Sun's light.

2 a) same bodies involved; both eclipses caused by movement   b) moon "behind" Earth in Step 1; moon "in front" of Earth in Step 2

3 models help us "see" how things happen; sometimes easier to see things than just to read or talk about them

Assess - Day 5

Suggestions for modifying assessments to reflect reading levels can be found under ASSESSMENT METHODS on page 12.

Show What You Know 1
(general assessment in Student Worktext)

Blanks: 1) lunar 2) solar
Also, the first eclipse should be circled in blue; the second should be circled in red.

Show What You Know 2
(optional test master in Teacher Guide)

1) S   2) L   3) S   4) S   5) L

To The Parent
Included at the bottom of all assessment tests, "To The Parent" provides a great way to solicit parent involvement. It not only gives parents an overview of the lesson, but also provides follow-up questions for home use.

NAME _____

Show What You Know 2

Read each sentence below. If it describes a **solar** eclipse, then circle **S**. If it describes a **lunar** eclipse, then circle **L**.

S   L   1. It is when the Moon's shadow falls on Earth.

S   L   2. It is when the Earth's shadow falls on the Moon.

S   L   3. It only covers a small part of Earth.

S   L   4. It may confuse birds into thinking night has come.

S   L   5. It can be seen from anywhere on Earth's night side.

To the Parent . . .   **Scripture Connection:** Psalms 91:4

Lesson Focus:
Eclipses

Lesson Objective:
To explore how solar and lunar eclipses occur.

National Science Education Standards:
Standard D2 — *"All students should develop an understanding of objects in the sky . . . the Sun, Moon, stars . . . all have properties, locations, and movements that can be observed and described . . ."*

Follow-up Questions:
Ask your child what causes a solar eclipse (the Moon gets between Earth and the Sun).
Ask your child what causes a lunar eclipse (the Earth gets between the Sun and Moon).
Ask your child which one is more commonly seen (lunar: they can be seen from anywhere on Earth's night side).

FOCUS Solar Energy

OBJECTIVE To explore how color can reflect or absorb sunlight

OVERVIEW Some colors reflect light. Some colors absorb light. When the light from the sun is absorbed, it can create heat energy.

WHAT TO DO

With your team, carefully follow each step below.

Observe

Look at the two tubes. Remove their caps and look inside. Think about how the tubes are similar. Think about how the tubes are different.

Describe

Describe the two tubes. What do they look like? What do they feel like? What shape are they? How strong are they? What color is each tube?

Discuss

What word can mean "bounce off"? reflect
What word can mean "to take in"? absorb
What can help reflect or absorb sunlight? color

EARTH · 97

National Standards
Focus: D2

Related: A1, A2, B2, D3

Category
Earth Science

Focus
Solar Energy

Objective
To explore how color can reflect or absorb sunlight

Overview
Read the overview aloud to your students. The goal is to create an atmosphere of curiosity and inquiry.

Say: *"Some colors reflect light. Some colors absorb light. When the light from the sun is absorbed, it can create heat energy."*

Additional Notes

To introduce this lesson, ask your students if they've ever stepped onto a parking lot barefoot in the middle of the summer. Say, *"Did it burn your feet? Did you quickly jump back onto the grass?"*

Compare the temperature of the soft green grass to the temperature of the hard black parking lot. Discuss a few of the reasons the surface of a lawn might be cooler than the surface of an asphalt parking lot, even though both are in direct sunlight (differences in color, differences in the materials, differences in the kind of surface, etc.).

Say, *"In this lesson we're going to explore how one characteristic, color, can make one thing get much hotter than another."*

What To Do

Once students are seated in "research teams" with materials in front of them, read the first section (OBSERVE) aloud.

Say, *"To start this lesson, we're going to **observe** some things. Good scientists always carefully examine the things they will be working with before beginning. First, I will read the instructions to you. Then you can follow the instructions as you **observe** the items in front of you."*

Monitor teams closely as they follow instructions. When teams are finished with this section, repeat the process with the DESCRIBE section. Conclude with the DISCUSS section.

Options

Expand the DISCUSS section by having students trace dotted "key words" using crayons or markers. Trace the word **reflect** in silver, the word **absorb** in black, and the word **color** using a different color for each letter.

FOCUS   Solar Energy

OBJECTIVE   To explore how color can reflect or absorb sunlight

OVERVIEW   Some colors reflect light. Some colors absorb light. When the light from the sun is absorbed, it can create heat energy.

WHAT TO DO

With your team, carefully follow each step below.

Observe

Look at the two tubes. **Remove** their caps and look inside. **Think** about how the tubes are similar. **Think** about how the tubes are different.

Describe

Describe the two tubes. What do they **look** like? What do they **feel** like? What **shape** are they? How **strong** are they? What **color** is each tube?

Discuss

What word can mean "bounce off"? reflect

What word can mean "to take in"? absorb

What can help reflect or absorb sunlight? color

EARTH · 97

Teacher to Teacher

Here's an opportunity to clear up a common misconception.

Since there's 93 million miles of freezingly cold space between the Earth and Sun, we don't actually get HEAT from the Sun.

What really happens is that the LIGHT from the Sun passes through our atmosphere and hits things. As this light is absorbed, it is changed into heat.

How much heat an object absorbs (and releases) depends on factors like color, composition, air flow, etc. Park a car with dark leather seats in direct sunlight — even on a cool day — and you'll quickly discover how extremely efficient some combinations can be!

READ THE STORY

Some colors **reflect** light. Some colors **absorb** light. Read the story below to find out what happens when sunlight strikes different colors.

Solar Energy

Scientists call energy from the Sun "solar energy." Solar energy is created by sunlight. When sunlight is absorbed, it can create heat (one form of energy). An object's color can affect how much light it absorbs.

Light can create heat.

Heat *cannot* travel through space.
Even though the Sun is very hot, it is too far away for its heat to affect Earth. The heat of the Sun cannot reach us.

But light *can* travel through space.
Light from the Sun travels through space to strike the Earth. This light is absorbed by many objects on Earth.

Colors absorb or reflect light.

Dark colors can absorb sunlight.
Dark, dull colors (like flat black) can absorb light. When sunlight is absorbed, it can create heat, making an object hot.

Light colors can reflect sunlight.
Light, shiny colors (like glossy white) reflect light. When sunlight is reflected, it can keep an object from getting hot.

Colors can affect comfort.

A white shirt can help keep you cool.
Since white reflects sunlight, a white shirt keeps you cooler if you're in the sun. Many people wear white clothes in summer.

A black shirt can help keep you warm.
Since black absorbs sunlight, a black shirt can be warmer than a white shirt. Many people prefer dark clothes in the fall.

98 · EARTH

Extended Teaching

1. To expand vocabulary, talk about "energy" as the capacity to do work. Solar energy (energy from the Sun) can be used for heating, generating electricity, and cooking. Scientists are constantly searching for new ways to harness the endless power of the Sun.

2. Encourage students to use the Internet to find out more about solar energy, solar houses, and ways of trapping solar energy.

3. Challenge students to wear different colored clothes to find out how color can affect comfort. Ask, *"Why do people usually wear light-colored clothes in the summer and darker clothes in the winter?"*

4. If your class is more advanced, challenge student research teams to paint the tubes from this activity with other colors (yellow, dark blue, etc.) and finishes (flat to glossy), then repeat the activity, recording how color and surface affect the efficiency of light's conversion to heat.

Inform - Day 2

Read The Story

Read the story aloud with your students. (See READING LEVELS on page 12.) After reading, monitor teams as they discuss what was read. Once you feel students have mastered the basic concepts, have them answer the comprehension questions (**What I Learned** - part 1) on the next page.

To introduce the story, say:

"The title of this story is 'Solar Energy.' Look at your story and follow along as we read it together."

If you wish, encourage Emergent readers to point to words and pictures as you read.

What I Learned (part 1)

These are basic fact-based comprehension questions. Student answers will vary, but suggested responses include:

① Dark colors absorb sunlight. When sunlight is absorbed, it is changed into heat

② a) both are colors b) black absorbs light; white reflects light

③ a) light yellow b) yellow is a much lighter color than dark blue, so it would reflect more light

Field Trip

Visit a greenhouse to find out the tricks they use to wring all the heat they can from sunlight and how they cool the greenhouse quickly on a day that's too sunny.

Guest Speaker

Invite a builder of energy-efficient homes, or a resident of a "solar home" to visit your class. Ask him/her to talk about ways the Sun can help reduce home energy costs.

Materials Needed*

black tube with lid   water
white tube with lid
construction paper - white

Safety Concerns

4. Slipping

There is a potential for spilled liquids. Remind students to exercise caution.

4. Other

Remind students to never look directly at the Sun!

Do the Activity

Read the activity in advance so you understand it thoroughly. (If time allows, try it yourself.) Before students begin, carefully go over the **Safety Concerns** together.

Pass out materials, then have your students follow along as you read the instructions for **Step 1**. Monitor teams closely as they complete this step.

Once teams have completed **Step 1**, read instructions for **Step 2**. Monitor teams as before. Repeat for **Step 3** and **Step 4**.

After the activity, allow time for each team to share their observations. To encourage higher-level thinking, encourage teams to not only share their observations with each other, but also with other teams.

Special Instructions

Step 1 - A paper cup (pinched to make a spout) may make pouring easier. You may substitute the phrase "finger width" for the "half inch" instruction if desired.

Step 2 - This step requires a sunny, protected location. A wide windowsill works great. Be sure the tubes are in direct sunlight (not just a bright spot)!

Step 3 - Remind students to remove the caps carefully to avoid spilling water.

Step 4 - Temperature variations may be minimal if air is cool or clouds interfere.

Bold-faced items supplied in kit.

  DO THE ACTIVITY
Working with your research team, carefully follow each step below. Before you start, be sure you know the **safety rules** for this activity.

STEP 1 Fill the black tube almost full of water. (**Leave** about a half inch of air at the top.) **Replace** the cap and tighten it. **Repeat** with the clear tube.

STEP 2 **Place** one sheet of white construction paper in the direct sun. **Lay** both tubes on the paper as shown. **Leave** the tubes in the sun for at least two hours.

STEP 3 **Touch** a finger to the water in the white tube to test its temperature. **Repeat** using the black tube. Make sure everyone on your team has a turn.

STEP 4 **Discuss** your findings. What was the only variable (difference) between the tubes? **Compare** your observations with those of other research teams.

100 · EARTH   Copyright ©2006 The Concerned Group, Inc. All rights reserved.

What Happened?

Immediately following the activity, help your students understand what they observed.

Say: "*In this activity, you explored how color can reflect or absorb sunlight, resulting in heat.*

In Step 1, you filled two tubes with water, and you observed that the only difference between the tubes was that they were different colors.

In Step 2, you exposed the tubes to direct sunlight for a period of time.

In Step 3, you tested the difference in heat absorbed by each tube. You discovered that dark colors absorb more light than light colors, resulting in more heat.

Finally in Step 4, you shared and compared findings with those of other research teams."

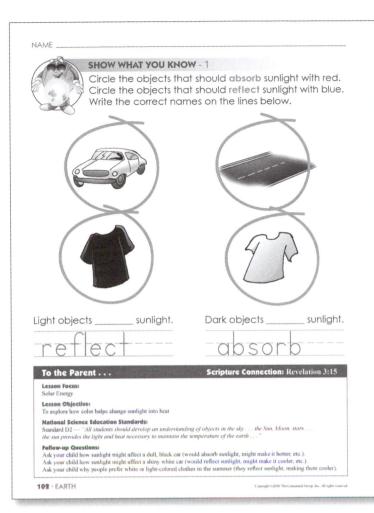

NAME _____

SHOW WHAT YOU KNOW - 1
Circle the objects that should **absorb** sunlight with red.
Circle the objects that should **reflect** sunlight with blue.
Write the correct names on the lines below.

Light objects _____ sunlight.
reflect

Dark objects _____ sunlight.
absorb

To the Parent . . .   **Scripture Connection:** Revelation 3:15

Lesson Focus:
Solar Energy

Lesson Objective:
To explore how color helps change sunlight into heat

National Science Education Standards:
Standard D2 — "All students should develop an understanding of objects in the sky . . . the Sun, Moon, stars . . . the sun provides the light and heat necessary to maintain the temperature of the earth . . ."

Follow-up Questions:
Ask your child how sunlight might affect a dull, black car (would absorb sunlight, might make it hotter, etc.).
Ask your child how sunlight might affect a shiny white car (would reflect sunlight, might make it cooler, etc.).
Ask your child why people prefer white or light-colored clothes in the summer (they reflect sunlight, making them cooler).

102 · EARTH

Food For Thought

A related "Scripture Object Lesson" you can share with your students.

Revelation 3:15

Do you like to drink hot chocolate on a cold winter's day? And when you come in from playing in the snow, doesn't soaking in a hot bath feel great?

But imagine what it would be like if the hot chocolate was only lukewarm . . . or if the bathtub was filled with water that wasn't hot at all. Ugh! That wouldn't be very nice, would it?

This Scripture talks about our relationship with God — whether our faith is hot, cold, or lukewarm. God doesn't want lukewarm relationships! He doesn't want us to just "sort of" believe in Him.

God wants enthusiastic believers who will share their faith and love for Him with others. What's the temperature of your faith today?

Expand - Day 4

Begin **Day 4** with a review of **Day 3**, then have students answer "part 2" questions.

What I Learned (part 2)

These are higher-level cognitive questions (explain, compare, predict). Student answers will vary but suggested responses may include:

1 light from the Sun

2 a) same size, same shape, same contents, etc. b) one black, one white

3 a) black car b) because black absorbs more sunlight, creating heat

Assess - Day 5

Suggestions for modifying assessments to reflect reading levels can be found under ASSESSMENT METHODS on page 12.

Show What You Know 1
(general assessment in Student Worktext)

Blanks: 1) reflect 2) absorb
Also, the shirt and road should be circled in red, the car and roof should be circled in blue

Show What You Know 2
(optional test master in Teacher Guide)

1) T   2) F   3) F   4) T   5) T

To The Parent
Included at the bottom of all assessment tests, "To The Parent" provides a great way to solicit parent involvement. It not only gives parents an overview of the lesson, but also provides follow-up questions for home use.

NAME _____

Show What You Know 2

Read each sentence below. If the sentence is true, circle the letter **T**. If the sentence is false, circle the letter **F**.

T   F   1. Energy that comes from the Sun is called "solar" energy.

T   F   2. Dark colors reflect sunlight. This makes objects hot.

T   F   3. Light colors absorb sunlight. This keeps objects cool.

T   F   4. Wearing white in the summer might keep you cooler.

T   F   5. Light from the Sun can be absorbed, resulting in heat.

To the Parent . . .   **Scripture Connection:** Revelation 3:15

Lesson Focus:
Solar Energy

Lesson Objective:
To explore how color helps change sunlight into heat.

National Science Education Standards:
Standard D2 — *"All students should develop an understanding of objects in the sky . . . the Sun, Moon, stars . . . the Sun provides the light and heat necessary to maintain the temperature of the Earth . . ."*

Follow-up Questions:
Ask your child how sunlight might affect a dull, black car (would absorb light, might make it hotter, etc.).
Ask your child how sunlight might affect a shiny white car (would reflect light, might make it cooler, etc.).
Ask your child why people prefer white or light-colored clothes in the summer (reflect sunlight, making them cooler).

Day & Night
Lesson 16

FOCUS	Day and Night
OBJECTIVE	To explore how Earth's rotation causes day and night
OVERVIEW	As the Earth spins (rotates), different parts of the Earth face the Sun. This makes it seem as if the Sun is moving across the sky, creating what we call day and night.

WHAT TO DO

With your team, carefully follow each step below.

Observe

Look at the sky in the early morning. Look at the sky at noon. Look at the sky in the evening. Think about where the Sun appears at each of these times.

Describe

Describe the Sun in the morning, noon, and evening. What does it look like? How does it make the sky change? Describe different sunsets you have seen.

Discuss

What is the Earth's spin called? rotation
Where does the Sun appear in the morning? east
Where does the Sun appear at sunset? west

EARTH · 103

Lesson 16

Introduction

National Standards
Focus: D3

Related: A1, A2, B2, D2, F4

Category
Earth Science

Focus
Day and Night

Objective
To explore how Earth's rotation causes day and night

Overview
Read the overview aloud to your students. The goal is to create an atmosphere of curiosity and inquiry.

Say: *"As the Earth spins (rotates), different parts of the Earth face the Sun. This makes it seem as if the Sun is moving across the sky, creating what we call day and night."*

Additional Notes

To introduce this lesson, ask your students, "How many of you enjoyed your ride last night?" Most students will look confused thinking, they missed something.

Explain that as they were sleeping last night, they were actually traveling at about 1,000 miles per hour as the surface of Earth was spin-ning around and around!

We don't notice this, of course, because everything around us is also "along for the ride." In this lesson, we'll take a look at how the ride provided by Earth's rotation gives us the time periods that we call "day and night."

Engage - Day 1

What To Do

Once students are seated in "research teams" with materials in front of them, read the first section (OBSERVE) aloud.

Say, *"To start this lesson, we're going to think about some things we've **observed**. Good scientists always spend time thinking about the things they will study, and looking for new details to learn. First, I will read the instructions to you. Then you can follow the instructions as you think about the things you have **observed**."*

Monitor teams closely as they follow instructions. When teams are finished with this section, repeat the process with the DESCRIBE section. Conclude with the DISCUSS section.

Options

Expand the DISCUSS section by having students trace dotted "key words" using crayons or markers. Trace the word **rotation** in red, the word **east** in yellow, and the word **west** in orange.

Day & Night
Lesson 16

FOCUS   Day and Night

OBJECTIVE   To explore how Earth's rotation causes day and night

OVERVIEW   As the Earth spins (rotates), different parts of the Earth face the Sun. This makes it seem as if the Sun is moving across the sky, creating what we call day and night.

WHAT TO DO

With your team, carefully follow each step below.

Observe

Look at the sky in the early morning. **Look** at the sky at noon. **Look** at the sky in the evening. **Think** about where the Sun appears at each of these times.

Describe

Describe the Sun in the morning, noon, and evening. What does it **look** like? How does it make the sky **change**? **Describe** different sunsets you have seen.

Discuss

What is the Earth's spin called? rotation

Where does the Sun appear in the morning? east

Where does the Sun appear at sunset? west

EARTH · 103

Teacher to Teacher

"Rotation" is a turning motion around a center axis. When the Earth makes one rotation and the Sun returns to the same place in the sky, scientists call it a "solar day." This is the measurement that most of us are familiar with.

Astronomers, however, measure time in a different way. When the Earth makes one rotation and the *stars* return to the same place in the sky, it is called a "sidereal day."

What's the difference? A solar day is 24 hours. A sidereal day is about four minutes shorter! This is because Earth is moving around the Sun, and it must turn a little bit farther each day to face the Sun.

READ THE STORY

When a place on Earth faces the Sun, it is **day**. When it faces away from the Sun, it is **night**. Read the story below to learn more.

Day and Night

Earth circles the Sun.
Like the other planets in our solar system, the Earth circles the Sun. But as it circles the Sun, it also spins around and around. Scientists call this spinning motion "rotation."

Earth rotates.

One rotation takes 24 hours.
Even though it seems to be sitting still, the Earth is constantly rotating. It takes Earth 24 hours to spin around one time.

The Sun shines on Earth.
The Sun is always shining on the Earth. But as the Earth rotates, different parts face the Sun. This causes day and night.

This is day.

In the day, the sky is full of light.
When a place on Earth faces the Sun, the sky is full of light. We call this the day.

Day is an active time.
Most animals are active and awake during the day. Day is also when most humans work and play.

This is night.

At night, the sky is dark.
When a place on Earth does not face the Sun, the sky is dark. We call this the night.

Night is a quiet time.
Most animals are quiet and asleep during the night. Night is also when most humans rest and sleep.

104 · EARTH

Copyright ©2006 The Concerned Group, Inc. All rights reserved.

Extended Teaching

1. To expand vocabulary, discuss "rotation" with words like "turning," "moving around," etc. Rotation refers to motion around a center axis. Talk about other types of rotation (wheels on axles, pulleys, etc.).

2. Discuss day and night activities as if the Sun and Moon could "see." Ask students what the Sun might see on Earth. Then ask what the Moon might see. (Don't forget nocturnal animals.) Talk about how the two views are different and why.

3. Show students two thermometers and explain how to read them. Place one in direct sunlight and the other in shade. After two hours, read the thermometers. Ask how this relates to the fact that nights are typically much cooler than days.

4. Twist open Oreos® to make a great "day or night" snack. (Cookie up = night; icing up = day.)

Inform - Day 2

Read The Story

Read the story aloud with your students. (See READING LEVELS on page 12.) After reading, monitor teams as they discuss what was read. Once you feel students have mastered the basic concepts, have them answer the comprehension questions (**What I Learned** - part 1) on the next page.

To introduce the story, say:

"The title of this story is 'Day and Night.' Look at your story and follow along as we read it together."

If you wish, encourage Emergent readers to point to words and pictures as you read.

What I Learned (part 1)

These are basic fact-based comprehension questions. Student answers will vary, but suggested responses include:

① As Earth spins, different parts of the Earth face the Sun.

② a) the sky is dark b) the area is still facing the Sun on a cloudy day; it is not facing the Sun at night.

③ a) days and nights would be longer b) it would take longer to spin around

Field Trip

Visit a local greenhouse. Find out how plants are affected by daylight and dark. Ask what happens when there are long periods of cloudy weather.

Guest Speaker

Invite an astronomer from a local observatory or university to visit your class. Ask him/her to discuss the measurement of time in a day using the stars. Have them bring pictures of a sidereal clock and explain its use.

Copyright ©2006 The Concerned Group, Inc. All rights reserved.

DAY & NIGHT · 113

Materials Needed*

polystyrene ball   paint brush
tempera paints   dowel rod
push pin   lamp

Safety Concerns

2. Thermal Burn

Keep students away from the lamp bulb.

4. Slipping

There is a potential for spilled liquids. Remind students to exercise caution.

4. Sharp Objects

Remind students to exercise caution when pushing the ball onto the dowel rod. Also carefully monitor use of push pins.

Do the Activity

Read the activity in advance so you understand it thoroughly. (If time allows, try it yourself.) Before students begin, carefully go over the **Safety Concerns** together.

Pass out materials, then have your students follow along as you read the instructions for **Step 1**. Monitor teams closely as they complete this step.

Once teams have completed **Step 1**, read instructions for **Step 2**. Monitor teams as before. Repeat for **Step 3** and **Step 4**.

After the activity, allow time for each team to share their observations. To encourage higher-level thinking, encourage teams to not only share their observations with each other, but also with other teams.

Special Instructions

Step 1 - You may wish to wait a day after Step 1 to let paint dry. Or have students insert the dowel rod (Step 2) before beginning Step 1 for easier painting.

Step 2 - Place a sticker on the classroom globe to show your town. This will help teams place push pins correctly on their "Earths."

Step 3 - Put tape on the floor to mark the 6' distance. Remind students to look at their "Earth," never at the lamp (or the Sun).

Bold-faced items supplied in kit.

DO THE ACTIVITY

Working with your research team, carefully follow each step below. Before you start, be sure you know the **safety rules** for this activity.

STEP 1
Paint your ball to look like Earth. Use blue for water and green for land. Paint a little white at the top and bottom (for ice at the North and South poles).

STEP 2
Look at a globe. Tilt your Earth slightly like the globe, then push your Earth gently down onto the dowel rod. Attach a push pin to show where you live.

STEP 3
Stand about six feet from the lamp (dark room). Slowly rotate your Earth. Look where the light ends and watch the push pin move into and out of the light.

STEP 4
Discuss what an ant standing on the push pin would have seen from your Earth. Compare your observations with those of other research teams.

What Happened?

Immediately following the activity, help your students understand what they observed.

Say: *"In this activity you were able to explore how Earth's rotation causes day and night.*

*In **Step 1**, you created a model of the Earth.*

*In **Step 2**, you marked where you live.*

*In **Step 3**, you modeled the rotation of the Earth as different parts of the Earth face the Sun.*

*In **Step 4**, you thought about what it would be like to be standing on your model and discussed what you might see from there. Finally, you compared the observations that you made with those of other research teams."*

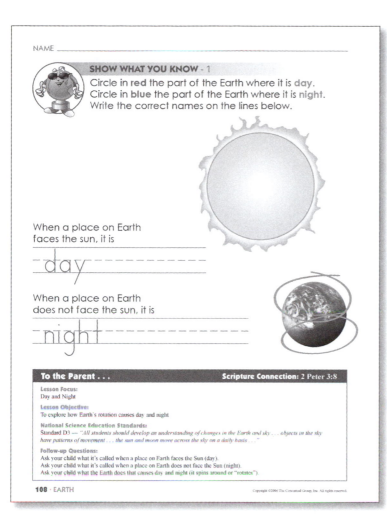

NAME _____

SHOW WHAT YOU KNOW - 1
Circle in **red** the part of the Earth where it is **day**.
Circle in **blue** the part of the Earth where it is **night**.
Write the correct names on the lines below.

When a place on Earth
faces the sun, it is

day

When a place on Earth
does not face the sun, it is

night

Food For Thought

A related "Scripture Object Lesson" you can share with your students.

2 Peter 3:8

Has there ever been a time when you could hardly wait for some special day? Maybe it was an upcoming birthday, or a vacation, or a holiday. Time seemed to drag by very, very slowly.

But when the long anticipated day finally arrived, you enjoyed it so much that the long wait was worth it!

Sometimes we have to wait on special things from God. Perhaps it's a prayer request or a change we need God to help us make. We may think God isn't being quick enough.

But God sees time in a different way — and His timing is always perfect! Put your trust in Him, and He will meet your need "just in time."

Expand - Day 4

Begin **Day 4** with a review of **Day 3**, then have students answer "part 2" questions.

What I Learned (part 2)

These are higher-level cognitive questions (explain, compare, predict). Student answers will vary but suggested responses may include:

1 a) Earth b) the Sun

2 a) it is marked like Earth; it is round, it moves; etc. b) it is not real; it is much smaller; nothing living on it; etc.

3 a) there would be only day or only night depending on where you were b) without rotation, the same part of the Earth would always face the Sun.

Assess - Day 5

Suggestions for modifying assessments to reflect reading levels can be found under ASSESSMENT METHODS on page 12.

Show What You Know 1

(general assessment in Student Worktext)

Blanks: 1) day 2) night
Also, the top part of Earth should be circled in red; the bottom part should be circled in blue.

Show What You Know 2

(optional test master in Teacher Guide)

1) Sun   2) night   3) day
4) Earth   5) rotation

To The Parent

Included at the bottom of all assessment tests, "To The Parent" provides a great way to solicit parent involvement. It not only gives parents an overview of the lesson, but also provides follow-up questions for home use.

NAME _____

Show What You Know 2

Read each sentence below. Draw a circle around the word that best completes the sentence.

1. Earth spins around as it circles the (Sun   Moon).

2. When a place on Earth does not face the Sun, it is (day   night).

3. Most animals are active and awake during the (night   day).

4. The Sun is always shining on the (Earth   Moon).

5. This spinning motion of Earth is called (circulation   rotation).

To the Parent . . .   **Scripture Connection:** 2 Peter 3:8

Lesson Focus:
Day and Night

Lesson Objective:
To explore how Earth's rotation causes day and night

National Science Education Standards:
Standard D3 — *"All students should develop an understanding of changes in the Earth and sky . . . objects in the sky have patterns of movement . . . the Sun and Moon move across the sky on a daily basis . . ."*

Follow-up Questions:
Ask your child what it's called when a place on Earth faces the Sun (day).
Ask your child what it's called when a place on Earth does not face the Sun (night).
Ask your child what the Earth does that causes day and night (it spins around or "rotates").

Months & Moons
Lesson 17

FOCUS	Moon Phases
OBJECTIVE	To explore how a month relates to the Moon's movement around Earth
OVERVIEW	A month is roughly equal to one complete trip (revolution) of the Moon around the Earth. Throughout the month, the Moon appears to change shapes.

WHAT TO DO

With your team, carefully follow each step below.

Observe

Look at the pictures of the Moon on page 110. Think about how these pictures are different. Look closely at the shape of the Moon in each picture.

Describe

Describe the Moon. What does it look like? What might its surface feel like? Describe different shapes or colors you've seen in the Moon on different nights.

Discuss

What large object circles around the Earth? Moon

About how long does one trip take? month

What seems to change about the Moon? shape

EARTH · 109

Lesson 17

Introduction

National Standards
Focus: D3

Related: A1, A2, B2, D2, F4

Category
Earth Science

Focus
Moon Phases

Objective
To explore how a month relates to the Moon's movement around Earth

Overview
Read the overview aloud to your students. The goal is to create an atmosphere of curiosity and inquiry.

Say: *"A month is roughly equal to one complete trip (revolution) of the Moon around the Earth. Throughout the month, the Moon appears to change shapes."*

Additional Notes

To introduce this lesson, ask your students what month they were born. As they say the names of the months, make a list on the board. When you're finished, ask them if any months are missing.

Now ask them what month contains the Thanksgiving holiday. Continue by connecting other holidays and events to months.

Once you have explored the relationship of time, events, and months, rhetorically ask students "Why is a month about 30 days? Why not 60 days? Why not 10?"

Then tell them, "In this lesson, we're going to learn how the movement of the Moon relates to the time periods that we call months."

What To Do

Once students are seated in "research teams" with materials in front of them, read the first section (OBSERVE) aloud.

Say, *"To start this lesson, we're going to* **observe** *some pictures. Although they are pictures of the same thing, notice that they are also different! First, I will read the instructions to you. Then you can follow the instructions as you look at the pictures in front of you."*

Monitor teams closely as they follow instructions. When teams are finished with this section, repeat the process with the DESCRIBE section. Conclude with the DISCUSS section.

Options

Expand the DISCUSS section by having students trace dotted "key words" using crayons or markers. Trace the word **Moon** in orange, the word **month** in blue, and the word **shape** in green.

Months & Moons
Lesson 17

FOCUS   Moon Phases

OBJECTIVE   To explore how a month relates to the Moon's movement around Earth

OVERVIEW   A month is roughly equal to one complete trip (revolution) of the Moon around the Earth. Throughout the month, the Moon appears to change shapes.

WHAT TO DO

With your team, carefully follow each step below.

Observe

Look at the pictures of the Moon on page 110. **Think** about how these pictures are different. **Look** closely at the shape of the Moon in each picture.

Describe

Describe the Moon. What does it **look** like? What might its surface **feel** like? **Describe** different **shapes** or **colors** you've seen in the Moon on different nights.

Discuss

What large object circles around the Earth? Moon

About how long does one trip take? month

What seems to change about the Moon? shape

EARTH · 109

Teacher to Teacher

A "moon" is a natural satellite of a planet. Scientists tell us that there are about 140 moons in our solar system. These moons come in a wide range of sizes and have many different characteristics.

Almost all of our solar system's moons are tidally locked to their planets. This means that the same side of the moon always faces its partner planet.

There are many variations. Earth has one of the biggest moons. Jupiter has four large moons and dozens of smaller ones. And Pluto's moon, Charon, is so big that some astronomers even refer to the combination as a double planet!

READ THE STORY

The time periods that we call **months** are roughly based on the movement of the **Moon** around the Earth. Read the story below to learn more.

Months and Moons

Ancient people used the Moon to measure time.
A month is a unit of time roughly based on how long it takes the Moon to circle Earth. In fact, the word "month" comes from an ancient word meaning "moon."

The Moon has phases.

The Moon seems to change shapes.
As it circles Earth, the Moon seems to change shapes. These different shapes are called "phases."

Each phase looks different.
This is because we see the bright part of the Moon from different angles. There are four major shapes in each cycle.

These are beginning phases.

This is the "new" Moon.
When the Moon is between the Sun and the Earth, we can not see the bright side of the Moon. The part facing us is dark.

This is the "first quarter" Moon.
A week after "new moon," the Moon is a quarter of the way around Earth. We can see only half of the bright part.

These are ending phases.

This is the "full" Moon.
Two weeks after "new moon," the Moon is halfway around Earth. Only now can we see all the bright side of the Moon.

This is the "last quarter" Moon.
Three weeks after "new moon," the Moon is three-quarters of the way around Earth. Soon the cycle will begin over again.

110 · EARTH

Copyright ©2006 The Concerned Group, Inc. All rights reserved.

Extended Teaching

1. To expand vocabulary, explain that the word "phase" means any stage in a series or cycle of changes.

2. Each moon cycle is actually 29.53 days long. It includes four minor phases not covered in the Student Worktext: Waxing Crescent (the first thin sliver of moon), Waxing Gibbous (a three-quarter moon), Waning Gibbous (back to three-quarters), and Waning Crescent (the last thin sliver before the next new moon).

3. A "new" Moon rises and sets with the Sun. It is only visible near sunrise and sunset, and then only as a dim darkened disk. A "full" Moon rises at sunset and sets at sunrise. It is very bright and dominates the night sky.

4. Using an almanac, help your students keep track of Moon phases. Encourage their parents to take them out each night to see the changing Moon. Have students draw a picture each night to record slight changes. Continue to keep a "Moon Journal" for 29 nights.

Inform - Day 2

Read The Story

Read the story aloud with your students. (See READING LEVELS on page 12.) After reading, monitor teams as they discuss what was read. Once you feel students have mastered the basic concepts, have them answer the comprehension questions (**What I Learned** - part 1) on the next page.

To introduce the story, say:

"The title of this story is 'Months and Moons.' Look at your story and follow along as we read it together."

If you wish, encourage Emergent readers to point to words and pictures as you read.

What I Learned (part 1)

These are basic fact-based comprehension questions. Student answers will vary, but suggested responses include:

(1) a month is about how long it takes the Moon to circle the Earth

(2) a "new" Moon is all dark; a "full" Moon is all bright

(3) because of the light reflected from the full Moon, it would be much brighter than other nights

Field Trip

Visit a local planetarium. Ask for a presentation about the phases of the Moon.

Guest Speaker

Invite an astronomer from an observatory or an astronomy professor from a university to visit your class. Ask him/her to bring slides of the phases of the Moon and discuss the relationship of the Moon and the Earth during each phase.

Copyright ©2006 The Concerned Group, Inc. All rights reserved.

Materials Needed*

polystyrene ball   paint brush
tempera paints   dowel rod
lamp

Safety Concerns

4. Slipping

There is a potential for falls in a dark room. Remind students to exercise caution.

4. Sharp Objects

Remind students to exercise caution when pushing the ball onto the dowel rod.

Do the Activity

Read the activity in advance so you understand it thoroughly. (If time allows, try it yourself.) Before students begin, carefully go over the **Safety Concerns** together.

Pass out materials, then have your students follow along as you read the instructions for **Step 1**. Monitor teams closely as they complete this step.

Once teams have completed **Step 1**, read instructions for **Step 2**. Monitor teams as before. Repeat for **Step 3** and **Step 4**.

After the activity, allow time for each team to share their observations. To encourage higher-level thinking, encourage teams to not only share their observations with each other, but also with other teams.

Special Instructions

Step 1 - Have students paint the entire ball tan, then use the brown for accents (craters, mountains, etc.).

Step 2 - Put tape on the floor to mark the six foot distance. Remind students to look at their "Moon," never directly at the lamp.

Step 3 - Demonstrate what "counter-clockwise" means, spinning slowly to your left.

DO THE ACTIVITY
Working with your research team, carefully follow each step below. Before you start, be sure you know the **safety rules** for this activity.

STEP 1
Push the ball gently down onto the dowel rod. **Paint** it to look like the Moon (browns and light tans). **Dry** it overnight. (This will be your moon model.)

STEP 2
Stand about six feet from the lamp (dark room). **Hold** your moon in front of you, slightly above your head (the Earth). Now **face** the "sun" (lamp).

STEP 3
Slowly **rotate** counter-clockwise, holding your moon in front of you. **Watch** your moon to see how it changes. **Repeat** until everyone has had a turn.

STEP 4
Discuss what happened to your moon. How did the light seem to change your moon's shape? **Compare** your observations with those of other research teams.

112 · EARTH   Copyright ©2006 The Concerned Group, Inc. All rights reserved.

What Happened?

Immediately following the activity, help your students understand what they observed.

Say: *"In this activity you were able to explore how the Moon's trip around Earth makes its shape appear to change, and that one cycle of changes takes about a month.*

*In **Step 1**, you created a model of the Moon.*

*In **Steps 2** and **3**, you modeled the Moon's orbit around the Earth, and you saw how the Moon appears to change shapes as time passes.*

*Finally, in **Step 4**, you discussed how light from the Sun creates the Moon's "phases," then you compared your observations about the Moon with those of other research teams."*

---

* Bold-faced items supplied in kit.

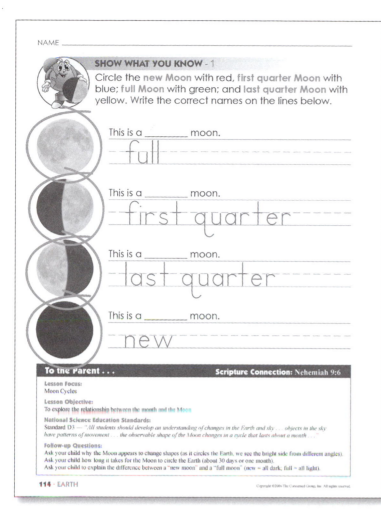

NAME _____

SHOW WHAT YOU KNOW - 1
Circle the **new Moon** with red, **first quarter Moon** with blue; **full Moon** with green; and **last quarter Moon** with yellow. Write the correct names on the lines below.

This is a _____ moon.
full

This is a _____ moon.
first quarter

This is a _____ moon.
last quarter

This is a _____ moon.
new

To the Parent . . .   **Scripture Connection:** Nehemiah 9:6

Lesson Focus:
Moon Cycles

Lesson Objective:
To explore the relationship between the month and the Moon

National Science Education Standards:
Standard D3 — "All students should develop an understanding of changes in the Earth and sky . . . objects in the sky have patterns of movement . . . the observable shape of the Moon changes in a cycle that lasts about a month . . ."

Follow-up Questions:
Ask your child why the Moon appears to change shapes (as it circles the Earth, we see the bright side from different angles).
Ask your child how long it takes for the Moon to circle the Earth (about 30 days or one month).
Ask your child to explain the difference between a "new moon" and a "full moon" (new = all dark, full = all light).

114 - EARTH

Food For Thought

A related "Scripture Object Lesson" you can share with your students.

Nehemiah 9:6

Have you heard the old phrase "once in a blue moon"?

People use these words to describe things that don't happen very often. The idea comes from the fact that sometimes a full Moon occurs twice during the same month. The second appearance is called a "blue" Moon.

Astronomers tell us this happens only once every two-and-a-half or three years!

Aren't you glad we can talk to God every day, not just "once in a blue moon"? We can see God through His handiwork of nature. We can hear Him in the words of Jesus. We can listen to Him through prayer and meditation. What a blessing daily contact with God can be!

Expand - Day 4

Begin **Day 4** with a review of **Day 3**, then have students answer "part 2" questions.

What I Learned (part 2)
These are higher-level cognitive questions (explain, compare, predict). Student answers will vary but suggested responses may include:

1 a) Moon (or ball) b) Sun (or lamp)

2 a) both are half moons b) first quarter moon lights up the right side of the Moon; last quarter moon lights up the left side

3 Earth's shadow would make the Moon dark; there would be an eclipse

Assess - Day 5

Suggestions for modifying assessments to reflect reading levels can be found under ASSESSMENT OPTIONS on page 12.

Show What You Know 1
(general assessment in Student Worktext)

Blanks: 1) full 2) first quarter 3) last quarter 4) new

Also, first illustration should be circled in green, second in blue, third in yellow, and fourth in red

Show What You Know 2
(optional test master in Teacher Guide)

1) Moon 2) month 3) shapes
4) new   5) full

To The Parent
Included at the bottom of all assessment tests, "To The Parent" provides a great way to solicit parent involvement. It not only gives parents an overview of the lesson, but also provides follow-up questions for home use.

NAME _____

Show What You Know 2

Read each sentence below. Using the **word bank**, choose the best word to complete each sentence, then write it on the line. (Some words will not be used.)

1. The _____ orbits (circles around) the Earth.

2. It takes about one _____ from one full Moon to the next.

3. Through the month, the Moon seems to change _____ .

4. A _____ Moon is very dark. We cannot see the light side.

5. A _____ Moon is very bright. It reflects the light of the Sun.

WORD BANK:

shapes　　Moon　　Earth　　full　　week　　new　　month　　year

To the Parent . . .　　　　**Scripture Connection:** Nehemiah 9:6

Lesson Focus:
Moon Cycles

Lesson Objective:
To explore the relationship between the month and the Moon

National Science Education Standards:
Standard D3 — *"All students should develop an understanding of changes in the Earth and sky . . . objects in the sky have patterns of movement . . . the observable shape of the Moon changes in a cycle that lasts about a month . . ."*

Follow-up Questions:
Ask your child why the Moon appears to change shapes (as it circles Earth, we see the bright side from different angles).
Ask your child how long it takes for the Moon to circle the Earth (about 30 days or 1 month).
Ask your child to explain the difference between a "new moon" and a "full moon" (new = all dark; full = all light).

Lesson 18

Introduction

National Standards
Focus: D3

Related: A1, A2, B2, D2, F4

Category
Earth Science

Focus
Seasons

Objective
To explore how seasons relate to Earth's movement around the Sun

Overview
Read the overview aloud to your students. The goal is to create an atmosphere of curiosity and inquiry.

Say: *"A year is equal to one complete trip (revolution) of the Earth around the Sun. During this 12-month cycle, the angle of sunlight hitting the Earth changes, creating weather patterns we call seasons."*

Years & Seasons
Lesson 18

FOCUS	Seasons
OBJECTIVE	To explore how seasons relate to Earth's movement around the Sun
OVERVIEW	A year is equal to one complete trip (revolution) of the Earth around the Sun. During this 12-month cycle, the angle of sunlight hitting the Earth changes, creating weather patterns we call seasons.

WHAT TO DO

With your team, carefully follow each step below.

Observe

Look at the pictures of the seasons on page 120. Think about how these pictures are different. Think about something you might do in each season.

Describe

Describe a day in spring. What would it **look** like? What would it **feel** like? Now describe a day for each of the other seasons (summer, fall, winter).

Discuss

What does the Earth revolve around? the Sun

How long does one complete trip take? a year

How long is a year? twelve months

EARTH · 115

Additional Notes

To introduce this lesson, begin by reciting this familiar line: *"April showers bring May flowers."*

Ask your students if they know what this is talking about. Discuss the fact that our lives are affected in many ways by the changing of the seasons.

We usually think of the seasons in terms of weather changes (winter, spring, summer, fall).

But tell students seasons actually come from the relationship of the Earth's tilt to the Sun. Weather is just one result. In this lesson, we'll find out how it all works!

What To Do

Once students are seated in "research teams" with materials in front of them, read the first section (OBSERVE) aloud.

Say, *"To start this lesson, we're going to **observe** some pictures. Notice that the pictures are all different! First, I will read the instructions to you. Then you can follow the instructions as you look at the pictures in front of you."*

Monitor teams closely as they follow instructions. When teams are finished with this section, repeat the process with the DESCRIBE section. Conclude with the DISCUSS section.

Options

Expand the DISCUSS section by having students trace dotted "key words" using crayons or markers. Trace the words **the Sun** in yellow, the words **a year** in red, and the words **twelve months** using a different color for each letter (for a total of 12 colors).

Years & Seasons
Lesson 18

FOCUS	Seasons
OBJECTIVE	To explore how seasons relate to Earth's movement around the Sun
OVERVIEW	A year is equal to one complete trip (revolution) of the Earth around the Sun. During this 12-month cycle, the angle of sunlight hitting the Earth changes, creating weather patterns we call seasons.

WHAT TO DO

With your team, carefully follow each step below.

Observe

Look at the pictures of the seasons on page 120.

Think about how these pictures are different. **Think** about something you might do in each season.

Describe

Describe a day in spring. What would it **look** like? What would it **feel** like? Now **describe** a day for each of the other seasons (summer, fall, winter).

Discuss

What does the Earth revolve around? the Sun

How long does one complete trip take? a year

How long is a year? twelve months

EARTH · 115

Teacher to Teacher

A common way to remember the number of days in each month is with the old rhyme that begins, *"Thirty days hath September."* But here's another method that may be even more helpful, especially for your kinesthetic learners!

Hold your left hand in front of you palm out. Fingers are months with 31 days; spaces are months with 30 days (except February). Start with your pinky as "January." Recite the months in order pointing to fingers and spaces until you reach your index finger and say "July." Point to it again and say "August" and begin going backwards. February is the exception (28 days or 29 in a leap year). But this is easy to remember because February's space is also the shortest!

READ THE STORY

The time periods that we call **years** are based on the movement of the **Earth** around the **Sun**. Read the story below to find out more.

Years & Seasons

The Earth circles the Sun.
It takes Earth one year (12 months) to circle the Sun. Since the Earth is tilted, the angle of sunlight hitting the Earth changes over time, creating the different seasons.

Earth moves.

One rotation takes 24 hours.
Even though it seems to be sitting still, the Earth is constantly rotating. It takes Earth one day to spin around one time.

One revolution takes 12 months.
The Earth is also moving around the Sun. It takes Earth one year (12 months) to complete its journey around the Sun.

Earth is tilted.

Earth's tilt affects the angle of sunlight.
As Earth moves around the Sun, the Earth's tilt causes sunlight to hit the Earth at different angles.

Less angle means more warmth.
Summers are warmer than winters because sunlight hits the Earth more directly. Also, the days are much longer in summer.

Seasons change.

The angle changes as Earth moves.
The angle of sunlight gradually changes because Earth is slowly moving around the Sun. This creates the seasons.

The angle creates the seasons.
Only one part of Earth tilts toward the Sun at a time. When it's summer in America, it's winter on the other side of Earth.

116 · EARTH

Extended Teaching

1. To help students better understand Earth's tilt, explain that Earth revolves on an "axis." Push a pencil through the center of a styrofoam ball. Tell students the pencil represents the axis from the North Pole to the South Pole. Show them that if the axis were straight up and down (tilt ball), then there would be no seasons because the angle of sunlight hitting Earth would always be the same.

2. To demonstrate the pulling forces of the Sun and Moon (related to Earth's tilt), use two bar magnets and a paper clip. Tell students that magnets have north and south poles. Demonstrate what happens when opposite poles and same poles come together. Now, place the paperclip (representing Earth) on the table. Slowly bring in the two magnets from opposite sides of the clip. Have students predict what might happen as the magnets get closer, then observe the power of these "invisible forces" on the paper clip.

Read The Story

Read the story aloud with your students. (See READING LEVELS on page 12.) After reading, monitor teams as they discuss what was read. Once you feel students have mastered the basic concepts, have them answer the comprehension questions (**What I Learned** - part 1) on the next page.

To introduce the story, say:

"The title of this story is 'Years and Seasons.' Look at your story and follow along as we read it together."

If you wish, encourage Emergent readers to point to words and pictures as you read.

What I Learned (part 1)

These are basic fact-based comprehension questions. Student answers will vary, but suggested responses include:

1 the Earth's tilt causes sunlight to hit the Earth at different angles. The more direct the sunlight, the warmer it gets

2 answers will vary, but should include the ideas about temperature and vegetation changes

3 there would be no seasons. The weather in one spot would be about the same all year round

Field Trip

Visit a local TV station and spend time with the meteorologist. Ask him/her to talk about how weather changes from season to season.

Guest Speaker

Invite a meteorologist to visit your class. Ask him/her to talk about how predictable weather patterns relate to seasons, but also about the unpredictable aspects of weather. Encourage him/her to bring slides to share.

YEARS & SEASONS· 125

Materials Needed*

polystyrene ball   chalk
tempera paints   paint brush
dowel rod   string

Safety Concerns

4. Slipping

There is a potential for spilled paint. Remind students to exercise caution.

4. Sharp Objects

Remind students to exercise caution when pushing the ball onto the dowel rod.

Do the Activity

Read the activity in advance so you understand it thoroughly. (If time allows, try it yourself.) Before students begin, carefully go over the **Safety Concerns** together.

Pass out materials, then have your students follow along as you read the instructions for **Step 1**. Monitor teams closely as they complete this step.

Once teams have completed **Step 1**, read instructions for **Step 2**. Monitor teams as before. Repeat for **Step 3** and **Step 4**.

After the activity, allow time for each team to share their observations. To encourage higher-level thinking, encourage teams to not only share their observations with each other, but also with other teams.

Special Instructions

Step 1 - You may wish to wait a day after Step 1 to let the paint on the ball dry.

Step 3 - Place a push pin in the "Earth" if students are having trouble determining one full rotation. Encourage a different team member to rotate the Earth for each month. (See "Teacher to Teacher," on page 124 for hints on helping students memorize how many days are in each month.)

DO THE ACTIVITY
Working with your research team, carefully follow each step below. Before you start, be sure you know the **safety rules** for this activity.

STEP 1 Paint the ball to look like Earth. Push the ball gently down onto a dowel rod. Now using the string and chalk, draw a 12-foot circle on the pavement.

STEP 2 Divide the circle in half, then divide the halves into quarters. Now divide the quarters into three equal parts. Label each section with a month's name.

STEP 3 Stand at the edge of January. As you move to the other edge, rotate your Earth once for each day in January (31). Repeat for each month in the year.

STEP 4 Discuss what this model shows us about Earth's trip around the sun. Discuss what it doesn't show us. Compare your observations with those of other teams.

118 · EARTH   Copyright ©2006 The Concerned Group, Inc. All rights reserved.

What Happened?

Immediately following the activity, help your students understand what they observed.

Say: "In this activity, you modeled Earth's twelve-month journey around the Sun.

In **Steps 1** and **2**, you divided the distance around the Sun into distinct parts, then labeled each part with the name of a month.

In **Step 3**, you showed how Earth makes a full rotation for each day in every month. By the time you finished your twelve-month trip around the Sun, your "Earth" had rotated 365 times!

In **Step 4**, you compared your observations with those of other research teams, and you shared what you'd learned about how Earth moves in its trip around the Sun."

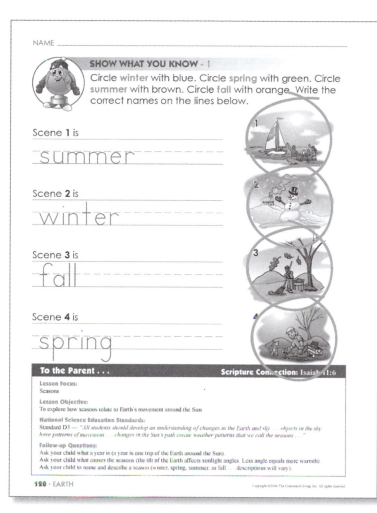

NAME _____

SHOW WHAT YOU KNOW - 1

Circle winter with blue. Circle spring with green. Circle summer with brown. Circle fall with orange. Write the correct names on the lines below.

Scene **1** is

summer

Scene **2** is

winter

Scene **3** is

fall

Scene **4** is

spring

To the Parent . . .

Scripture Connection: Isaiah 11:6

Lesson Focus:
Seasons

Lesson Objective:
To explore how seasons relate to Earth's movement around the Sun

National Science Education Standards:
Standard D3 — "All students should develop an understanding of changes in the Earth and sky . . . objects in the sky have patterns of movement . . . changes in the Sun's path create weather patterns that we call the seasons . . ."

Follow-up Questions:
Ask your child what a year is (a year is one trip of the Earth around the Sun).
Ask your child what causes the seasons (the tilt of the Earth affects sunlight angles. Less angle equals more warmth).
Ask your child to name and describe a season (winter, spring, summer, or fall . . . descriptions will vary).

Food For Thought

A related "Scripture Object Lesson" you can share with your students.

Isaiah 11:6

Have you ever heard the old phrase "March comes in like a lion, but goes out like a lamb"?

People say this because March often has the biggest weather extremes — from bitter cold winds to warm spring-like breezes.

March's beginning can be like a lion, fierce and strong. But its quieter end is more like a lamb, peaceful and calm.

Scripture talks about a place where the lion and the lamb can lie down together in peace . . . a place filled with God's love . . . a place with no more suffering and no more pain . . . a place that we know as "heaven."

Best of all, Jesus will be in Heaven, and we can spend eternity with Him!

Expand - Day 4

Begin **Day 4** with a review of **Day 3**, then have students answer "part 2" questions.

What I Learned (part 2)

These are higher-level cognitive questions (explain, compare, predict). Student answers will vary but suggested responses may include:

1 it spun around and around (rotated), and it circled the Sun (revolved)

2 a) same number of days b) tilt of Earth is different, making our Augusts hotter and our Januarys colder

3 using an "Earth" that was tilted at the correct angle; adding a bright light in the center of the circle; etc.

Assess - Day 5

Suggestions for modifying assessments to reflect reading levels can be found under ASSESSMENT METHODS on page 12.

Show What You Know 1

(general assessment in Student Worktext)

Blanks: 1) summer 2) winter 3) fall
4) spring
Also, scene 1 should be circled in brown, scene 2 in blue, scene 3 in orange, and scene 4 in green

Show What You Know 2

(optional test master in Teacher Guide)

1) F   2) T   3) F   4) T   5) T

To The Parent

Included at the bottom of all assessment tests, "To The Parent" provides a great way to solicit parent involvement. It not only gives parents an overview of the lesson, but also provides follow-up questions for home use.

NAME _____

Show What You Know 2

Read each sentence below. If the sentence is true, then circle **T**. If the sentence is false, then circle **F**.

T   F   1. It takes Earth one week to completely spin around one time.

T   F   2. The seasons occur because Earth is tilted on its axis.

T   F   3. It is hotter in the summer because Earth is closer to the Sun.

T   F   4. Earth constantly rotates on its axis as it revolves around the Sun.

T   F   5. It takes Earth one year to revolve around the Sun.

To the Parent . . .   **Scripture Connection:** Isaiah 11:6

Lesson Focus:
Seasons

Lesson Objective:
To explore how seasons relate to Earth's movement around the Sun

National Science Education Standards:
Standard D3 — *"All students should develop an understanding of changes in the Earth and sky . . . objects in the sky have patterns of movement . . . changes in the Sun's path create weather patterns that we call the seasons . . ."*

Follow-up Questions:
Ask your child what a year is (a year is one trip of the Earth around the Sun).
Ask your child what causes the seasons (the tilt of the Earth affects sunlight angles ... less angle equals more warmth).
Ask your child to name and describe a season (winter, spring, summer, or fall ... descriptions will vary).

FOCUS   States of Matter

OBJECTIVE   To explore Earth's three most common states of matter.

OVERVIEW   Everything is made of matter. Matter comes in different forms that scientists call "states." The three most common states on Earth are solid, liquid, and gas.

WHAT TO DO

With your team, carefully follow each step below.

Observe

Look at the antacid tablet. Look at the water. Think about the three most common states of matter (solid, liquid, gas). Which state describes each item?

Describe

Describe the tablet and the water. What does each one look like? What does each one feel like? What color is each item. What shape is each item?

Discuss

What state of matter best describes wood?   solid

What state of matter best describes oil?   liquid

What state of matter best describes air?   gas

PHYSICAL 123

Introduction

National Standards
Focus: B1

Related: A1, A2, B2

Category
Physical Science

Focus
States of Matter

Objective
To explore Earth's three most common states of matter

Overview
Read the overview aloud to your students. The goal is to create an atmosphere of curiosity and inquiry.

Say: *"Everything is made of matter. Matter comes in different forms that scientists call "states." The three most common states on Earth are solid, liquid, and gas."*

Additional Notes

To introduce this lesson, tell your students that you are going to "pour you a glass full of the three most common states of matter."

Now demonstrate by pouring a carbonated soda pop into a glass full of ice. Challenge students to discover the three states of matter that are present. (The soda pop is **liquid**, the bubbles are **gas**, and the ice is **solid**.)

Discuss the differences between the three states. Talk about the fact that water is unusual because it can easily be found in all three states (ice, steam, water). Remind students that *everything* on Earth is made of matter in some state.

What To Do

Once students are seated in "research teams" with materials in front of them, read the first section (OBSERVE) aloud.

Say, *"To start this lesson, we're going to observe some things. Good scientists always carefully examine the things they will be working with before beginning. First, I will read the instructions to you. Then you can follow the instructions as you observe the items in front of you."*

Monitor teams closely as they follow instructions. When teams are finished with this section, repeat the process with the DESCRIBE section. Conclude with the DISCUSS section.

Options

Expand the DISCUSS section by having students trace dotted "key words" using crayons or markers. Trace the word **solid** in red, the word **liquid** in blue, and the word **gas** in green.

FOCUS	States of Matter
OBJECTIVE	To explore Earth's three most common states of matter.
OVERVIEW	Everything is made of matter. Matter comes in different forms that scientists call "states." The three most common states on Earth are solid, liquid, and gas.

WHAT TO DO

With your team, carefully follow each step below.

Observe

Look at the antacid tablet. Look at the water. Think about the three most common states of matter (solid, liquid, gas). Which state describes each item?

Describe

Describe the tablet and the water. What does each one look like? What does each one feel like? What color is each item. What shape is each item?

Discuss

What state of matter best describes wood? *solid*

What state of matter best describes oil? *liquid*

What state of matter best describes air? *gas*

PHYSICAL · **123**

Teacher to Teacher

Solid, liquid, and gas are the three most common states of matter on Earth. For students this age, that's a significant concept to master.

But don't forget there's more to the story. When it comes to the universe, *plasma* is the most common state of matter. (That's what stars are made from.)

And advanced physics research continues to find new states of matter. Bose-Einstein Condensate (the "fifth state of matter") was discovered in 1996. Then in 2004, a related form called "Fermionic Condensate" was proven.

Who knows what other exciting discoveries lie ahead?

READ THE STORY

The three most common states of matter on Earth are **solid**, **liquid**, and **gas**. Read the story below to find out more about the states of matter.

States of Matter

Everything is made of matter. Matter has different states. The state of an object's matter determines what the object is like. Matter has three common states on Earth: solid, liquid, and gas. Matter sometimes changes states.

This is a solid.

Sugar is a solid state of matter.
A substance is "solid" when it is firm and has a definite shape. Examples include rocks, wood, glass — or even your lunch!

Dissolving can change the state of sugar.
Mixing sugar with water makes it dissolve. The particles of sugar seem to disappear! The sugar changes from solid to liquid.

This is a liquid.

Water is a liquid state of matter.
A substance is "liquid" when it can flow. Examples include oil, water, or even milk. Some liquids flow easier than others.

Heating can change the state of water.
Heating water makes it boil. When water boils, it turns into a type of gas (steam). The water changes from liquid to gas.

This is a gas.

Propane is a gaseous state of matter.
A substance is a "gas" when it is not a solid or liquid. Examples include air, carbon dioxide, and fuels like propane.

Compression can change the state of gas.
When propane gas is compressed, it turns into a type of liquid. Compressing gas into a liquid makes it easier to transport.

124 · PHYSICAL

Extended Teaching

1. For a closer look at a gas, pour a carbonated beverage into a glass. Have students observe the bubbles in the liquid. Explain that "soda pop" is made by dissolving carbon dioxide in flavored water. The carbon dioxide is pushed with high pressure into the bottle which is immediately sealed. When the bottle is opened, bubbles of carbon dioxide begin to rush to the surface. (Shaking a bottle makes them rush much faster!)

2. Students easily grasp that solids and liquids on Earth have mass and weight, but gas is not so obvious. To demonstrate, blow up two balloons and tie them so one hangs from each end of a yardstick. Suspend the yardstick by a string in the middle so it is balanced and level. Now use a pin to pop one balloon, allowing the air to escape. The other balloon will sink down, demonstrating the fact that air really does have weight.

Inform - Day 2

Read The Story

Read the story aloud with your students. (See READING LEVELS on page 12.) After reading, monitor teams as they discuss what was read. Once you feel students have mastered the basic concepts, have them answer the comprehension questions (**What I Learned - part 1**) on the next page.

To introduce the story, say:

"The title of this story is 'States of Matter.' Look at your story and follow along as we read it together."

If you wish, encourage Emergent readers to point to words and pictures as you read.

What I Learned (part 1)

These are basic fact-based comprehension questions. Student answers will vary, but suggested responses include:

1 solid, liquid, gas

2 Solids are firm and have a definite shape; Liquids can "flow"

3 It would turn into a liquid (water)

Field Trip

Take a "Matter March" outdoors. Challenge students to find examples of solids, liquids, and gases (trees, rocks; water, gas in cars; steam, air; etc.). Have each team keep a list. When you return to the classroom, make three "states of matter" columns on the board. Now compile the findings of the class by having teams write objects in the correct column.

Guest Speaker

Invite the school nurse to visit your class. Ask her/him to explain how an antacid can help when you have a stomachache.

Materials Needed*

antacid tablet   plastic cup
film canister (with lid)   water

Safety Concerns

3. Poison Hazard

Warn students not to put the antacid tablets in their mouths.

4. Slipping

There is a potential for spilled liquids. Remind students to exercise caution.

4. Other

Warn students not to stand over the film can. The lid could hit them!

Do the Activity

Read the activity in advance so you understand it thoroughly. (If time allows, try it yourself.) Before students begin, carefully go over the **Safety Concerns** together.

Pass out materials, then have your students follow along as you read the instructions for **Step 1**. Monitor teams closely as they complete this step.

Once teams have completed **Step 1**, read instructions for **Step 2**. Monitor teams as before. Repeat for **Step 3** and **Step 4**.

After the activity, allow time for each team to share their observations. To encourage higher-level thinking, encourage teams to not only share their observations with each other, but also with other teams.

Special Instructions

Step 2 - Although this activity is very safe when conducted as shown, safety goggles are a reasonable precaution when working with gases and flying lids.

Step 3 - The lid must be snapped on very quickly! Depending on developmental readiness, some students may need assistance. Warn students to not stand over the film can — the lid will pop off without warning! Keep paper towels handy for immediate cleanup.

* Bold-faced items supplied in kit.

DO THE ACTIVITY
Working with your research team, carefully follow each step below. Before you start, be sure you know the **safety rules** for this activity.

STEP 1 **Examine** the antacid tablets, the water, the cup, and the film can. Now **discuss** which state of matter (solid, liquid, or gas) best describes each item.

STEP 2 **Fill** a clear plastic cup half full of water. **Drop** one antacid tablet into the water. **Watch** the surface of the water and **observe** what happens.

STEP 3 **Fill** the film can half full of water. **Drop** half an antacid tablet into the water, then quickly **snap** on the lid. **Wait** a few moments and **observe** what happens.

STEP 4 **Review** steps 2 and 3. **Discuss** which states of matter were present in each step. **Compare** your observations with those of other research teams.

What Happened?

Immediately following the activity, help your students understand what they observed.

Say: *"In this activity you explored three common states of matter.*

*In **Step 2**, you saw what can happen when certain solids are mixed with certain liquids. The result was a type of gas that became visible as bubbles or foam.*

*In **Step 3**, you saw that mixing states of matter can sometimes result in a significant amount of force. Sealing these interacting materials in a closed container led to a small explosion!*

*Finally, in **Step 4** you discussed the various states of matter shown in this activity. Like all good scientists, you also compared your findings with those of other teams."*

SHOW WHAT YOU KNOW - 1

Circle the **solid** matter in red. Circle the **liquid** matter in blue. Circle the matter that is a **gas** in green. Write the correct "state" on the lines below.

This matter is a

liquid

This matter is a

solid

This matter is a

gas

To the Parent . . .

Scripture Connection: Colossians 3:1-4

Lesson Focus:
States of Matter

Lesson Objective:
To explore Earth's three most common states of matter

National Science Education Standards:
Standard B1 — "All students should understand that materials have observable (and measurable) properties . . .
Materials exist in different states . . . some materials can be changed from one state to another . . ."

Follow-up Questions:
Ask your child to describe the solid state of matter, then give at least one example (rock, wood, ice, etc.).
Ask your child to describe the liquid state of matter, then give at least one example (water, oil, milk, etc.).
Ask your child to describe the gaseous state of matter, then give at least one example (steam, propane, etc.).

Food For Thought

A related "Scripture Object Lesson" you can share with your students.

Colossians 3:1-4

Just as Earth has different states of matter, we can have different states of mind.

Your mind can be in a state of forgiveness or it can be unforgiving. It can be in a state of pride or it can be humble. It can be willing, or grateful, or prayerful — or any one of many different states.

Remember that your state of mind reflects attitudes about yourself, about others, and about God.

That's why it's important to keep your mind focused on Jesus. The more time we spend *thinking* about Him, the more we *become* like Him. A mind filled with Jesus' love is in the best state of all!

Expand - Day 4

Begin **Day 4** with a review of **Day 3**, then have students answer "part 2" questions.

What I Learned (part 2)

These are higher-level cognitive questions (explain, compare, predict). Student answers will vary but suggested responses may include:

① solid, liquid, gas

② a) mixed the same materials together
b) the container in Step 3 was sealed, causing a small explosion

③ might turn back into a liquid; compressing gas can change its state (see this week's "story")

Assess - Day 5

Suggestions for modifying assessments to reflect reading levels can be found under ASSESSMENT METHODS on page 12.

Show What You Know

(general assessment in Student Worktext)

Blank: 1) liquid 2) solid 3) gas
Also, the water faucet should be circled in blue, the ice cubes in red, and the teapot in green.

Show What You Know 2

(optional test master in Teacher Guide)

1) G   2) S   3) L   4) S   5) G

To The Parent

Included at the bottom of all assessment tests, "To The Parent" provides a great way to solicit parent involvement. It not only gives parents an overview of the lesson, but also provides follow-up questions for home use.

NAME _____

Read the sentences below. Each sentence describes a specific state of matter. If it describes a solid, circle **S**. If it describes a liquid, circle **L**. If it describes a gas, circle **G**.

S L G 1. This common substance is not a solid or a liquid.

S L G 2. This common substance is firm and has a definite shape.

S L G 3. This common substance has the ability to flow.

S L G 4. Rocks and trees are examples of this substance.

S L G 5. Steam from boiling water is an example of this substance.

To the Parent . . .   **Scripture Connection:** Colosians 3:1-4

Lesson Focus:
States of Matter

Lesson Objective:
To explore Earth's three most common states of matter

National Science Education Standards:
Standard B1 — *"All students should understand that materials have observable (and measureable) properties . . . Materials exist in different states . . . some materials can be changed from one state to another . . ."*

Follow-up Questions:
Ask your child to describe the solid state of matter, then give at least one example (rock, wood, ice, etc.).
Ask your child to describe the liquid state of matter, then give at least one example (water, oil, milk, etc.).
Ask your child to describe the gaseous state of matter, then give at least one example (steam, propane, etc.).

BiCarb Balloon
Lesson 20

FOCUS   Chemical & Physical change

OBJECTIVE   To explore how matter can change from one state to another

OVERVIEW   Matter comes in different forms called "states". But sometimes matter changes from one state to another. Common changes in state are caused by chemical or physical actions.

WHAT TO DO
With your team, carefully follow each step below.

Observe

Look at the baking soda. Look at the salt. Look at the vinegar. Think about what common state of matter (solid, liquid, gas) best describes each item.

Describe

Describe the baking soda, salt, and vinegar. What does each one look like? What does each one feel like? What does each one smell like?

Discuss

What state of matter best describes salt? solid
What state of matter best describes vinegar? liquid
What state of matter best describes air? gas

PHYSICAL · **129**

Lesson 20

Introduction

National Standards
Focus: B1

Related: A1, A2, B2

Category
Physical Science

Focus
Chemical/Physical change

Objective
To explore how matter can change from one state to another

Overview
Read the overview aloud to your students. The goal is to create an atmosphere of curiosity and inquiry.

Say: *"Matter comes in different forms called 'states.' But sometimes matter changes from one state to another. The most common changes in state are caused by chemical or physical actions."*

Additional Notes

Introduce this lesson by asking students if they have ever traveled from one state to another. You'll probably discover that many students have traveled from their home state to another state to visit someone or some place.

Now ask students how long it took for them to reach the other state, and how far they had to travel.

Once you have allowed sufficient time for answers, tell students that in this activity they will see something change from one state to another . . . and it won't even have to leave the classroom!

You can use this introduction to highlight the fact that many words in the English language have more than one meaning.

What To Do

Once students are seated in "research teams" with materials in front of them, read the first section (OBSERVE) aloud.

Say, *"To start this lesson, we're going to **observe** some things. Good scientists always carefully examine the things they will be working with before beginning. First, I will read the instructions to you. Then you can follow the instructions as you **observe** the items in front of you."*

Monitor teams closely as they follow instructions. When teams are finished with this section, repeat the process with the DESCRIBE section. Conclude with the DISCUSS section.

Options

Expand the DISCUSS section by having students trace dotted "key words" using crayons or markers. Trace the word **solid** in brown, the word **liquid** in blue, and the word **gas** in green.

FOCUS   Chemical & Physical change

OBJECTIVE   To explore how matter can change from one state to another

OVERVIEW   Matter comes in different forms called "states". But sometimes matter changes from one state to another. Common changes in state are caused by chemical or physical actions.

WHAT TO DO

With your team, carefully follow each step below.

Observe

Look at the baking soda. Look at the salt. Look at the vinegar. Think about what common state of matter (solid, liquid, gas) best describes each item.

Describe

Describe the baking soda, salt, and vinegar. What does each one look like? What does each one feel like? What does each one smell like?

Discuss

What state of matter best describes salt? solid
What state of matter best describes vinegar? liquid
What state of matter best describes air? gas

PHYSICAL · **129**

Teacher to Teacher

For students in this age group, it's best to focus only on the most common states of matter on Earth — solid, liquid, and gas.

But as students enter high school, they'll find there are other states of matter beyond our planet. In fact, *plasma* is the most common state of matter in the universe. (That's what stars are made from.)

And back here on Earth, advanced physics research has been discovering other states of matter.

Through super-conductivity experiments, Bose-Einstein Condensate was discovered in 1996. A related form called Fermionic Condensate was discovered in 2004. That makes SIX states of matter that scientists have discovered to date.

Extended Teaching

1. To expand vocabulary, explain that "bicarb" is an abbreviation for "bicarbonate of soda." Most people know it as "baking soda." Baking soda is primarily used to make baked goods, and sometimes to help relieve excess stomach acid.

2. Explain that "change" is an action verb. We can expect something to happen when there is a change. Physical changes include grinding, chopping, breaking, melting, freezing, cutting, and so on. Chemical changes include rotting, rusting, food digesting, etc.

3. Physics: Discuss the concept of "forces." A force always pushes or pulls, usually resulting in change. Both chemical and physical forces "force" changes to occur.

4. Make "States of Matter" Jello©! Point out that the powder is a solid; the steam from the boiling water is a gas; mixing the powder with water creates a liquid; and finally, cooling the gel creates a solid again.

Read The Story
Read the story aloud with your students. (See READING LEVELS on page 12.) After reading, monitor teams as they discuss what was read. Once you feel students have mastered the basic concepts, have them answer the comprehension questions (**What I Learned** - part 1) on the next page.

To introduce the story, say:

"The title of this story is 'Changes in Matter.' Look at your story and follow along as we read it together."

If you wish, encourage Emergent readers to point to words and pictures as you read.

What I Learned (part 1)
These are basic fact-based comprehension questions. Student answers will vary, but suggested responses include:

① chemical; physical

② a) both physical changes   b) freezing changes a liquid to a solid; boiling changes a liquid to a gas

③ Answers will vary, but should include freezing or boiling. Some students may also refer to "chemical" changes, such as mixing in another substance

Field Trip
Visit a manufacturer that makes synthetic products such as plastics. Talk about the chemical changes taking place.

Guest Speaker
Invite a chemisty teacher from a local college to visit your class. Ask him/her to demonstrate some simple chemical changes.

Materials Needed*

plastic tube - clear   salt
balloons -2   funnel
baking soda (sodium bicarbonate)
vinegar (acedic acid)

Safety Concerns

3. Poison Hazard

Keep materials out of mouths and away from eyes. Balloons can pose a choking hazard.

4. Slipping

There is a potential for spilled liquids. Remind students to exercise caution.

Do the Activity

Read the activity in advance so you understand it thoroughly. (If time allows, try it yourself.) Before students begin, carefully go over the **Safety Concerns** together.

Pass out materials, then have your students follow along as you read the instructions for **Step 1**. Monitor teams closely as they complete this step.

Once teams have completed **Step 1**, read instructions for **Step 2**. Monitor teams as before. Repeat for **Step 3** and **Step 4**.

After the activity, allow time for each team to share their observations. To encourage higher-level thinking, encourage teams to not only share their observations with each other, but also with other teams.

Special Instructions

Step 1 - Have one team member hold the funnel while another adds the salt. Note: "a little" means half a spoonful or less!

Step 2 - Differences in motor skills development may make it difficult for some teams to attach the balloon to the tube. Balloon must be tight! If you see problems, join the group and demonstrate. This will shift the focus from the skill to the observation process.

Step 3 - Keep paper towels on hand for immediate cleanup of spills.

* Bold-faced items supplied in kit.

DO THE ACTIVITY
Working with your research team, carefully follow each step below. Before you start, be sure you know the **safety rules** for this activity.

STEP 1
Examine the salt, baking soda, and vinegar. Discuss which state of matter (solid, liquid, or gas) best describes each item. Pour a little salt into one balloon.

STEP 2
Pour an inch of vinegar into the tube. Attach the balloon to the top of the tube. Now quickly tip the balloon so the salt falls in the tube. Observe what happens.

STEP 3
Empty the tube and rinse with clean water. Now pour a little baking soda in the other balloon. Repeat step 2. Carefully observe what happens.

STEP 4
Compare steps 2 and 3. Discuss what states of matter were shown in each step. Compare your observations with those of other research teams.

What Happened?

Immediately following the activity, help your students understand what they observed.

Say: *"In this activity you explored the changes in matter caused by various chemical actions.*

*In **Step 1**, you classified each material according to its state of matter.*

*In **Step 2**, you saw a solid (salt) change into a liquid — a physical change.*

*In **Step 3**, you observed a solid (baking soda) change into a gas — a chemical change.*

Remember, never try an activity like this at home unless an adult is present to help you."

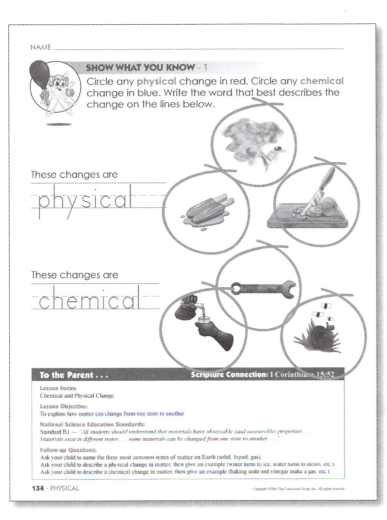

NAME _____

SHOW WHAT YOU KNOW - 1

Circle any *physical* change in red. Circle any *chemical* change in blue. Write the word that best describes the change on the lines below.

These changes are

physical

These changes are

chemical

To the Parent . . .   Scripture Connection: I Corinthians 15:52

Lesson Focus:
Chemical and Physical Change

Lesson Objective:
To explore how matter can change from one state to another

National Science Education Standards:
Standard B1 — *"All students should understand that materials have observable (and measurable) properties . . . Materials exist in different states . . . some materials can be changed from one state to another . . ."*

Follow-up Questions:
Ask your child to name the three most common states of matter on Earth (solid, liquid, gas).
Ask your child to describe a physical change in matter, then give an example (water turns to ice, water turns to steam, etc.).
Ask your child to describe a chemical change in matter, then give an example (baking soda and vinegar make a gas, etc.).

Food For Thought

A related "Scripture Object Lesson" you can share with your students.

I Corinthians 15:52

We often use the word "change" in our daily lives. We change our clothes, change our surroundings, and even change our minds. When we travel, we may have to change buses, or planes, or trains. If we buy something, our money may make a sudden change from big bills to small coins. And sometimes we may even need a change of attitude.

In this text, God promises us the ultimate change. One day everyone who believes in God will be changed from an earthly body to a heavenly one!

In our new bodies, we will never again worry about sickness, pain, or death. And best of all, we will live forever with God, sharing in the wonders of this amazing universe He has created.

Expand - Day 4

Begin **Day 4** with a review of **Day 3**, then have students answer "part 2" questions.

What I Learned (part 2)

These are higher-level cognitive questions (explain, compare, predict). Student answers will vary but suggested responses may include:

1 a) solid, liquid, gas b) salt and baking soda began as solids; salt mixed with vinegar became liquid; baking soda mixed with vinegar became a gas

2 a) did the same things b) answers should reflect the fact that different ingredients produced different results

3 adds gas; makes it expand or "rise"

Assess - Day 5

Suggestions for modifying assessments to reflect reading levels can be found under ASSESSMENT METHODS on page 12.

Show What You Know 1

(general assessment in Student Worktext)

Top scenes are physical (circle in red); Bottom scenes are chemical (circle in blue).

Show What You Know 2

(optional test master in Teacher Guide)

1) chemical   2) physical   3) chemical
4) physical   5) physical

To The Parent

Included at the bottom of all assessment tests, "To The Parent" provides a great way to solicit parent involvement. It not only gives parents an overview of the lesson, but also provides follow-up questions for home use.

NAME _____

Show What You Know 2

Read each sentence below. If it describes a chemical change, fill in the word **chemical**. If it describes a physical change, fill in the word **physical**.

1. Mixing baking soda and vinegar creates a _____ change.

2. Boiling water creates a _____ change.

3. Unprotected iron rusts. This is a _____ change.

4. Turning liquid water into solid ice is a _____ change.

5. Turning solid ice into liquid water is a _____ change.

To the Parent . . .   **Scripture Connection:** 1 Corinthians 15:52

Lesson Focus:
Chemical and Physical change

Lesson Objective:
To explore how matter can change from one state to another

National Science Education Standards:
Standard B1 — *"All students should understand that materials have observable (and measurable) properties . . .*
Materials exist in different states . . . some materials can be changed from one state to another . . ."

Follow-up Questions:
Ask your child to name the three most common states of matter on Earth (solid, liquid, gas).
Ask your child to describe a physical change in matter, then give an example (water turns to ice, water turns to steam, etc.).
Ask your child to describe a chemical change in matter, then give an example (baking soda and vinegar make a gas, etc.).

Bubble Bonds
Lesson 21

FOCUS Bonds

OBJECTIVE To explore how the bonds between atoms hold things together

OVERVIEW Atoms are tiny particles of matter. Atoms can link together. Scientists call this link a "bond." The stronger the bond, the stronger the material.

WHAT TO DO

With your team, carefully follow each step below.

Observe

Look at the bubble solution. Think about what it is made from (water and liquid soap). How is this material like other liquids you have seen? How is it different?

Describe

Describe the bubble solution. What does it look like? What color is it? What does it smell like? What does it feel like? How is it different from bottled water?

Discuss

What is one tiny particle of matter called? a t o m
What word means "to link things together"? b o n d
What is a mix of different liquids called? s o l u t i o n

PHYSICAL ·135

Lesson 21

Introduction

National Standards
Focus: B1

Related: A1, A2

Category
Physical Science

Focus
Bonds

Objective
To explore how the bonds between atoms hold things together

Overview
Read the overview aloud to your students. The goal is to create an atmosphere of curiosity and inquiry.

Say: *"Atoms are tiny particles of matter. Atoms can link together. Scientists call this link a 'bond.' The stronger the bond, the stronger the material."*

Additional Notes

Introduce this lesson on the playground. Have students form two parallel lines facing each other about two yards apart. Have them keep their arms at their sides. Ask a student from one line to run through the opposite line. Point out how easy this was.

Now have them link arms firmly and repeat. Point out that this time the student either could not break through or had difficulty doing it. Allow more students to try.

Explain that when the students linked arms, the line formed a "bond." Say, *"Bonds make things stronger. In this lesson, we're going to explore how bonds work."*

What To Do

Once students are seated in "research teams" with materials in front of them, read the first section (OBSERVE) aloud.

Say, *"To start this lesson, we're going to **observe** some things. Good scientists always carefully examine the things they will be working with before beginning. First, I will read the instructions to you. Then you can follow the instructions as you **think** about each question."*

Monitor teams closely as they follow instructions. When teams are finished with this section, repeat the process with the DESCRIBE section. Conclude with the DISCUSS section.

Options

Expand the DISCUSS section by having students trace dotted "key words" using crayons or markers. Trace the word **atom** in blue, the word **bond** in green, and the word **solution** in a different color for each letter to make rainbow shades.

Bubble Bonds
Lesson 21

FOCUS   Bonds

OBJECTIVE   To explore how the bonds between atoms hold things together

OVERVIEW   Atoms are tiny particles of matter. Atoms can link together. Scientists call this link a "bond." The stronger the bond, the stronger the material.

WHAT TO DO

With your team, carefully follow each step below.

Observe

Look at the bubble solution. Think about what it is made from (water and liquid soap). How is this material like other liquids you have seen? How is it different?

Describe

Describe the bubble solution. What does it look like? What color is it? What does it smell like? What does it feel like? How is it different from bottled water?

Discuss

What is one tiny particle of matter called?   a t o m

What word means "to link things together"?   b o n d

What is a mix of different liquids called?   s o l u t i o n

PHYSICAL · 135

Teacher to Teacher

There are many types of bonds between atoms. These include ionic bonds (uneven sharing of electrons), covalent bonds (more even sharing of electrons), and hydrogen bonds (the ones that cause surface tension in water).

When bonds are made or broken, it causes change. Physical changes affect the appearance of the material. Chemical changes result in entirely new materials.

But regardless of the type of change, energy is being taken in or given off. Managing the exchange of energy has become a major focus of modern life. Just look at the amount of time and effort required just to provide energy for our homes and cars!

Atoms are tiny particles of matter. Atoms can link together to create a **bond**. Read the story below to find out more about bonds.

Atoms & Bonds

Atoms link together to form bonds.

An atom is a tiny particle of matter. It is far too small to see. Everything is made from atoms. Atoms can link together. Scientists call this link a "bond."

Liquids have bonds.

Water is held together by bonds.
The atoms in water link together to form surface tension. This is a very weak kind of bond. Otherwise we could walk on water!

Soap is held together by bonds.
Blow air into soap and its bonds hold it together as bubbles. Soap's bonds are stronger than water's, but still break easily.

Solids have bonds.

Wood is held together by bonds.
Wood atoms have strong bonds. Steel atoms have even stronger bonds! The stronger the bond, the stronger the material.

Bonds make materials useful.
Different materials like soap, water, wood, metal, plastic, or glass are used in different ways because of their bonds.

Bonds can be broken.

Physical actions break bonds.
Bonds can be broken by physical actions. Sawing a board, boiling water, and melting steel are good examples.

Chemical actions break bonds.
Bonds can be broken by chemical actions. When you eat an apple, chemicals break it into the nutrients your body needs.

Extended Teaching

1. To expand vocabulary, explain that a "bond" is anything that fastens or holds together. In science, bonds refer to atoms joining together to make bigger particles called molecules. Everything on Earth is made of atoms and molecules bonded together.

2. A bubble is a ball of air or gas surrounded by a solid or liquid. Soap bubbles are simple bubbles made from bonding water and soap.

3. To expand vocabulary, explain that a "chemist" is a special kind of scientist who studies how different types of materials behave, change, and bond together.

4. Have a Bubble Party! Provide bubble solution and different items such as straws, funnels, wands, etc. Have contests for the biggest bubble, highest pile of bubbles, prettiest bubble, bubble inside a bubble, farthest floating bubble, and so forth.

Inform - Day 2

Read The Story

Read the story aloud with your students. (See READING LEVELS on page 12.) After reading, monitor teams as they discuss what was read. Once you feel students have mastered the basic concepts, have them answer the comprehension questions (**What I Learned** - part 1) on the next page.

To introduce the story, say:

"The title of this story is 'Atoms and Bonds.' Look at your story and follow along as we read it together."

If you wish, encourage Emergent readers to point to words and pictures as you read.

What I Learned (part 1)

These are basic fact-based comprehension questions. Student answers will vary, but suggested responses include:

(1) its atoms have a very weak bond

(2) the atoms in a plastic knife have a stronger bond that the atoms in a paper towel

(3) a) paper b) because steel atoms have strong bonds; you could not easily open a package wrapped in steel!

Field Trip

Visit a factory that makes or uses large amounts of soap. Find out how the soap is helpful. If there is a children's science museum in your area, find out if they have interactive bubble experiments.

Guest Speaker

Invite a local chemist or high school chemistry teacher to visit your class. Ask him/her to bring some models showing chemical bonds. Discuss how bonds can be helpful.

BUBBLE BONDS· 143

Materials Needed*

petri dish   large straw
medium straw   small straw
bubble solution

Safety Concerns

3. Poison Hazard

Keep bubble solution out of mouths and away from eyes. Do not inhale.

3. Hygiene

Don't share straws without disinfecting.

4. Slipping

There is a potential for spilled liquids. Remind students to exercise caution.

Do the Activity

Read the activity in advance so you understand it thoroughly. (If time allows, try it yourself.) Before students begin, carefully go over the **Safety Concerns** together.

Pass out materials, then have your students follow along as you read the instructions for **Step 1**. Monitor teams closely as they complete this step.

Once teams have completed **Step 1**, read instructions for **Step 2**. Monitor teams as before. Repeat for **Step 3** and **Step 4**.

After the activity, allow time for each team to share their observations. To encourage higher-level thinking, encourage teams to not only share their observations with each other, but also with other teams.

Special Instructions

Note: Goggles are a reasonable safety precaution to avoid soap in the eyes.

Step 1 - Pour a shallow layer of bubble solution into each team's petri dish before beginning this step. Remind students to blow gently and not to inhale!

* Bold-faced items supplied in kit.

DO THE ACTIVITY
Working with your research team, carefully follow each step below. Before you start, be sure you know the **safety rules** for this activity.

STEP 1 Look at the bubble solution in your petri dish. Place the end of the largest straw into the solution. Blow through the straw gently. Observe what happens.

STEP 2 Repeat step 1 using the medium straw. Observe any changes in the bubbles. Repeat again using the small straw. Observe what happens.

STEP 3 Gently insert the small straw into the large bubble. Blow gently. Try to make a small bubble inside the large bubble. Observe what happens.

STEP 4 Review each step. Discuss how bubbles are made and what holds them together. Compare your findings with those of other research teams.

138 · PHYSICAL   Copyright ©2006 The Concerned Group, Inc. All rights reserved.

What Happened?

Immediately following the activity, help your students understand what they observed.

Say: *"In this activity you explored how bonds between atoms hold things together.*

In Step 1, you blew air into the solution. The soap and water bonded together to create a bubble.

In Steps 2 and 3, you discovered that straw size affects bubble size, and that you can make bubbles inside of bubbles!

Finally, in Step 4 you compared your findings with those of other research teams."

Bubble Solution

To make "homemade" bubble solution, just combine one cup of liquid detergent (Dawn® or Joy® recommended), one teaspoon of glycerin (available at any pharmacy), and ten cups of water.

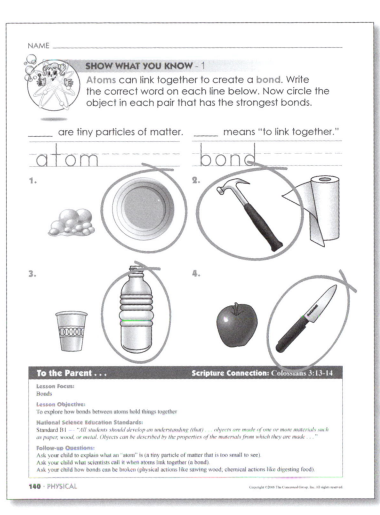

NAME _____

SHOW WHAT YOU KNOW - 1

Atoms can link together to create a **bond**. Write the correct word on each line below. Now circle the object in each pair that has the strongest bonds.

_____ are tiny particles of matter.   _____ means "to link together."

atom   bond

1.
2.
3.
4.

To the Parent . . .   **Scripture Connection:** Colossians 3:13-14

Lesson Focus:
Bonds

Lesson Objective:
To explore how bonds between atoms hold things together

National Science Education Standards:
Standard B1 — "All students should develop an understanding (that) . . . objects are made of one or more materials such as paper, wood, or metal. Objects can be described by the properties of the materials from which they are made . . ."

Follow-up Questions:
Ask your child to explain what an "atom" is (a tiny particle of matter that is too small to see).
Ask your child what scientists call it when atoms link together (a bond).
Ask your child how bonds can be broken (physical actions like sawing wood; chemical actions like digesting food).

140 · PHYSICAL

Food For Thought

A related "Scripture Object Lesson" you can share with your students.

Colossians 3:13-14

In this study we learned that atoms can link together to form bonds, and these bonds hold things together.

Scripture talks about a special kind of bond that holds people together. It's the bond of love.

There is no problem so great that love cannot solve it, no wound so great that love cannot heal it.

Are you having a problem with a friend or family member? Why not ask God to step in and heal the relationship with His infinite love?

Don't dwell on the past or focus on the problem. Let God's love bind you back together.

Expand - Day 4

Begin **Day 4** with a review of **Day 3**, then have students answer "part 2" questions.

What I Learned (part 2)

These are higher-level cognitive questions (explain, compare, predict). Student answers will vary but suggested responses may include:

① the straws were smaller in step 2

② a) they all were tubes you could blow air through b) there were different sizes of straws

③ a) wouldn't make bubbles as well
b) because the atoms in the soapy water have stronger bonds than the atoms in plain water

Assess - Day 5

Suggestions for modifying assessments to reflect reading levels can be found under ASSESSMENT METHODS on page 12.

Show What You Know 1

(general assessment in Student Worktext)

Blanks: 1) atom 2) bond
1) circle the plate 2) circle the hammer
3) circle the plastic bottle 4) circle the knife

Show What You Know 2

(optional test master in Teacher Guide)

1) plain water 2) soapy water 3) bread
4) wood 5) steel

To The Parent

Included at the bottom of all assessment tests, "To The Parent" provides a great way to solicit parent involvement. It not only gives parents an overview of the lesson, but also provides follow-up questions for home use.

NAME _____

Show What You Know 2

Look at the materials in the "word bank" below. Think about how strong the **bonds** are in each material. Now list them in order from the weakest bond to the strongest.

1. _____   weakest bond

▲

2. _____

3. _____

4. _____

▼

5. _____   strongest bond

WORD BANK:

plain water   wood   steel   soapy water   a loaf of bread

To the Parent . . .   **Scripture Connection:** Colossians 3:13-14

Lesson Focus:
Bonds

Lesson Objective:
To explore how bonds between atoms hold things together

National Science Education Standards:
Standard B1 — *"All students should develop an understanding (that) . . . objects are made of one or more materials such as paper, wood, or metal. Objects can be described by the properties of the materials from which they are made . . ."*

Follow-up Questions:
Ask your child to explain what an "atom" is (a tiny particle of matter that is too small to see).
Ask your child what scientists call it when atoms link together (a bond).
Ask your child how bonds can be broken (physical actions like sawing wood; chemical actions like digesting food).

Lesson 22

Introduction

The following is the student-facing worksheet shown on the left:

Soap Boat
Lesson 22

FOCUS   Surface Tension

OBJECTIVE   To explore the concept of surface tension

OVERVIEW   Surface tension happens because water molecules stick to each other. Scientists call connections like this a "bond." But when a bond is broken, interesting things can happen!

WHAT TO DO

With your team, carefully follow each step below.

Observe

Look at the soap, water, and paper. Think about the three most common states of matter on Earth (solid, liquid, gas). Which state describes each item?

Describe

Describe the water and the soap. What does each one look like? What does each one feel like? How are they similar? How are they different?

Discuss

What word means "to stick to each other"? bond
What word is "a tiny piece of matter"? molecule
Where might you find "surface tension"? water

PHYSICAL **141**

National Standards
Focus: B1

Related: A1, A2

Category
Physical Science

Focus
Surface Tension

Objective
To explore the concept of surface tension

Overview
Read the overview aloud to your students. The goal is to create an atmosphere of curiosity and inquiry.

Say: *"Surface tension happens because water molecules stick to each other. Scientists call connections like this a 'bond'. But when a bond is broken, interesting things can happen!"*

Additional Notes

To introduce this lesson, ask students how the clothes they are wearing got so clean. Most will answer that someone (usually a parent) washed the clothes.

Now ask, *"What did this person use to wash your clothes?"* Focus on the fact that water alone usually doesn't get clothes really clean.

Continue by saying, *"Something unique happens when soap is added to water. In a way, soap actually helps water become wetter!*

In this lesson, we'll look at a kind of bond called 'surface tension.' And we'll discover that when surface tension is broken, interesting things can happen!"

What To Do

Once students are seated in "research teams" with materials in front of them, read the first section (OBSERVE) aloud.

Say, *"To start this lesson, we're going to **observe** some things. Good scientists always carefully examine the things they will be working with before beginning. First, I will read the instructions to you. Then you can follow the instructions as you **observe** the items in front of you."*

Monitor teams closely as they follow instructions. When teams are finished with this section, repeat the process with the DESCRIBE section. Conclude with the DISCUSS section.

Options

Expand the DISCUSS section by having students trace dotted "key words" using crayons or markers. Trace the word **bond** in green, the word **molecule** in black, and the word **water** in blue.

FOCUS	Surface Tension
OBJECTIVE	To explore the concept of surface tension
OVERVIEW	Surface tension happens because water molecules stick to each other. Scientists call connections like this a "bond." But when a bond is broken, interesting things can happen!

WHAT TO DO

With your team, carefully follow each step below.

Observe

Look at the soap, water, and paper. **Think** about the three most common states of matter on Earth (solid, liquid, gas). Which state describes each item?

Describe

Describe the water and the soap. What does each one **look** like? What does each one **feel** like? How are they **similar**? How are they **different**?

Discuss

What word means "to stick to each other"? b o n d
What word is "a tiny piece of matter"? m o l e c u l e
Where might you find "surface tension"? w a t e r

PHYSICAL · 141

Teacher to Teacher

Surface tension is all around us!

Surface tension makes water "bead up" on waxed cars because water molecules are more attracted to each other than to waxed metal.

The shape of raindrops is affected by surface tension. Small raindrops are almost completely round (not teardrop-shaped as they are often drawn), and large raindrops are round with a flat side facing the area of air resistance.

Surface tension is strong enough to float a needle if you carefully lay it flat on very smooth water.

And a "belly flop" into a pool is a great (although painful) reminder of surface tension!

Extended Teaching

1. To expand vocabulary, define "molecules" as tiny bits of matter too small to see. A drop of water is made up of millions of water molecules! Water molecules are formed when atoms of hydrogen and oxygen join together.

2. For an advanced class, you may want to point out that there is always a certain amount of space between molecules. For instance, the molecules in liquids are much more closely packed than the molecules in gases — but not nearly as closely packed as the molecules in most solids.

3. Demonstrate surface tension with a penny, an eye dropper, and water. Fill the eye dropper with water. Slowly, drip a drop of water onto a penny. Carefully add one drop at a time. Have students observe the water drawing together into a tiny sphere. Continue until the sphere breaks. Now repeat and count the number of drops the penny will hold until the surface tension breaks.

Read The Story

Read the story aloud with your students. (See READING LEVELS on page 12.) After reading, monitor teams as they discuss what was read. Once you feel students have mastered the basic concepts, have them answer the comprehension questions (**What I Learned** - part 1) on the next page.

To introduce the story, say:

"The title of this story is 'Surface Tension.' Look at your story and follow along as we read it together."

If you wish, encourage Emergent readers to point to words and pictures as you read.

What I Learned (part 1)

These are basic fact-based comprehension questions. Student answers will vary, but suggested responses include:

1 water molecules pull toward each other and cling together

2 a) soapy water b) soap breaks surface tension, allowing water to attach to dirt and wash it away

3 it might sink, since soap would break the surface tension holding it up

Field Trip

Visit a local factory that manufactures soap, or one that uses a lot of soap for cleaning. Find out how soap is helpful to the factory.

Guest Speaker

Invite a biologist or amateur bug collector to visit your class. Have them bring examples of mayflies, water striders, and similar insects, or show a film about these interesting creatures. Discuss how they use surface tension to "walk on water."

Materials Needed*

petri dish	**toothpick**
wax paper	**paper boats** - 2
liquid soap	water
scissors	pencil

Safety Concerns

3. Poison Hazard

Keep soap out of mouths and away from eyes.

4. Slipping

There is a potential for spilled liquids. Remind students to exercise caution.

4. Sharp Objects

Remind students to exercise caution with the toothpick and the scissors.

Do the Activity

Read the activity in advance so you understand it thoroughly. (If time allows, try it yourself.) Before students begin, carefully go over the **Safety Concerns** together.

Pass out materials, then have your students follow along as you read the instructions for **Step 1**. Monitor teams closely as they complete this step.

Once teams have completed **Step 1**, read instructions for **Step 2**. Monitor teams as before. Repeat for **Step 3** and **Step 4**.

After the activity, allow time for each team to share their observations. To encourage higher-level thinking, encourage teams to not only share their observations with each other, but also with other teams.

Special Instructions

Step 1 - Cut wax paper into two-inch squares before giving it to students. Assist with cutting out boats if needed.

Step 2 - For best results, touch the toothpick to the water in the center of the notch.

Step 3 - For this to work, the toothpick only needs a light coating of soap on the tip. Too much soap can make placement hard to control.

Bold-faced items supplied in kit.

  DO THE ACTIVITY
Working with your research team, carefully follow each step below. Before you start, be sure you know the **safety rules** for this activity.

STEP 1 Fill the petri dish with water. **Place** a drop of liquid soap on the wax paper. Now **cut out** the two boat shapes from the sheet of paper your teacher gives you.

STEP 2 Carefully **place** the first boat on the water. **Touch** the tip of the toothpick to the water in the center of the notch. **Observe** what happens. **Remove** the boat.

STEP 3 Carefully **place** the second boat in the water. **Dip** the toothpick in the liquid soap. **Stick** the tip of the soapy toothpick in the notch again. **Observe** what happens.

STEP 4 **Review** steps 2 and 3. **Discuss** how they were similar and how they were different. **Compare** your observations with those of other research teams.

144 · PHYSICAL

What Happened?

Immediately following the activity, help your students understand what they observed.

Say: *"When you touched the soap to water at the back of the boat in Step 3, you started a chain of events!*

The soap broke the surface tension, and the water molecules began to rush apart. But since they were in the notch, they could only move one way. As they shot out of the notch backward, the reaction pushed the boat forward.

If we wanted to do this again, however, we'd have to use clean water and a new boat because the surface tension in the petri dish is now broken."

SHOW WHAT YOU KNOW - 1

Show what you know about surface tension. Circle the correct answers to each question. (Note: Some of the questions have more than one right answer!)

Which pictures are good illustrations of surface tension?

Which object can stay on top of the water without floating?

Which makes cleaning easier by breaking surface tension?

To the Parent . . . **Scripture Connection:** Ephesians 4:2-3

Lesson Focus:
Surface Tension

Lesson Objective:
To explore the concept of surface tension

National Science Education Standards:
Standard B1 — *"All students should understand that materials have observable (and measureable) properties . . . Materials exist in different states . . . some materials can be changed from one state to another . . ."*

Follow-up Questions:
Ask your child how surface tension makes water into drops (causes water molecules to cling together, pull closer).
Ask your child how some insects can use surface tension. (They can stay on top of the water without floating.)
Ask your child how soap can make cleaning easier (breaks surface tension).

146 · PHYSICAL

Food For Thought

A related "Scripture Object Lesson" you can share with your students.

Ephesians 4: 2-3

Think about someone you really enjoy being with. What do you like to do together? How do you feel when you are together? The closeness of being with people we like is a very special kind of bond.

But sometimes the bonds of friendship can be broken. Something may be said or done that causes feelings to be hurt.

This Scripture reminds us that God wants us to be humble and patient, always striving for unity "in the bond of peace." Remember that God always wants us to forgive others, just as Christ has forgiven us.

Why not ask God to help you develop a kind and gentle spirit? Strengthen the bonds of friendship through His love.

Expand - Day 4

Begin **Day 4** with a review of **Day 3**, then have students answer "part 2" questions.

What I Learned (part 2)

These are higher-level cognitive questions (explain, compare, predict). Student answers will vary but suggested responses may include:

(1) a) nothing b) boat moved forward

(2) a) soap was added b) soap broke the surface tension

(3) answers will vary; common examples include things held together with glue or nails or screws, things melted together, things frozen together, etc.

Assess - Day 5

Suggestions for modifying assessments to reflect reading levels can be found under ASSESSMENT METHODS on page 12.

Show What You Know 1

(general assessment in Student Worktext)

1) circle water on leaf and water on twig
2) circle mayfly only
3) circle bar soap and liquid soap

Show What You Know 2

(optional test master in Teacher Guide)

1) weak 2) break down 3) molecules
4) sit 5) drops

To The Parent

Included at the bottom of all assessment tests, "To The Parent" provides a great way to solicit parent involvement. It not only gives parents an overview of the lesson, but also provides follow-up questions for home use.

NAME _____

Show What You Know 2

Read the sentences about **surface tension** below, then circle the word in the parenthesis that best completes each sentence.

1. Surface tension is a (strong, weak) kind of bond.

2. Soap can help (break down, build up) surface tension.

3. Water (materials, molecules) are tiny pieces of matter.

4. Surface tension helps mayflies (float, sit) on top of the water.

5. Surface tension causes water to form into (drops, steam).

To the Parent . . .   **Scripture Connection:** Ephesians 4: 2-3

Lesson Focus:
Surface Tension

Lesson Objective:
To explore the concept of surface tension

National Science Education Standards:
Standard B1 — *"All students should understand that materials have observable (and measureable) properties . . .*
Materials exist in different states . . . some materials can be changed from one state to another . . ."

Follow-up Questions:
Ask your child how surface tension causes water to form into drops (causes water molecules to cling together, pull closer).
Ask your child how some insects can use surface tension (they can stay on top of the water without floating).
Ask your child how soap can make cleaning easier (breaks surface tension).

Milk Color Mix
Lesson 23

FOCUS Properties of Matter

OBJECTIVE To explore how mixing two colors can make a third color

OVERVIEW Every material is different. We can see something's size or color. We can feel its weight or its temperature. Scientists call these "properties." A material's properties determine how it affects other materials.

WHAT TO DO
With your team, carefully follow each step below.

Observe

Look at the white milk, the blue food coloring, and the yellow food coloring. Think about what these three things have in common.

Describe

Describe all three liquids. What does each one look like? What color is each one? How are they similar? How are they different?

Discuss

What makes materials different? p r o p e r t i e s
How is a baseball different from a softball? s i z e
How are glass and paper cups different? w e i g h t

PHYSICAL · 147

Lesson 23

Introduction

National Standards
Focus: B1

Related: A1, A2

Category
Physical Science

Focus
Properties of Matter

Objective
To explore how mixing two colors can make a third color

Overview
Read the overview aloud to your students. The goal is to create an atmosphere of curiosity and inquiry.

Say: *"Every material is different. We can see something's size or color. We can feel its weight or its temperature. Scientists call these 'properties.' A material's properties determine how it affects other materials."*

Additional Notes

To introduce this lesson, hold up a piece of paper. Ask the students to use as many words as they can to describe this object. Write these words on the board.

Explain to students that they were listing the "properties" of paper. These are the things that make paper different from all other materials (like cloth or water or sand).

Now repeat the activity with a pair of scissors. Once you are finished, cut the paper into pieces with the scissors. Explain that the properties of each material is what made this possible. (You can't cut scissors with paper!)

Say, *"In this lesson, we'll explore how properties determine the way materials affect other materials."*

What To Do

Once students are seated in "research teams" with materials in front of them, read the first section (OBSERVE) aloud.

Say, *"To start this lesson, we're going to* **observe** *some different liquids. Good scientists always carefully examine the things they will be working with before beginning. First, I will read the instructions to you. Then you can follow the instructions as you* **observe** *the liquids in front of you."*

Monitor teams closely as they follow instructions. When teams are finished with this section, repeat the process with the DESCRIBE section. Conclude with the DISCUSS section.

Options

Expand the DISCUSS section by having students trace dotted "key words" using crayons or markers. Trace the word **properties** in light green, the word **size** in bright blue, and the word **weight** in yellow.

Milk Color-Mix
Lesson 23

FOCUS   Properties of Matter

OBJECTIVE   To explore how mixing two colors can make a third color

OVERVIEW   Every material is different. We can see something's size or color. We can feel its weight or its temperature. Scientists call these "properties." A material's properties determine how it affects other materials.

WHAT TO DO

With your team, carefully follow each step below.

Observe

Look at the white milk, the blue food coloring, and the yellow food coloring. **Think** about what these three things have in common.

Describe

Describe all three liquids. What does each one **look** like? What **color** is each one? How are they **similar**? How are they **different**?

Discuss

What makes materials different? properties

How is a baseball different from a softball? size

How are glass and paper cups different? weight

PHYSICAL · 147

Teacher to Teacher

Properties are used to identify things. An object's properties help us decide how to use it.

In sports, we often focus on an athlete's physical properties — like height and weight. In matter, there are physical properties like boiling point, freezing point, and density.

We also may focus on an athlete's performance — how well he bats, how fast she runs, etc. In matter, there are chemical properties — how a substance reacts with other substances, whether it is flammable or corrodes easily, etc.

By looking at both the physical and chemical properties of a substance, scientists can not only determine potential hazards, but also identify valuable characteristics that make a material useful.

READ THE STORY
Every kind of material is different. Scientists call these differences **properties**. Read the story below to find out more about properties.

Different Things

Materials are different in many ways.
Differences can include size, color, weight, or even temperature. Scientists call these differences "properties." Properties determine how materials affect other materials.

Toys can be different.
A bowling ball is heavy and hard.
A bowling ball's properties make it perfect for bowling. But imagine using a bowling ball to play volleyball. Ouch!

A pool toy is large and light.
The properties of a pool toy make it great for floating on the water. But a pool toy wouldn't work at all to build a treehouse.

Food can be different.
Peanuts come in many forms.
Roasted peanuts are hard and crunchy. Boiled peanuts are soft like peas. Ground up peanuts make sticky peanut butter.

Peanuts can be used in many ways.
The properties of peanuts make them useful in making paint, soap, plastics, bug sprays, and even some cosmetics!

Color can be different.
Color is one kind of property.
Color tells us many things. A yellow banana tastes different from a brown one. A black shirt gets hotter than a white one in the sun.

Properties have properties, too!
A color can be light or dark. A color can have different shades. When colors are mixed together, they can make other colors.

148 · PHYSICAL

Extended Teaching

1. To expand vocabulary, explain that words often have more than one meaning. For instance, in this lesson the term "property" refers to a characteristic or trait (as opposed to "something owned"). This helps introduce students to the concept of homophones —words that sound the same but have different meanings. Challenge students to look for other examples (rule = to reign over, or a guide for conduct; play = a theatrical performance, or to take part in a game, or to operate a musical instrument; etc.).

2. Peanuts are a good example of a material with many properties. George Washington Carver was an amazing agricultural chemist who discovered over 300 uses for peanuts. Peanuts can be used to make everything from peanut butter to paper to ink! Read students a biography about this amazing American. (Note: Many of Carver's discoveries were never patented. He believed food products were a gift from God.)

Inform - Day 2

Read The Story
Read the story aloud with your students. (See READING LEVELS on page 12.) After reading, monitor teams as they discuss what was read. Once you feel students have mastered the basic concepts, have them answer the comprehension questions (**What I Learned** - part 1) on the next page.

To introduce the story, say:

"The title of this story is 'Different Things.' Look at your story and follow along as we read it together."

If you wish, encourage Emergent readers to point to words and pictures as you read.

What I Learned (part 1)
These are basic fact-based comprehension questions. Student answers will vary, but suggested responses include:

1 size, weight, color, temperature

2 answers will vary, but should demonstrate different properties . . . example from story is bowling ball and volleyball (bowling ball is hard, heavy; volleyball is softer, lighter)

3 a) cold, white, etc. b) if it gets hot, it will melt into water; it may get dirty and change colors; it will change shapes if it is molded into a snowman; etc.

Field Trip
Visit a factory that manufactures some kind of food. Ask your guide to talk about how the different properties of the ingredients help or hinder the process.

Guest Speaker
Invite a chef to visit your class. Ask him/her to prepare a simple dish and talk about how the properties of the different ingredients interact.

Materials Needed*

petri dish   liquid soap
paper towels   whole milk
food coloring (yellow & blue)

Safety Concerns

3. Poison Hazard

Keep soap out of mouths and away from eyes.

4. Slipping

There is a potential for spilled liquids. Remind students to exercise caution.

Do the Activity

Read the activity in advance so you understand it thoroughly. (If time allows, try it yourself.) Before students begin, carefully go over the **Safety Concerns** together.

Pass out materials, then have your students follow along as you read the instructions for **Step 1**. Monitor teams closely as they complete this step.

Once teams have completed **Step 1**, read instructions for **Step 2**. Monitor teams as before. Repeat for **Step 3** and **Step 4**.

After the activity, allow time for each team to share their observations. To encourage higher-level thinking, encourage teams to not only share their observations with each other, but also with other teams.

Special Instructions

Note: Goggles are a reasonable safety precaution to avoid soap in the eyes.

Step 1 - Warn students not to drink or taste the milk. Also, food coloring can stain clothing. Exercise appropriate precautions.

DO THE ACTIVITY
Working with your research team, carefully follow each step below. Before you start, be sure you know the **safety rules** for this activity.

STEP 1
Place the petri dish on a paper towel. **Fill** the petri dish with milk. Carefully **place** one drop of blue food coloring in the middle of the dish.

STEP 2
Now carefully **place** one drop of yellow food coloring about 1 inch away from the spot of blue food coloring. (An inch is about the width of your thumb.)

STEP 3
Quicky **add** one or two drops of liquid soap between the two spots of color. **Observe** what happens as the soap changes the properties of the milk.

STEP 4
Review the steps in this activity. **Discuss** what caused the colors to mix together. **Compare** your observations with those of other research teams.

What Happened?

Immediately following the activity, help your students understand what they observed.

Say: *"In this activity, you observed how a material's properties can determine how it affects other materials.*

*In **Steps 1** and **2**, you added drops of blue and yellow coloring to a petri dish full of milk.*

*Then in **Step 3**, you added a drop of soap to the area between the colors. The soap broke the surface tension of the milk, allowing the two colors to mix. This changed the properties "blue" and "yellow" into the new property "green"!*

*Finally in **Step 4**, you checked your results by discussing your findings with other teams."*

* Bold-faced items supplied in kit.

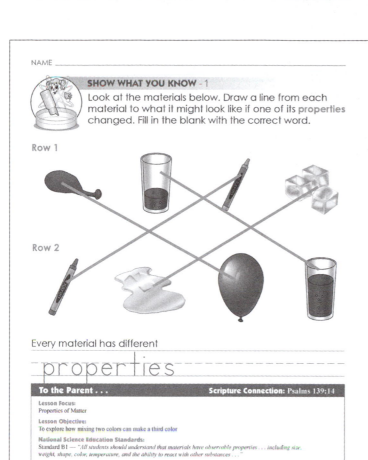

NAME _____

SHOW WHAT YOU KNOW - 1

Look at the materials below. Draw a line from each material to what it might look like if one of its **properties** changed. Fill in the blank with the correct word.

Row 1

Row 2

Every material has different

properties

To the Parent . . .   **Scripture Connection:** Psalms 139:14

Lesson Focus:
Properties of Matter

Lesson Objective:
To explore how mixing two colors can make a third color

National Science Education Standards:
Standard B1 — *"All students should understand that materials have observable properties . . . including size, weight, shape, color, temperature, and the ability to react with other substances . . ."*

Follow-up Questions:
Every material is different. Ask your child what scientists call these differences (properties).
Ask your child to list some properties that materials might have (size, weight, shape, color, temperature, etc.).
Ask your child how freezing water changes its properties (makes it hard, makes it colder, etc.).

Food For Thought

A related "Scripture Object Lesson" you can share with your students.

Psalms 139:14

Every human being has similar properties. We all have a heart and a brain. We all have skin and hair and fingers and toes.

But every one of us is very different, too. That's the way God made us!

Sometimes you might feel a little uncomfortable around people who are different from you. But Scripture reminds us that God made every person unique. We simply need to learn to recognize and celebrate what makes that person special.

Never let someone's outside appearance keep you from getting to know them better. Ask God to help you discover their special gift. Enjoy your differences, and thank the Creator — the one who made each of us unique and special!

Expand - Day 4

Begin **Day 4** with a review of **Day 3**, then have students answer "part 2" questions.

What I Learned (part 2)

These are higher-level cognitive questions (explain, compare, predict). Student answers will vary but suggested responses may include:

① blue and yellow make green

② everything was the same, except a drop of soap was added in step 3

③ if it turned to snow, it would change colors; if it turned to ice it would get harder; etc.

Assess - Day 5

Suggestions for modifying assessments to reflect reading levels can be found under ASSESSMENT METHODS on page 12.

Show What You Know 1

(general assessment in Student Worktext)

1) line from balloon to balloon (changed size); glass to glass (changed weight); crayon to crayon (changed color); and ice cubes to puddle (changed temperature)
2) fill in word = properties

Show What You Know 2

(optional test master in Teacher Guide)

1) temperature 2) shape 3) color
4) weight 5) size (color or smell are more obscure, but also acceptable for #5)

To The Parent

Included at the bottom of all assessment tests, "To The Parent" provides a great way to solicit parent involvement. It not only gives parents an overview of the lesson, but also provides follow-up questions for home use.

NAME _____

Show What You Know 2

Read each sentence below. Using the **word bank** below, choose a word to tell what property is being described, then write it on the line. (Some words will not be used.)

1. My hands are cold from playing in the snow. _____

2. That strange cloud looks a lot like a rabbit! _____

3. We painted my bedroom green and white. _____

4. This box is too heavy for me to lift without help. _____

5. Grandmother made a very big chocolate cake. _____

WORD BANK:

sound   shape   temperature   size   weight   color   smell

FOCUS Density

OBJECTIVE To explore how density affects matter

OVERVIEW "Density" means how tightly molecules are packed together. (Molecules are the tiny particles everything is made from.) An object's density can affect how it behaves, or even how its matter affects other matter.

WHAT TO DO

With your team, carefully follow each step below.

Observe

Look at the tablet, the water, and the oil. Think about the three most common states of matter on Earth (solid, liquid, gas). Which state describes each item?

Describe

Describe the water and the oil. What does each one look like? What does each one feel like? How are they similar? How are they different?

Discuss

What state of matter is the tint tablet? solid
What state of matter is the water or oil? liquid
What state of matter best describes a bubble? gas

PHYSICAL · 153

Lesson 24

Introduction

National Standards
Focus: B1

Related: A1, A2, B2

Category
Physical Science

Focus
Density

Objective
To explore how density affects matter

Overview
Read the overview aloud to your students. The goal is to create an atmosphere of curiosity and inquiry.

Say: *"Density means how tightly molecules are packed together. (Molecules are the tiny particles everything is made from.) An object's density can determine how its matter behaves, or even how its matter affects other matter."*

Additional Notes

To help introduce this lesson, have your students lightly tap different objects with their knuckles (the top of a desk, a pencil box, a chair, a thick book, a toy drum, etc.).

Have them listen closely to the sound that each object makes. Give them time to test several.

Now ask students to compare the sounds they heard to the "heaviness" of each object they tapped.

As you discuss their findings (heavy objects sound different from light objects of the same size) use the word "density" to describe the difference in objects tested.

Engage - Day 1

What To Do

Once students are seated in "research teams" with materials in front of them, read the first section (OBSERVE) aloud.

Say, *"To start this lesson, we're going to **observe** some things. Observe is a word good scientists use often. It means 'to look at closely.' First, I will read the instructions to you. Then you can follow the instructions as you **observe** the items in front of you."*

Monitor teams closely as they follow instructions. When teams are finished with this section, repeat the process with the DESCRIBE section. Conclude with the DISCUSS section.

Options

Expand the DISCUSS section by having students trace the dotted "key words" using crayons or markers. Have students trace the word **solid** in yellow (like the tint tablet), **liquid** in blue (like water), and **gas** in pink (like a bubble-gum bubble).

Little Lava-Lamp
Lesson 24

FOCUS	Density
OBJECTIVE	To explore how density affects matter
OVERVIEW	"Density" means how tightly molecules are packed together. (Molecules are the tiny particles everything is made from.) An object's density can affect how it behaves, or even how its matter affects other matter.

WHAT TO DO

With your team, carefully follow each step below.

Observe

Look at the **tablet**, the **water**, and the **oil**. **Think** about the three most common states of matter on Earth (solid, liquid, gas). Which state describes each item?

Describe

Describe the **water** and the **oil**. What does each one **look** like? What does each one **feel** like? How are they similar? How are they different?

Discuss

What state of matter is the tint tablet? *solid*

What state of matter is the water or oil? *liquid*

What state of matter best describes a bubble? *gas*

PHYSICAL · **153**

Teacher to Teacher

All matter is made of atoms and molecules. The interaction of these particles depends on the state of the matter (and vice versa).

In order to better understand how density affects matter, it's helpful to know more about matter's three most common states.[1]

In a **solid**, molecules are very close. They vibrate, but always remain in a fixed position.

In a **liquid**, molecules are not as close, but they can move around.

In a **gas**, molecules are farther apart and they move randomly.

[1] *Currently there are six known states of matter: solid, liquid, gas, plasma, and two kinds of "condensates" (Bose-Einstein and Fermionic).*

Density

Everything on Earth has a certain density.
Density is a word scientists use to tell how tightly molecules are packed together. Things that are more dense are heavier. Things that are less dense are lighter.

This is iron

Iron is matter in a solid state.
A solid is usually more dense than a liquid or gas. Iron molecules are more tightly packed together than water or air molecules.

Solids can have different density.
Iron is very dense. Foam is not very dense. A piece of iron is much heavier than the same size piece of foam.

This is water.

Water is matter in a liquid state.
Liquids are usually less dense than solids, but more dense than gases. This makes water lighter than iron, but heavier than air.

Liquids can have different density.
If the density of two liquids is different, they may not mix together. The lighter liquid will usually float to the top.

This is air.

Air is matter in a gaseous state.
Gases are usually less dense than solids or liquids. When air is released in water, it forms a bubble and rises to the surface.

Air can have different density.
Cold air is more dense than hot air. The warmest air in a room will be at the ceiling. Air density can even affect weather.

154 · PHYSICAL

Extended Teaching

1. To extend vocabulary, use other words to describe "density" such as "compact" or "tightly packed." Since density describes an object's mass as it relates to volume, you may also use words related to "weight." (This is an oversimplification, but useful at this level.)

2. Some things seem to defy logic. For instance, rocks do not float because they are denser than water. But pumice (a volcanic rock) FLOATS! This is because pumice is full of air (which is less dense than water). Also, steel is much denser than water. So why does a battleship float? The ship's shape displaces water with air.

3. Give each student a glass of milk, chocolate mix, a spoon, and a straw. Ask students to pour the mix (solid) into the milk (liquid) and stir. Now have them softly blow air (gas) through the straw into the cup and observe the bubbles. Ask, "Which one is more dense — milk or air?"

Inform - Day 2

Read The Story

Read the story aloud with your students. (See READING LEVELS on page 12.) After reading, monitor teams as they discuss what was read. Once you feel students have mastered the basic concepts, have them answer the comprehension questions (**What I Learned** - part 1) on the next page.

To introduce the story, say:

"The title of this story is 'Density.' Look at your story and follow along as we read it together."

If you wish, encourage Emergent readers to point to words and pictures as you read.

What I Learned (part 1)

These are basic fact-based comprehension questions. Student answers will vary, but suggested responses include:

1 how tightly its molecules are packed together

2 a) both gas, both less dense than liquid or solid b) cold air is more dense than hot air

3 they will not mix; the water will sink to the bottom (or the oil will float to the top)

Field Trip

If there is a hot air balloonist in your area, try to arrange a demonstration. Also, many science museums offer hands-on displays about the most common states of matter.

Guest Speaker

Invite a balloon artist to visit your class. Ask him/her to bring helium-filled balloons as well as air-filled balloons. Have the artist talk about differences in balloons and demonstrate the art to your students.

LITTLE LAVA LAMP · 161

Materials Needed*

clear tube (plastic)   **tint tablet**
vegetable oil   water
paper towels

Safety Concerns

3. Poison Hazard

Do not eat the tablet! Also, improper handling may stain fingers or clothes.

4. Slipping

There is a potential for spilled liquids. Remind students to exercise caution.

Do the Activity

Read the activity in advance so you understand it thoroughly. (If time allows, try it yourself.) Before students begin, carefully go over the **Safety Concerns** together.

Pass out materials, then have your students follow along as you read the instructions for **Step 1**. Monitor teams closely as they complete this step.

Once teams have completed **Step 1**, read instructions for **Step 2**. Monitor teams as before. Repeat for **Step 3** and **Step 4**.

After the activity, allow time for each team to share their observations. To encourage higher-level thinking, encourage teams to not only share their observations with each other, but also with other teams.

Special Instructions

Step 1 - Make certain students recognize the "half full" point. You may wish to mark tubes with a line before beginning.

Step 2 - Students must keep the tube very still! Shaking will delay step 3!

Step 3 - Confirm lids are screwed on tight before students turn tubes upside down.

Step 4 - Rotate between groups. Guide if needed. Encourage them to use the scientific terms they have learned.

 DO THE ACTIVITY
Working with your research team, carefully follow each step below. Before you start, be sure you know the **safety rules** for this activity.

STEP 1 Fill the tube half full of water. Now slowly **add** oil until the tube is full. **Hold** the tube very still until the two liquids have completely stopped moving.

STEP 2 **Drop** the tint tablet into the tube. Carefully **observe** what happens. At what point did the tablet begin to dissolve? **Discuss** what you see happening.

STEP 3 Once the bubbles are gone, fasten the lid on the tube. Slowly **turn** it upside down. **Observe** what happens. **Repeat** until everyone has had a turn.

STEP 4 **Review** each step in this activity. **Discuss** the states of matter present in each step. **Compare** your observations with those of other teams.

What Happened?

Immediately following the activity, help your students understand what they observed.

Say: "**Step 1** of this activity showed that some liquids of different densities do not mix. The lighter liquid floated to the top of the tube.

In **Steps 2** and **3**, the solid tint tablet fell through the liquid oil, but did not dissolve until it hit the denser liquid water. As it dissolved, it gave off gas bubbles. Water molecules stuck to these bubbles, and rode them to the surface.

But when the bubbles popped, releasing the gas, the water molecules sank back down.

In this activity we were able to see the difference in density between a solid (like the tablet), the liquids (like the oil and water), and a gas (like the air bubbles)."

NAME _____

SHOW WHAT YOU KNOW - 1

Circle the **solid** matter in red. Circle the **liquid** matter in blue. Circle the matter that is a **gas** in green. Write the correct "state" on the lines below.

The least dense matter is

gas

The most dense matter is

solid

The medium dense matter is

liquid

Food For Thought

*A related "Scripture Object Lesson"
you can share with your students.*

Job 37:16

When your friends or family sense you have a problem, they may ask, "What's the matter?" That's just another way of asking, "What's wrong?" The problem that you face may be no bigger than a tiny bubble in a pond (gas). Or it may be a lot bigger, causing you to shed a few tears (liquid). It might even be a huge problem, so that you feel like you're carrying a basket of bricks (solid)! But as surely as God controls all the matter in the universe, He knows your problem and He has a plan for you.

Whatever your problem, big or small, learn to trust in God — and let Him take control of your life.

Expand - Day 4

Begin **Day 4** with a review of **Day 3**, then have students answer "part 2" questions.

What I Learned (part 2)

These are higher-level cognitive questions (explain, compare, predict). Student answers will vary, but suggested responses may include:

1 a) didn't dissolve; fell through oil
b) dissolved in water; colored water; started to bubble

2 a) water is more dense b) water fell to the bottom (or oil floated to the top)

3 a) to the bottom of the tube b) a BB is more dense than water or oil

Assess - Day 5

Suggestions for modifying assessments to reflect reading levels can be found under ASSESSMENT METHODS on page 12.

Show What You Know 1

(general assessment in Student Worktext)

Blanks: 1) gas 2) solid 3) liquid
Also, the scales should be circled in red, the oil and water in blue, and the air bubbles in green (students may also circle the diver in blue since the diver is in the water)

Show What You Know 2

(optional test master in Teacher Guide)

1) S   2) L   3) G   4) S   5) G

To The Parent

Included at the bottom of all assessment tests, "To The Parent" provides a great way to solicit parent involvement. It not only gives parents an overview of the lesson, but also provides follow-up questions for home use.

NAME _____

Show What You Know 2

Read each sentence below. If it describes the solid state of matter, circle **S**. If it describes liquid matter, circle **L**. If it describes gaseous matter, circle **G**.

S L G   1. I am the most dense state of matter.

S L G   2. I am water. What state of matter am I?

S L G   3. I can form a bubble when I am in a liquid.

S L G   4. My molecules are the most tightly packed.

S L G   5. I am the least dense state of matter.

To the Parent . . .   **Scripture Connection:** Job 37:16

Lesson Focus:
Density

Lesson Objective:
To explore how density affects matter

National Science Education Standards:
Standard B1 — *"All students should understand that materials have observable (and measurable) properties . . . Materials exist in different states . . . some materials can be changed from one state to another . . ."*

Follow-up Questions:
Ask your child which state of matter is the most dense (solid). Ask for an example of a solid.
Ask your child which state of matter is the least dense (gas). Ask for an example of a gas.
Ask your child to give an example of how density affects matter (oil floats on water; bubbles rise to surface; etc.).

Lesson 25

Spoonful of Sound
Lesson 25

FOCUS Sound

OBJECTIVE To explore how sound is created by vibration

OVERVIEW Vibration is when an object moves back and forth very rapidly. When this movement makes a noise we can hear, we call it "sound."

WHAT TO DO

With your team, carefully follow each step below.

Observe
Look at the three spoons. Think about how these spoons are similar. Think about how these spoons are different. Discuss what each spoon might be used for.

Describe
Describe each spoon. What does it **look** like? What does it **feel** like? What **color** is it? What **shape** is it? How is each spoon **different** from the others?

Discuss
What is the hardest spoon made from? metal
What is the white spoon made from? plastic
What is the odd-shaped spoon made from? wood

PHYSICAL · 159

Introduction

National Standards
Focus: B2

Related: A1, A2, B1, E1, E2, F1

Category
Physical Science

Focus
Sound

Objective
To explore how sound is created by vibration

Overview
Read the overview aloud to your students. The goal is to create an atmosphere of curiosity and inquiry.

Say: *"Vibration is when an object moves back and forth very rapidly. When this movement makes a noise we can hear, we call it sound."*

Additional Notes

To introduce this lesson, ask your students which sense or senses (sight, hearing, touch, taste, smell) they can use to detect sounds.

Once they have focused on hearing, tell them you're going to show them another way to detect sound. Have them place their fingertips against the front of their throats. Now have them slowly say "ah" (just like a doctor). Explain that they are not only *hearing* the sound, but also *feeling* the vibration of air in their vocal cords. Repeat using other short vowel sounds. This will help students understand that we not only *hear* sounds, but sometimes also *feel* the vibrations that create sound.

What To Do

Once students are seated in "research teams" with materials in front of them, read the first section (OBSERVE) aloud.

Say, *"To start this lesson, we're going to **observe** some similar things. Good scientists always carefully examine the things they will be working with before beginning. First, I will read the instructions to you. Then you can follow the instructions as you **observe** the items in front of you."*

Monitor teams closely as they follow instructions. When teams are finished with this section, repeat the process with the DESCRIBE section. Conclude with the DISCUSS section.

Options

Expand the DISCUSS section by having students trace dotted "key words" using crayons or markers. Trace the word **metal** in silver or gray, the word **plastic** in blue, and the word **wood** in brown.

FOCUS	Sound
OBJECTIVE	To explore how sound is created by vibration
OVERVIEW	Vibration is when an object moves back and forth very rapidly. When this movement makes a noise we can hear, we call it "sound."

Spoonful of Sound
Lesson 25

WHAT TO DO

With your team, carefully follow each step below.

Observe

Look at the three spoons. **Think** about how these spoons are similar. **Think** about how these spoons are different. **Discuss** what each spoon might be used for.

Describe

Describe each spoon. What does it **look** like? What does it **feel** like? What **color** is it? What **shape** is it? How is each spoon **different** from the others?

Discuss

What is the hardest spoon made from? *metal*
What is the white spoon made from? *plastic*
What is the odd-shaped spoon made from? *wood*

PHYSICAL · 159

Teacher to Teacher

Help your students research how animals use sound/vibration to communicate. Here are some ideas to get you started:

Cats use a smooth vibrating sound (purring) to show that they are contented. Elephants use a deep, vibrating sound (rumbling) to show they are frightened. This sound is often impossible for the human ear to hear, but elephant riders certainly can feel it! Bats rely on very high pitched sounds (echolocation) to avoid obstacles or find each other as they fly. Many marine animals (like whales and dolphins) use whistling sounds to communicate, as well as clicking sounds that work like sonar.

Extended Teaching

1. Demonstrate the variety of sounds made by different musical instruments by playing recordings. Show pictures of the instruments as they are played, and discuss how the sound is made (banging, air flow, plucked strings, etc.). The classic *Peter and the Wolf* is ideal for this activity!

2. Give each student a large rubber band. Demonstrate how to stretch the band and pluck it to create a vibration. Stretch and relax the band to make different sounds. Try thicker and thinner bands for variety. Point out that not only can you hear and feel the vibration, but in this case you can actually *see* it too!

3. Play "Snack Sounds." Choose fun food items that usually make a lot of noise (carrots, corn chips, large pretzels, dry cereals, etc.). Encourage teams to have fun trying to eat these very noisy foods *quietly*!

Read The Story

Read the story aloud with your students. (See READING LEVELS on page 12.) After reading, monitor teams as they discuss what was read. Once you feel students have mastered the basic concepts, have them answer the comprehension questions (**What I Learned** - part 1) on the next page.

To introduce the story, say:

"The title of this story is 'Sound.' Look at your story and follow along as we read it together."

If you wish, encourage Emergent readers to point to words and pictures as you read.

What I Learned (part 1)

These are basic fact-based comprehension questions. Student answers will vary, but suggested responses include:

(1) 1) back/forth movement 2) sound

(2) a) both make sound through vibration b) answers will vary, but should include the idea that a drum requires banging and a trumpet requires blowing air

(3) It would make little noise b) drum skin must be tight to produce vibration

Field Trip

Take a trip to "stalk sounds." Have the group walk around the playground without talking, listening carefully to the sounds they hear and taking notes. When you return to class, compile their findings on the board into categories like "natural," "man-made," "loud," "soft," "short," "long," etc.

Guest Speaker

Invite a musician to visit your class. Have him/her bring various instruments and demonstrate how vibration can be used to create many different kinds of sounds.

Materials Needed*

spoons (1 metal, 1 plastic, 1 wooden)
binder clip   string

Safety Concerns

4. Other

Caution students not to wrap the string around their finger too tightly.

Do the Activity

Read the activity in advance so you understand it thoroughly. (If time allows, try it yourself.) Before students begin, carefully go over the **Safety Concerns** together.

Pass out materials, then have your students follow along as you read the instructions for **Step 1**. Monitor teams closely as they complete this step.

Once teams have completed **Step 1**, read instructions for **Step 2**. Monitor teams as before. Repeat for **Step 3** and **Step 4**.

After the activity, allow time for each team to share their observations. To encourage higher-level thinking, encourage teams to not only share their observations with each other, but also with other teams.

Special Instructions

Step 1 - The "end" of the spoon refers to the top of the handle (see illustration). You may need to define "index finger" if some have not heard this term before. Also, emphasize the difference between "tapping" and "banging," and remind students to avoid horseplay.

Step 2 - To help students better describe what they hear, suggest words like high/low, soft/loud, short/long, etc. Also, encourage them to make comparisons with other sounds they have heard.

DO THE ACTIVITY

Working with your research team, carefully follow each step below. Before you start, be sure you know the **safety rules** for this activity.

STEP 1 — **Clip** the center of the string to the end of a spoon. **Wrap** the ends of the string around your index fingers. **Tap** the spoon on a chair. **Record** what you hear.

STEP 2 — **Place** your index fingers in your ears. **Tap** the spoon on a chair again. **Record** what you hear. **Compare** this to the sound you heard in Step 1.

STEP 3 — **Repeat** steps 1 and 2 using the other two spoons. **Record** what you hear with each change. Make sure everyone on your team has a turn.

STEP 4 — **Compare** all the sounds you heard in this activity. **Discuss** your observations with your team, then **compare** findings with other research teams.

162 · PHYSICAL

What Happened?

Immediately following the activity, help your students understand what they observed.

Say: *"In this activity you created vibrations in different kinds of materials (like metal, plastic, and wood). These vibrations produced different kinds of sounds.*

*In **Step 1**, you tested the power of the air to carry a faint sound to your ears. The sound was not very easy to hear.*

*In **Step 2**, you made a more direct connection from the vibration to your ears, helping you hear the sound much better.*

*In **Step 3**, you compared the sounds made by different materials. You discovered that different materials vibrate in different ways, resulting in different sounds.*

*Finally in **Step 4**, you compared your findings with those of the other research teams."*

---

* Bold-faced items supplied in kit.

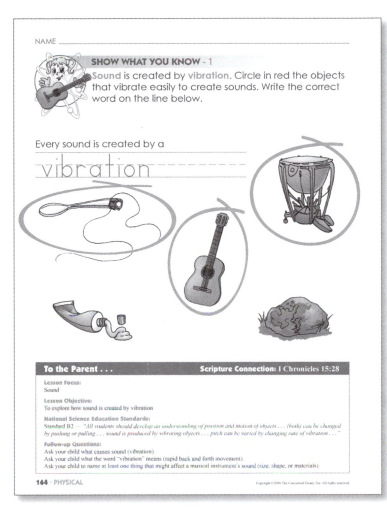

NAME _____

SHOW WHAT YOU KNOW - 1
Sound is created by vibration. Circle in red the objects that vibrate easily to create sounds. Write the correct word on the line below.

Every sound is created by a

vibration

To the Parent . . .   Scripture Connection: I Chronicles 15:28

Lesson Focus:
Sound

Lesson Objective:
To explore how sound is created by vibration

National Science Education Standards:
Standard B2 — "All students should develop an understanding of position and motion of objects . . . (both) can be changed by pushing or pulling . . . sound is produced by vibrating objects . . . pitch can be varied by changing rate of vibration . . ."

Follow-up Questions:
Ask your child what causes sound (vibration).
Ask your child what the word "vibration" means (rapid back and forth movement).
Ask your child to name at least one thing that might affect a musical instrument's sound (size, shape, or materials).

164 · PHYSICAL

Food For Thought

A related "Scripture Object Lesson" you can share with your students.

I Chronicles 15:28

This Scripture shows how important music was to the Children of Israel. They used this gift from God as a way to praise and worship Him.

Scripture contains many examples of God's people honoring Him by singing or playing musical instruments.

But some music does not honor God. It can even lead to feelings of anger, jealousy, or pain.

Like the children's song says, "Be careful little ears what you hear!" Make sure the music you sing or play or hear is always the kind that God would choose for you.

Expand - Day 4

Begin **Day 4** with a review of **Day 3**, then have students answer "part 2" questions.

What I Learned (part 2)

These are higher-level cognitive questions (explain, compare, predict). Student answers will vary, but suggested responses may include:

1 a) answers will vary, but should describe shape, color, size, etc. b) metal, plastic, wood

2 a) all came from vibrations b) some higher, some lower, etc.

3 a) no b) answers will vary, but should include the idea that vibration would be different for different sizes, shapes, or types of metal

Assess - Day 5

Suggestions for modifying assessments to reflect reading levels can be found under ASSESSMENT METHODS on page 12.

Show What You Know 1
(general assessment in Student Worktext)

Blank: vibration
The guitar, spoon on a string, and drum should be circled in red

Show What You Know 2
(optional test master in Teacher Guide)

1) pluck strings
2) beat with a drumstick
3) blow air through a mouthpiece
4) crash two halves together
5) tap with a metal rod

To The Parent

Included at the bottom of all assessment tests, "To The Parent" provides a great way to solicit parent involvement. It not only gives parents an overview of the lesson, but also provides follow-up questions for home use.

NAME _____

Show What You Know 2

Look at the list of musical instruments below. On each line, write a phrase that best describes what you would need to do to create a vibration. (Example: flute = blow air through a mouthpiece.)

Guitar _____

Drum _____

Trumpet _____

Cymbals _____

Triangle _____

To the Parent . . .   **Scripture Connection:** 1 Chronicles 15:28

Lesson Focus:
Sound

Lesson Objective:
To explore how sound is created by vibration

National Science Education Standards:
Standard B2 — *"All students should develop an understanding of position and motion of objects . . . (both) can be changed by pushing or pulling . . . sound is produced by vibrating objects . . . pitch can be varied by changing rate of vibration . . ."*

Follow-up Questions:
Ask your child what causes sound (vibration).
Ask your child what the word "vibration" means (rapid back and forth movement).
Ask your child to name at least one thing that might affect a musical instrument's sound (size, shape, or materials).

Lesson 26

FOCUS Pitch

OBJECTIVE To explore how "changing the rate of vibration changes the sound"

OVERVIEW Sounds are created by vibration. If the rate of vibration changes, then the pitch (tone) of the sound changes, too.

WHAT TO DO

With your team, carefully follow each step below.

Observe

Hold the string in your hand. Look at the string closely.

Now ask a team member to stretch the string tightly.

Pluck the string and listen to the result.

Describe

Describe the string. What does it look like? What does it feel like? What can you do to make the string make a sound? What might change the sound?

Discuss

What do we call noise we can hear? sound

What is it that creates sound? vibration

What are changes in sound called? pitch

PHYSICAL · 165

National Standards
Focus: B2

Related: A1, A2, B1, E1, E2

Category
Physical Science

Focus
Pitch

Objective
To explore how changing the rate of vibration changes the sound

Overview
Read the overview aloud to your students. The goal is to create an atmosphere of curiosity and inquiry.

Say: *"Sounds are created by vibration. If the rate of vibration changes, then the pitch or 'tone' of the sound changes, too."*

Additional Notes

To introduce this lesson, ask your students to think about a guitar. Discuss what it is made from, what its basic parts are, and how it is shaped.

Show them a picture of a guitar — or a real guitar if you have one. Point out the different parts (the hole in the front, the strings, the tuning keys, etc.).

Ask students how a guitar makes sound. Explain that when someone strikes the strings, the strings vibrate, and these vibrations create the noises we call sound.

Say, *"In this lesson, we'll discover where sounds come from, what causes sounds to change, and even some ways that those changes can be controlled."*

What To Do

Once students are seated in "research teams" with materials in front of them, read the first section (OBSERVE) aloud.

Say, *"To start this lesson, we're going to **observe** a familiar object. Good scientists always carefully examine the things they will be working with before beginning. First, I will read the instructions to you. Then you can follow the instructions as you **observe** the object in front of you."*

Monitor teams closely as they follow instructions. When teams are finished with this section, repeat the process with the DESCRIBE section. Conclude with the DISCUSS section.

Options

To expand the DISCUSS section, have students feel slight variations in vibration by tracing the dotted "key word" **sound** with a pencil, the word **vibration** with a crayon, and the word **pitch** with a felt-tip marker. Take some time to discuss the tiny differences in how each one felt.

String-Thing

FOCUS	Pitch
OBJECTIVE	To explore how "changing the rate of vibration changes the sound"
OVERVIEW	Sounds are created by vibration. If the rate of vibration changes, then the pitch (tone) of the sound changes, too.

WHAT TO DO

With your team, carefully follow each step below.

Observe

Hold the string in your hand. **Look** at the string closely.

Now **ask** a team member to stretch the string tightly.

Pluck the string and **listen** to the result.

Describe

Describe the string. What does it **look** like? What does it **feel** like? What can you do to make the string make a sound? What might **change** the sound?

Discuss

What do we call noise we can hear? *sound*

What is it that creates sound? *vibration*

What are changes in sound called? *pitch*

PHYSICAL · **165**

Teacher to Teacher

Sound is created by vibration, but there are vibrations that are beyond the range of the human ear.

Infrasound refers to vibrations of less than 20 Hertz (cycles per second). These "low frequency" sounds include earthquake waves, underground explosions, avalanches, volcanoes, ocean waves, and even meteors hitting Earth.

Studies have shown that although they can't hear them, some people can sense these sounds, making them feel uneasy.

Ultrasound refers to vibrations that take place above 20,000 Hertz. Although humans can't, many animals hear these "high frequency" sounds. Ultrasound can also be used as a medical diagnostic tool.

READ THE STORY
Vibration creates sound. If the rate of vibration changes, then the sound changes, too. Read the story below to find out more.

Changes in Sound
Different vibrations create different sounds.
Vibration is a rapid back and forth movement. If the speed of the vibration changes, then the sound changes, too. The tone a sound makes is called its "pitch."

These are handbells.
Handbells make sound through vibration.
When you ring a handbell, a clapper strikes the shell of the bell, making it vibrate. We hear this vibration as sound.

Different bells have different sounds.
A bell's sound is determined by its size and shape. Every bell is designed to play only one very specific pitch.

This is a violin.
A violin makes sound through vibration.
The bow vibrates the violin's strings. The tighter the string, the faster it vibrates, the higher the pitch.

Changing vibration changes pitch.
By moving his fingers, a musician can tighten or loosen a string. This changes the vibration, which changes the pitch.

This is your voice.
People make sound through vibration.
Your throat contains "vocal chords." When you speak, air passes through your vocal chords, making them vibrate.

Changing vocal chords changes pitch.
If you tighten your vocal chords, the pitch is higher. If you loosen your vocal chords, the pitch is lower.

Extended Teaching

1. To expand vocabulary, talk about "frequency" (a word used to describe the speed of vibration). Humans can sing notes with low frequencies (about 60 vibrations/second) to high frequencies (over 4,000 vibrations/second). Let students try to sing at their highest and lowest frequencies.

2. A fun variation on this lesson's activity is to use your String Thing as a "clucker"! Simply hold the cup securely, wrap a damp paper towel around the string, pinch the string tightly, and jerk downward gently. With a little practice, the resulting squawks sound remarkably like a chicken!

3. To show how size and shape affect vibration and sound, repeat this activity using different size cups (from medicine cups to 20 oz. cups) and different thicknesses of string. Point out that the cup is the "amplifier" (new vocabulary term) that makes the sound of the string easier to hear. Connect this idea to how musical instruments work.

Read The Story
Read the story aloud with your students. (See READING LEVELS on page 12.) After reading, monitor teams as they discuss what was read. Once you feel students have mastered the basic concepts, have them answer the comprehension questions (**What I Learned** - part 1) on the next page.

To introduce the story, say:

"The title of this story is 'Changes in Sound.' Look at your story and follow along as we read it together."

If you wish, encourage Emergent readers to point to words and pictures as you read.

What I Learned (part 1)
These are basic fact-based comprehension questions. Student answers will vary, but suggested responses include:

1 a) the rate of vibration b) the tone a sound makes

2 a) both make sound by vibration
b) answers will vary

3 a) pitch gets higher b) the tighter something is, the faster it vibrates, and the higher the tone

Field Trip
Attend a performance by a handbell choir. Arrange for a demonstration after the performance. (Note: Handbells are unusual instruments since they only have one pitch. You can't play a tune with just one!)

Guest Speaker
Invite a concert musician with a cello or double bass (or bluegrass musician with a "washtub bass") to visit your class. Ask him/her to demonstrate how tightening or loosening a string can change the pitch or tone. Encourage your guest to play a pattern or two for your students.

Materials Needed*

portion cup (pre-drilled)
string (thin)   **string** (thick)
paperclip

Safety Concerns

4. Other

Remind students to be good scientists and to work cooperatively.

Do the Activity

Read the activity in advance so you understand it thoroughly. (If time allows, try it yourself.) Before students begin, carefully go over the **Safety Concerns** together.

Pass out materials, then have your students follow along as you read the instructions for **Step 1**. Monitor teams closely as they complete this step.

Once teams have completed **Step 1**, read instructions for **Step 2**. Monitor teams as before. Repeat for **Step 3** and **Step 4**.

After the activity, allow time for each team to share their observations. To encourage higher-level thinking, encourage teams to not only share their observations with each other, but also with other teams.

Special Instructions

Step 1 - Depending on developmental readiness, some teams may need help tying the knot and threading the string through the hole.

Step 2 - For even better vibration, a second team member can hold the cup at the top with their fingertips. Monitor to make sure cups are being held correctly for best results.

DO THE ACTIVITY

Working with your research team, carefully follow each step below. Before you start, be sure you know the **safety rules** for this activity.

STEP 1 Tie the paperclip to the end of the string. **Slide** the knot to the center of the paperclip. **Push** the other end of the string through the hole in the bottom of the cup.

STEP 2 Pull the string until the paperclip rests on the bottom of the cup. **Ask** a team member to hold the cup firmly, then **pull** the string until it is tight.

STEP 3 Pluck the string and listen to the result. Now **loosen** or **tighten** the string and repeat. **Compare** the sounds the string makes as you loosen and tighten the string.

STEP 4 The tighter the string, the faster it vibrated. **Discuss** the effect this had on the sound, then **compare** your team's findings with other research teams.

168 · PHYSICAL

What Happened?

Immediately following the activity, help your students understand what they observed.

Say: *"In this activity you were able to change sound by changing the rate of vibration.*

In Steps 1 and 2, you made your own stringed instrument in order to conduct your experiments.

In Step 3, you observed changes in pitch created by tightening and loosening the string. A tight string vibrates faster, making the pitch higher. A loose string vibrates slower, making the pitch lower.

Finally in Step 4, you shared and compared your findings with those of other research teams."

* *Bold-faced items supplied in kit.*

NAME _____

SHOW WHAT YOU KNOW - 1

Vibration creates **sound**. The rate of vibration changes the **pitch**. Circle the objects that can change their pitch easily. Write the correct word on the line below.

Vibration rate changes the

pitch

To the Parent . . .   Scripture Connection: Proverbs 15:1

Lesson Focus:
Pitch (or tone)

Lesson Objective:
To explore how changing the rate of vibration changes pitch

National Science Education Standards:
Standard B2 — "*All students should develop an understanding of position and motion of objects . . . (both) can be changed by pushing or pulling . . . sound is produced by vibrating objects . . . pitch can be varied by changing rate of vibration . . .*"

Follow-up Questions:
Ask your child what causes sound (vibration). Ask your child to describe some common sounds.
Ask your child what changes in vibration are called (pitch).
Ask your child what causes pitch to go up or down as we speak (vocal chords get tighter or looser).

170 · PHYSICAL

Food For Thought

A related "Scripture Object Lesson" you can share with your students.

Proverbs 15:1

In this lesson, we learned that the rate of vibration affects the pitch or "tone" of a sound. Putting different tones together can create beautiful music. Music is not only pleasing to the ear, but it can also communicate emotions like happiness, sadness, anger, or joy.

This Scripture reminds us that our words can have the same kind of effect on others. The tone we use in speaking can affect the message we are sending to someone.

Do you think about how something sounds before you say it? Are you always aware of your tone? Make a special effort today to make your words vibrate with a tone that is pleasing to others. This kind of talk can be music to God's ears!

Expand - Day 4

Begin **Day 4** with a review of **Day 3**, then have students answer "part 2" questions.

What I Learned (part 2)

These are higher-level cognitive questions (explain, compare, predict). Student answers will vary, but suggested responses may include:

1 a) up b) the tighter the string, the faster it vibrates; the faster it vibrates, the higher the pitch

2 a) both have strings that vibrate, both are plucked, etc.   b) guitar bigger, has more strings, etc.

3 if a string is not tight enough to vibrate, there is no sound because there is no vibration

Assess - Day 5

Suggestions for modifying assessments to reflect reading levels can be found under ASSESSMENT METHODS on page 12.

Show What You Know 1

(general assessment in Student Worktext)

Blank: pitch
Also, the singer and violin, should be circled. (Handbells vibrate, but don't change pitch.)

Show What You Know 2

(optional test master in Teacher Guide)

1) bow   2) air   3) clapper
4) lower   5) higher

To The Parent

Included at the bottom of all assessment tests, "To The Parent" provides a great way to solicit parent involvement. It not only gives parents an overview of the lesson, but also provides follow-up questions for home use.

NAME _____

Show What You Know 2

Read each sentence below. Using the **word bank** below, choose the best word to complete each sentence, then write it on the line. (Some words will not be used.)

1. A violin's strings vibrate when stroked by a _____ .

2. Vocal chords vibrate when _____ passes through.

3. A handbell vibrates when the _____ strikes the bell.

4. When a violin's strings are looser, pitch is _____ .

5. When your vocal chords tighten, the pitch gets _____ .

WORD BANK:

hand   higher   bow   string   clapper   cup   lower   air

To the Parent . . .   **Scripture Connection:** Proverbs 15:1

Lesson Focus:
Pitch (or tone)

Lesson Objective:
To explore how changing the rate of vibration changes pitch

National Science Education Standards:
Standard B2 — "*All students should develop an understanding of position and motion of objects . . . (both) can be changed by pushing or pulling . . . sound is produced by vibrating objects . . . pitch can be varied by changing rate of vibration . . .*"

Follow-up Questions:
Ask your child what causes sound (vibration). Ask your child to describe some common sounds.
Ask your child what changes in vibration are called (pitch).
Ask your child what causes pitch to go up or down as we speak (vocal chords get tighter or looser).

Speedy Sounds
Lesson 27

FOCUS   Sound and Density

OBJECTIVE   To explore how density affects the speed of sound

OVERVIEW   Sound can travel at different speeds depending on what it's traveling through. Generally, the denser the substance (the closer its molecules), the faster sound can travel.

WHAT TO DO

With your team, carefully follow each step below.

Observe

Look at the two balloons. Think about how they are similar. Think about how they are different. Discuss some things that balloons might be used for.

Describe

Describe each balloon. What does it look like? What does it feel like? What color is it? What are some ways you might change a balloon's shape?

Discuss

What substance will be inside Balloon 1? air

What substance will be inside Balloon 2? water

What word means "closer molecules"? dense

Lesson 27

Introduction

National Standards
Focus: B2

Related: A1, A2, B1, E1, E2

Category
Physical Science

Focus
Sound and Density

Objective
To explore how density affects the speed of sound

Overview
Read the overview aloud to your students. The goal is to create an atmosphere of curiosity and inquiry.

Say: *"Sound can travel at different speeds depending on what it's traveling through. Generally, the denser the substance (the closer its molecules), the faster sound can travel."*

Additional Notes

Introduce this lesson by saying, *"Have you ever watched a thunderstorm far in the distance? Which did you see or hear first — the lightning or the thunder?"*

Talk about the fact that if a storm is a few miles away, you always see the lightning first. This is because sound is a lot slower than light. (You can estimate a storm's distance by the delay between the lightning and thunder. Every five seconds is about one mile.)

Both light and sound have to travel to get to you! That means that sound has a certain speed — and in this lesson, your students will discover that the speed that sound travels *changes* depending on what it's traveling through!

What To Do

Once students are seated in "research teams" with materials in front of them, read the first section (OB-SERVE) aloud.

Say, *"To start this lesson, we're going to **observe** some things. Good scientists always carefully examine the things they will be working with before beginning. First, I will read the instructions to you. Then you can follow the instructions as you **observe** the items in front of you."*

Monitor teams closely as they follow instructions. When teams are finished with this section, repeat the process with the DE-SCRIBE section. Conclude with the DISCUSS section.

Options

Expand the DISCUSS section by having students trace dotted "key words" using crayons or markers. Trace the word **air** in yellow or gold, the word **water** in blue, and the word **dense** in brown or black.

FOCUS	Sound and Density
OBJECTIVE	To explore how density affects the speed of sound
OVERVIEW	Sound can travel at different speeds depending on what it's traveling through. Generally, the denser the substance (the closer its molecules), the faster sound can travel.

WHAT TO DO

With your team, carefully follow each step below.

Observe

Look at the two balloons. **Think** about how they are similar. **Think** about how they are different. **Discuss** some things that balloons might be used for.

Describe

Describe each balloon. What does it **look** like? What does it **feel** like? What **color** is it? What are some ways you might **change** a balloon's shape?

Discuss

What substance will be inside Balloon 1? air
What substance will be inside Balloon 2? water
What word means "closer molecules"? dense

PHYSICAL · **171**

Teacher to Teacher

Normally, the denser a material is, the faster sound travels though it. However, it's a bit more complex when it comes to air.

The temperature of air can change the speed of sound slightly (about 740 mph at 32°, about 770 mph at 72°). But wait a minute! Shouldn't the speed be *slower* at 72° since colder air is more dense?

Normally, yes — but air molecules are much more active at higher temperatures. This offsets the fact that hot air is a bit less dense.

This example illustrates the fact that although sound almost always travels faster in solids than in liquids or gases, there *are* some exceptions, since other properties may also affect sound waves.

The Speed of Sound

Sound can travel at different speeds.
Sound travels at different speeds depending on what it's traveling through. Generally the denser the substance (the closer its molecules are), the faster sound can travel.

Sounds are slow in gases.

Air is a gas. It is not very dense.
Vibration causes molecules to "bump together," making sound. Since air molecules are far apart, sound is slower through air.

Sound travels slowly through air.
Sound travels through the air at about 750 miles per hour. The temperature of air can affect sound speeds slightly.

Sounds are faster in liquids.

Water is a liquid. It is much denser than air.
Molecules in liquids are closer together than those in gases. This allows sound to travel much faster through water than air.

Sound travels faster through water.
Sound travels through water at about 3,300 miles per hour. This lets some sea creatures communicate over long distances.

Sounds are fastest in solids.

Copper is a solid. It is much denser than water.
The particles in solids like copper are very tightly packed. This allows the vibrations that create sound to travel very rapidly.

Sound travels very fast through copper.
Sound travels through copper at about 13,000 miles per hour. Copper wire is used to transfer audio signals (a form of sound).

Extended Teaching

1. Pile various objects on a table (marshmallow, rock, piece of wood, eraser, ball, cotton, etc.). Ask teams to place the objects in order according to density. (Clue: if two objects are similar in size, the heavier one is usually more dense.)

2. Fill a child's wading pool with water. Wait until the water is completely still. Have students observe closely as you drop a large marble in the center of the pool. The waves that ripple out from the center show water molecules colliding to create a wave pattern. Although we can't see sound, it is very similar. A vibration causes molecules to collide, creating a moving ripple that scientists call a "sound wave."

3. For a snack, serve a "Density Dinner." Offer students food items of various densities such as carrots, marshmallows, bananas, crackers, etc. Have them group the items according to density. Encourage them to observe how a food's density affects the sound it makes when chewed.

Inform - Day 2

Read The Story

Read the story aloud with your students. (See READING LEVELS on page 12.) After reading, monitor teams as they discuss what was read. Once you feel students have mastered the basic concepts, have them answer the comprehension questions (**What I Learned** - part 1) on the next page.

To introduce the story, say:
"The title of this story is 'The Speed of Sound.' Look at your story and follow along as we read it together."

If you wish, encourage Emergent readers to point to words and pictures as you read.

(Author's Note: The story refers to sound traveling through copper. This is an oversimplifaction suitable for this age group. Moving audio signals is actually a very complex process by which sound is transferred through copper wire using electricity.)

What I Learned (part 1)

These are basic fact-based comprehension questions. Student answers will vary, but suggested responses include:

(**1**) air molecules are farther apart

(**2**) a) both are solids b) the particles in copper are packed more closely than the particles in cotton

(**3**) a) steel b) because sound travels more rapidly through a solid than a liquid

Field Trip

Visit a local telephone company. Have them explain how the sound waves of your voice are transferred through a copper wire (as an audio signal), then changed back into sound waves on the other end so the listener can hear you!

Guest Speaker

Invite a diver to visit your class. Have him/her share stories about sounds heard underwater. Talk about how sound moves easier through water than through air.

Materials Needed*

ballons - 2   **pencil** (unsharpened)
water   paper towels

Safety Concerns

3. Choking

Balloons can pose a choking hazard. Exercise caution when inflating. Also, see pencil cautions in Step 1 below.

4. Slipping

There is a potential for spilled liquids. Remind students to exercise caution.

Do the Activity

Read the activity in advance so you understand it thoroughly. (If time allows, try it yourself.) Before students begin, carefully go over the **Safety Concerns** together.

Pass out materials, then have your students follow along as you read the instructions for **Step 1**. Monitor teams closely as they complete this step.

Once teams have completed **Step 1**, read instructions for **Step 2**. Monitor teams as before. Repeat for **Step 3** and **Step 4**.

After the activity, allow time for each team to share their observations. To encourage higher-level thinking, encourage teams to not only share their observations with each other, but also with other teams.

Special Instructions

Step 1 - Clean pencils (unsharpened!) before beginning. *Students must remain seated while pencils are in their mouths!* Monitor this closely to avoid accidents.

Step 2 - Filling the balloon with water is easier if you attach it to a sink faucet. Be sure not to overfill.

Other - You may wish to appoint a "safety monitor" for each team to help you watch for inappropriate behavior. Avoid anything that may cause a balloon to burst. Also, be sure to disinfect or discard pencils after use.

* Bold-faced items supplied in kit.

DO THE ACTIVITY

Working with your research team, carefully follow each step below. Before you start, be sure you know the **safety rules** for this activity.

STEP 1

Scratch the pencil eraser with a fingernail. **Record** what you hear. **Hold** the pencil in your teeth and scratch it again. **Compare** this to the first sound.

STEP 2

Fill Balloon 1 with air. **Tie** it shut. **Fill** Balloon 2 with water. **Tie** it shut. **Place** Balloon 1 against your ear. **Tap** it lightly with the pencil. **Re-cord** what you hear.

STEP 3

Place Balloon 2 against your ear. **Tap** it lightly with the pencil. **Com-pare** the sound you hear to Balloon 1. Make sure everyone on your team has a turn.

STEP 4

Compare all the sounds you heard in this activity. **Discuss** your observations with your team, then **compare** findings with other research teams.

174 · PHYSICAL

What Happened?

Immediately following the activity, help your students understand what they observed.

Say: *"In this activity, you were able to explore how density affects the speed of sound.*

*In **Step 1**, you could barely hear the scratch on the pencil when the sound had to travel through the air. But when you grasped the pencil in your teeth, the sound traveled through the solids much more clearly.*

*In **Step 2**, you could hear the sound of the tapping pencil through the air in the balloon. But in **Step 3**, the sound traveling through the denser water in Balloon 2 was much louder and clearer.*

*Finally in **Step 4**, you shared and compared your observations with those of other research teams. By comparing results, you discovered that sound usually travels much better through solids and liquids than it does through air."*

NAME _____

SHOW WHAT YOU KNOW - 1

Sound travels at different speeds through a **solid**, a **liquid**, or a **gas**. Circle the objects to show how fast sound travels. Use red for slow, blue for faster, green for fastest. Write the correct word on the lines below.

The least dense matter is

gas

The most dense matter is

solid

The medium dense matter is

liquid

To the Parent . . .   Scripture Connection: I Peter 1:14

Lesson Focus:
Sound and Density

Lesson Objective:
To explore how density affects the transfer of sound

National Science Education Standards:
Standard B2 — "All students should develop an understanding of position and motion of objects . . . (both) can be changed by pushing or pulling . . . sound is produced by vibrating objects . . . pitch can be varied by changing rate of vibration . . ."

Follow-up Questions:
Ask your child to name one thing that can affect the speed of sound (the substance the sound is traveling through).
Ask your child to compare sound speeds through a gas, a liquid, and a solid (gas = slow, liquid = faster, solid = fastest).
Ask your child why sound travels faster through water than air (water is more dense; its molecules are closer together).

176 · PHYSICAL

Food For Thought

A related "Scripture Object Lesson" you can share with your students.

I Peter 1:14

We've learned that the speed of sound is affected by the density of the substance the sound is traveling through. In this case "dense" means how tightly the molecules are packed together.

But there's another meaning for the word dense — "stubborn or slow to understand." If we're determined to get our own way, or we refuse to do something we know God wants us to do, then we're being dense.

A dense attitude can slow our communication with God. But the more time you spend in prayer and reading God's word, the more you learn to trust Him. And the more you trust Him, the easier it is to let Him lead in your daily life. Don't be dense! Learn to trust God.

Expand - Day 4

Begin **Day 4** with a review of **Day 3**, then have students answer "part 2" questions.

What I Learned (part 2)

These are higher-level cognitive questions (explain, compare, predict). Student answers will vary, but suggested responses may include:

1 a) the one filled with water b) water is denser than air

2 a) same shape, same material b) one filled with air; one filled with water

3 a) dolphin b) it lives in the water and sounds travel better through water

Assess - Day 5

Suggestions for modifying assessments to reflect reading levels can be found under ASSESSMENT METHODS on page 12.

Show What You Know 1
(general assessment in Student Worktext)

Blanks: 1) gas 2) solid 3) liquid
Also, the teapot/steam illustration should be circled in red, the coins in green, and the water in blue

Show What You Know 2
(optional test master in Teacher Guide)

1) F 2) T 3) F 4) T 5) T

To The Parent

Included at the bottom of all assessment tests, "To The Parent" provides a great way to solicit parent involvement. It not only gives parents an overview of the lesson, but also provides follow-up questions for home use.

Show What You Know 2

Read each sentence below. If the sentence is true, then circle the letter **T**. If the sentence is false, then circle the letter **F**.

T F   1. Sound travels at the same speed through all materials.

T F   2. Sound travels faster through water than through air.

T F   3. Sound travels faster through air than through copper.

T F   4. Air's temperature can affect the speed of sound.

T F   5. Some sea creatures can hear sounds at great distances.

To the Parent . . .   Scripture Connection: 1 Peter 1:14

Lesson Focus:
Sound and Density

Lesson Objective:
To explore how density affects the transfer of sound

National Science Education Standards:
Standard B2 — *"All students should develop an understanding of position and motion of objects . . . (both) can be changed by pushing or pulling . . . sound is produced by vibrating objects . . . pitch can be varied by changing rate of vibration . . ."*

Follow-up Questions:
Ask your child to name one thing that can affect the speed of sound (the substance the sound is traveling through).
Ask your child to compare sound speeds through a gas, a liquid, and a solid (gas = slow, liquid = faster, solid = fastest).
Ask your child why sound travels faster through water than air (water is more dense; its molecules are closer together).

Lesson 28

FOCUS
Action/Reaction

OBJECTIVE
To understand Newton's third law of motion

OVERVIEW
Forces always come in pairs. When an object pushes (or pulls) another object, the second object reacts with equal force in the opposite direction.

WHAT TO DO

With your team, carefully follow each step below.

Observe

Look at the pictures on page 178. Talk about how these things are different from each other. Now discuss some ways that these things might be similar.

Describe

Describe each thing on page 178. What does it look like? What might it feel like? What color is it? What shape is it? What is it doing?

Discuss

Where might you see birds moving fast? a i r
Where might you see fish moving fast? w a t e r
Where might you see cars moving fast? r o a d

PHYSICAL · **177**

Introduction

National Standards
Focus: B2

Related: A1, A2, B1, E1, E2

Category
Physical Science

Focus
Action/Reaction

Objective
To understand Newton's third law of motion

Overview
Read the overview aloud to your students. The goal is to create an atmosphere of curiosity and inquiry.

Say: *"Forces always come in pairs. When an object pushes or pulls another object, the second object reacts with equal force in the opposite direction."*

Additional Notes

To introduce this lesson, have your students sit on the floor in pairs facing each other, feet to feet and holding onto their partner's hands. (Make certain the area behind their backs is clear.)

Begin slowly singing "Row, Row, Row Your Boat." On the first "Row," one should lean forward and the other back. Reverse this on the second "Row." Have them continue rocking back and forth "rowing" as they sing the song together several times.

Point out that as one student pulled, the other pushed. Say, *"Forces are like this — they always come in pairs. In this lesson we'll discover that this kind of motion is a physical 'law' and that it has a name!"*

What To Do

Once students are seated in "research teams" with materials in front of them, read the first section (OBSERVE) aloud.

Say, *"To start this lesson, we're going to **observe** some pictures. Carefully examine the details, then discuss what you see with your team. First, I will read the instructions to you. Then you can follow the instructions as you **observe** the pictures."*

Monitor teams closely as they follow instructions. When teams are finished with this section, repeat the process with the DESCRIBE section. Conclude with the DISCUSS section.

Options

Expand the DISCUSS section by having students trace dotted "key words" using crayons or markers. Trace the word **air** in light blue, the word **water** in dark blue, and the word **road** in black.

FOCUS   Action/Reaction

OBJECTIVE   To understand Newton's third law of motion

OVERVIEW   Forces always come in pairs. When an object pushes (or pulls) another object, the second object reacts with equal force in the opposite direction.

WHAT TO DO

With your team, carefully follow each step below.

Observe

Look at the pictures on page 178. **Talk** about how these things are different from each other. Now **discuss** some ways that these things might be similar.

Describe

Describe each thing on page 178. What does it **look** like? What might it **feel** like? What **color** is it? What **shape** is it? What is it doing?

Discuss

Where might you see birds moving fast? air

Where might you see fish moving fast? water

Where might you see cars moving fast? road

PHYSICAL · **177**

Teacher to Teacher

Isaac Newton is one of the most famous scientists and mathematicians of all times. He explained the movement of large objects (mechanics) with three basic laws.

The first law states that if an object is stopped or moving, it stays stopped or moving unless a force acts on it. Also called "the law of inertia," it's why seatbelts are necessary!

The second law explains how force affects an object's velocity. The bigger the object and the stronger the force, the more the object accelerates — and the greater the force it takes to stop it!

Finally, Newton's third law states for every action there is an equal and opposite reaction. And that's what is explored in this lesson.

READ THE STORY
Newton's third law says, "For every action, there is an equal and opposite reaction." Read the story below to find out what this means.

Newton's Third Law

For every action, there is an equal and opposite reaction.
Forces always come in pairs. When an object pushes (or pulls) another object, the second object reacts with equal force in the opposite direction.

Birds use action/reaction.

A bird's wings push the air down.
When a bird beats its wings, the action pushes air downward. When the air goes down, something else must go up!

The reaction pushes the bird up.
The downward force on the air creates an upward force on the bird. This reaction helps birds climb high into the sky.

Fish use action/reaction.

A fish's fins push the water backward.
When a fish flips its fins, the action pushes water backward. When the water goes back, something else must go forward.

The reaction pushes the fish forward.
The backward force on the water creates a forward force on the fish. This reaction helps fish swim rapidly through the sea.

Cars use action/reaction.

A car's wheels push the road backward.
As a car's wheels turn, they push backward against the road. A backward push means something else must go forward.

The reaction pushes the car forward.
The backward force on the road creates a forward force on the car. This reaction can help cars go very fast.

178 · PHYSICAL

Extended Teaching

1. To expand vocabulary and comprehension, explain that "Newton" refers to Sir Isaac Newton (1642-1727), an English mathematician and natural philosopher. Newton is considered by many to be the greatest scientist who ever lived. He theorized that there were three basic "laws of motion." This lesson is about the third of these "laws."

2. Remind students that a "force" is a push or pull which changes the motion of an object. Ask them to think about a swing on a playground. Unless someone pushes the swing, it will just hang there without moving. But when a person pushes it (force), it begins to move.

3. Newton made many of his discoveries just by being a good observer. Take your class outdoors and have them sit quietly, observing movement of any kind. Challenge them to determine what caused the movement, and to make notes about how it might demonstrate Newton's Third Law.

Inform - Day 2

Read The Story

Read the story aloud with your students. (See READING LEVELS on page 12.) After reading, monitor teams as they discuss what was read. Once you feel students have mastered the basic concepts, have them answer the comprehension questions (**What I Learned** - part 1) on the next page.

To introduce the story, say:

"The title of this story is 'Newton's Third Law.' Look at your story and follow along as we read it together."

If you wish, encourage Emergent readers to point to words and pictures as you read.

What I Learned (part 1)

These are basic fact-based comprehension questions. Student answers will vary, but suggested responses include:

① a) "For every action, there is an equal and opposite reaction." b) answers should reflect examples in story

② a) both are forces that "push" b) bird wings push air; fish fins push water

③ the car will go backwards

Field Trip

Take your students to a baseball batting cage or golf driving range. Watch people swinging the bat or club and talk about the reaction of the ball to this force.

Guest Speaker

Invite a high school physics teacher to visit your class. Ask him/her to bring items to help demonstrate Newton's third law of motion.

Materials Needed*

long balloons - 2   string
large straw   tape
stopwatch (optional)

Safety Concerns

3. Choking

Remind students to exercise caution when inflating balloons as they can pose a choking hazard.

Do the Activity

Read the activity in advance so you understand it thoroughly. (If time allows, try it yourself.) Before students begin, carefully go over the **Safety Concerns** together.

Pass out materials, then have your students follow along as you read the instructions for **Step 1**. Monitor teams closely as they complete this step.

Once teams have completed **Step 1**, read instructions for **Step 2**. Monitor teams as before. Repeat for **Step 3** and **Step 4**.

After the activity, allow time for each team to share their observations. To encourage higher-level thinking, encourage teams to not only share their observations with each other, but also with other teams.

Special Instructions

Step 1 - Differences in motor skills development may make parts of this step difficult for some teams. If you see problems, join the group and demonstrate. This shifts the focus from the skill to the observation process. (A knitting needle makes it easier to thread the string through the straw.)

Step 2 - Don't let students touch the balloon while blowing. They may run out of air and have to take turns!

Step 3 - To keep the balloon from deflating prematurely, twist the end and hold it in a pinch. Make sure a team member is ready to track the time . . . it will go quickly!

* Bold-faced items supplied in kit.

DO THE ACTIVITY
Working with your research team, carefully follow each step below. Before you start, be sure you know the **safety rules** for this activity.

STEP 1
Inflate and tie Balloon 1. Tape the straw parallel to the balloon. Run the string through the straw, then hold the ends of the string and stretch it tight.

STEP 2
Blow Balloon 1 from one end of the string to the other. Time how long it takes. Now repeat Step 1 with Balloon 2, but don't tie the end! (Just hold it shut for now.)

STEP 3
Release the end of Balloon 2. Time how long it takes to reach the end of the string. Compare this to Balloon 1's trip. Repeat if desired.

STEP 4
Review the different ballon trips. Discuss your observations with your team, then compare your findings with those of other research teams.

What Happened?

Immediately following the activity, help your students understand what they observed.

Say: *"In this activity, we were able see Newton's third law of motion in action.*

In Step 2, team members blew air to push the balloon down the string. But the force of that air was not focused. Some of it hit the balloon and some of it just flowed around it. Since the 'action' was fairly weak, the 'reaction' was weak, too, and the balloon moved slowly.

In Step 3, the force of the air was much more focused. The air released from the balloon created a strong backward force (action), which pushed the balloon forward rapidly (reaction).

Finally in Step 4, you were able to share and compare your observatoins with those of other research teams."

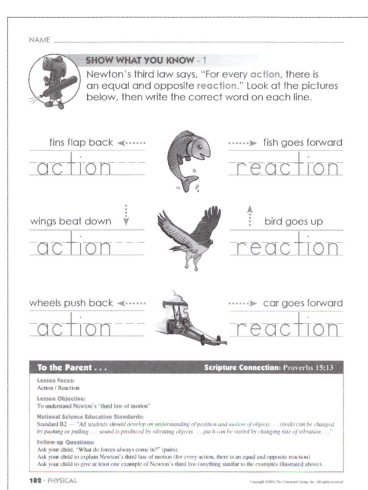

NAME _____

SHOW WHAT YOU KNOW - 1

Newton's third law says, "For every **action**, there is an equal and opposite **reaction**." Look at the pictures below, then write the correct word on each line.

fins flap back ◄······
action

······► fish goes forward
reaction

wings beat down
action

bird goes up
reaction

wheels push back ◄······
action

······► car goes forward
reaction

To the Parent . . .   Scripture Connection: Proverbs 15:13

Lesson Focus:
Action / Reaction

Lesson Objective:
To understand Newton's "third law of motion"

National Science Education Standards:
Standard B2 — "All students should develop an understanding of position and motion of objects . . . (both) can be changed by pushing or pulling . . . sound is produced by vibrating objects . . . pitch can be varied by changing rate of vibration . . ."

Follow-up Questions:
Ask your child, "What do forces always come in?" (pairs).
Ask your child to explain Newton's third law of motion (for every action, there is an equal and opposite reaction).
Ask your child to give at least one example of Newton's third law (anything similar to the examples illustrated above).

182 · PHYSICAL

Food For Thought

A related "Scripture Object Lesson" you can share with your students.

Proverbs 15:13

Newton's Third Law says, *"for every action, there is an equal and opposite reaction"*. This refers to physical actions.

But Scripture reminds us that God has created a kind of action/reaction, too. We might say, *"For every action we take, there's usually a reaction in someone else."*

When you smile at someone, don't they usually smile back? But if you're grouchy or irritable, it often makes those around you feel that way, too.

Remember, you may have the power to create positive reactions just by the way you behave!

Why not start using God's law of action/reaction to start making your world a better place?

Expand - Day 4

Begin **Day 4** with a review of **Day 3**, then have students answer "part 2" questions.

What I Learned (part 2)

These are higher-level cognitive questions (explain, compare, predict). Student answers will vary, but suggested responses may include:

1   a) second balloon   b) second balloon

2   a) both same materials, both same direction, both pushed by air, etc.   b) second balloon had greater force and went faster

3   a) might go even faster   b) more air to provide a greater force; bigger "action" causes bigger "reaction," etc.

Assess - Day 5

Suggestions for modifying assessments to reflect reading levels can be found under ASSESSMENT METHODS on page 12.

Show What You Know 1

(general assessment in Student Worktext)

all blanks in first column: action
all blanks in second column: reaction

Show What You Know 2

(optional test master in Teacher Guide)

1) F   2) T   3) T   4) F   5) F

To The Parent

Included at the bottom of all assessment tests, "To The Parent" provides a great way to solicit parent involvement. It not only gives parents an overview of the lesson, but also provides follow-up questions for home use.

NAME _____

Show What You Know 2

Read each sentence below. If the sentence is true, then circle the letter **T**. If the sentence is false, then circle the letter **F**.

T F 1. Sir Isaac Newton talked about five "laws of motion."

T F 2. For every action, there is an equal and opposite reaction.

T F 3. When a bird's wings push down, it can make the bird go up.

T F 4. Forces always come in groups of three or more.

T F 5. When a fish's fins push up, it usually makes the fish go up.

To the Parent . . .   **Scripture Connection:** Proverbs 15:13

Lesson Focus:
Action / Reaction

Lesson Objective:
To understand Newton's third law of motion

National Science Education Standards:
Standard B2 — *"All students should develop an understanding of position and motion of objects . . . (both) can be changed by pushing or pulling . . . sound is produced by vibrating objects . . . pitch can be varied by changing rate of vibration . . ."*

Follow-up Questions:
Ask your child, "What do forces always come in?" (pairs)
Ask your child to explain Newton's third law of motion (for every action, there is an equal and opposite reaction).
Ask your child to give at least one example of Newton's third law (answers will vary).

Introduction

The following reproduces the student page:

FOCUS   Flight

OBJECTIVE   To explore how forces relate to flight

OVERVIEW   Nothing moves without some kind of force (push or pull). Flight can happen when the upward push of air is stronger than the downward pull of gravity.

WHAT TO DO

With your team, carefully follow each step below.

Observe

Look at the pictures on page 184. Observe how these objects are different from each other. Now talk about some things these objects might have in common.

Describe

Describe each object on page 184. What does it look like? What color is it? What shape is it? What is it doing? How heavy is it compared to the other objects?

Discuss

What force does a bulldozer use to move dirt? push
What force does a truck use to tow a trailer? pull
What is the "upward push" airplanes use to fly? lift

PHYSICAL · 183

National Standards
Focus: B2

Related: A1, A2, B1, E1, E2

Category
Physical Science

Focus
Flight

Objective
To explore how forces relate to flight

Overview
Read the overview aloud to your students. The goal is to create an atmosphere of curiosity and inquiry.

Say: *"Nothing moves without some kind of force . . . some type of push or pull. Flight can happen when the upward* **push** *of air is stronger than the downward* **pull** *of gravity."*

Additional Notes

To introduce this lesson, ask your students to raise their hands if they've ever flown in an airplane. Now ask them to raise their hands if they've ever seen an airplane on TV or in a book. (This should be everyone.)

Have students name or describe some of the parts of an airplane.

Ask, *"How much do you think a large airplane weighs? Is it heavier than a car? How can such a heavy object fly through the air?"*

Focus on the fact that there must be some kind of "force" to keep an airplane in the air. Say, *"In this lesson, we'll explore how forces can create flight."*

What To Do

Once students are seated in "research teams" with materials in front of them, read the first section (OB-SERVE) aloud.

Say, *"To start this lesson, we're going to **observe** some pictures. Carefully examine the details, then discuss what you see with your team. First, I will read the instructions to you. Then you can follow the instructions as you **observe** the pictures."*

Monitor teams closely as they follow instructions. When teams are finished with this section, repeat the process with the DE-SCRIBE section. Conclude with the DISCUSS section.

Options

To expand the DISCUSS section, have students trace dotted "key words" using crayons or markers. Trace the word **push** in yellow, the word **pull** in red, and the word **lift** in blue.

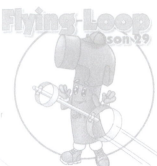

FOCUS	Flight
OBJECTIVE	To explore how forces relate to flight
OVERVIEW	Nothing moves without some kind of force (push or pull). Flight can happen when the upward push of air is stronger than the downward pull of gravity.

WHAT TO DO

With your team, carefully follow each step below.

Observe

Look at the pictures on page 184. Observe how these objects are different from each other. Now talk about some things these objects might have in common.

Describe

Describe each object on page 184. What does it **look** like? What **color** is it? What **shape** is it? What is it doing? How **heavy** is it compared to the other objects?

Discuss

What force does a bulldozer use to move dirt? p u s h

What force does a truck use to tow a trailer? p u l l

What is the "upward push" airplanes use to fly? l i f t

PHYSICAL · **183**

Teacher to Teacher

Men and women have dreamed of flying for centuries. In the 1500s, Leonardo da Vinci made several sketches of flying machines. However, his designs were not practical since they relied on human muscle for power. (Engines didn't exist.)

In 1903, Professor Samuel Langley of the Smithsonian Institute built what is recognized as the first engine-powered plane using a $50,000 government grant. However, both attempts to fly his very expensive plane resulted in it crashing on takeoff!

Then just eight days after Langley's second crash, the Wright brothers' plane (built for less than $1,000) flew 852 feet — and landed safely. The rest is history.

Extended Teaching

1. To expand vocabulary, explain that "lift" means to raise from a lower to a higher position. Use words such as "raise," "elevate," and "hoist" as you discuss the concept. Ask students to use the word "lift" in a sentence that does not involve flight. Talk about the difference between the verb form (to move from a lower to a higher position) and the noun form (a machine designed to raise something). Point out that the noun form is also used to describe the kind of aerodynamic force that is discussed in this lesson.

2. Talk about the difference between "push" and "pull." Push is to exert force resulting in motion *away* from the force. Pull is to exert force resulting in motion *toward* the force. Discuss ways we use these different forces to move objects.

3. Have students research the history of the Frisbee®. (It all started with pies and rowdy college students!) Bring various flying discs to school and practice throwing them.

Inform - Day 2

Read The Story

Read the story aloud with your students. (See READING LEVELS on page 12.) After reading, monitor teams as they discuss what was read. Once you feel students have mastered the basic concepts, have them answer the comprehension questions (**What I Learned** - part 1) on the next page.

To introduce the story, say:

"The title of this story is 'How Things Fly.' Look at your story and follow along as we read it together."

If you wish, encourage Emergent readers to point to words and pictures as you read.

What I Learned (part 1)

These are basic fact-based comprehension questions. Student answers will vary, but suggested responses include:

1 air on top must flow faster to go the same distance

2 a) both round, both are a kind of wing, both use shape to create lift, etc.
b) answers will vary but should include ideas like, "disc spins, loop doesn't," "loop has more parts," etc.

3 there would be no lift, the wing would be pushed downward, etc.

Field Trip

Visit a flight museum. (Many airports, even small ones, have museums or major displays dedicated to flight.) Have students make notes about what they see, then share their findings when you return.

Guest Speaker

Invite a pilot to visit your class. Ask him or her to talk about lift and how it relates to flying.

Materials Needed*

paper strips **straw**
scissors tape
measuring tape

Safety Concerns

4. Sharp Objects

Remind students to exercise caution when using scissors.

4. Other

Flying loops should only be used outdoors (on a calm day) or in a gym. Students should never throw loops toward anyone.

Do the Activity

Read the activity in advance so you understand it thoroughly. (If time allows, try it yourself.) Before students begin, carefully go over the **Safety Concerns** together.

Pass out materials, then have your students follow along as you read the instructions for **Step 1**. Monitor teams closely as they complete this step.

Once teams have completed **Step 1**, read instructions for **Step 2**. Monitor teams as before. Repeat for **Step 3** and **Step 4**.

After the activity, allow time for each team to share their observations. To encourage higher-level thinking, encourage teams to not only share their observations with each other, but also with other teams.

Special Instructions

Step 1 - Demonstrate a precise "half fold" by lining up the edges of the strip, holding them in place with one hand, and pressing down to the fold with the other hand.

Step 3 - Demonstrate how to throw the Flying Loop. (First see safety instructions above.) Simply hold the straw parallel to the floor with the small loop in front. Aim slightly upwards and throw as you would a paper airplane.

DO THE ACTIVITY
Working with your research team, carefully follow each step below. Before you start, be sure you know the **safety rules** for this activity.

STEP 1
Fold one paper strip in half. Cut it along the fold line and discard half. Tape the ends together to make a loop. Now tape the long strip to make a second loop.

STEP 2
Tape the loops to the straw as shown. Be sure the ends of the straw are flush with the edges of the loops, and that both loops are straight.

STEP 3
Following directions from your teacher, throw the "flying loop." Measure how far it goes. Repeat until everyone on your team has had a turn.

STEP 4
Review the flights from step 3. Discuss your observations with your research team, then compare your findings with those of other teams.

186 · PHYSICAL   Copyright ©2009 The Concerned Group, Inc. All rights reserved.

What Happened?

Immediately following the activity, help your students understand what they observed.

Say: *"In this activity you were able to see how the forces of push and pull relate to flight.*

*In **Steps 1** and **2**, you built an unusual structure with a shape that created the potential for lift.*

*In **Step 3**, you watched your 'loop' fly. Air moved faster over the outside of the top half and the inside of the bottom half, creating lift.*

*In **Step 4**, you shared and compared your observations with other research teams. You discovered that in spite of its unusual shape, a 'flying loop' can still create lift."*

* Bold-faced items supplied in kit.

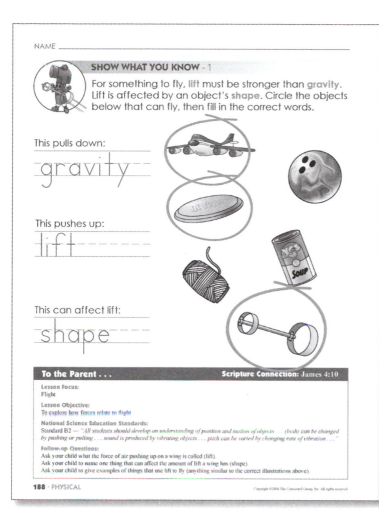

NAME _____

SHOW WHAT YOU KNOW - 1

For something to fly, **lift** must be stronger than **gravity**. Lift is affected by an object's **shape**. Circle the objects below that can fly, then fill in the correct words.

This pulls down:

gravity

This pushes up:

lift

This can affect lift:

shape

To the Parent . . .   Scripture Connection: James 4:10

Lesson Focus:
Flight

Lesson Objective:
To explore how forces relate to flight

National Science Education Standards:
Standard B2 — "All students should develop an understanding of position and motion of objects . . . (both) can be changed by pushing or pulling . . . sound is produced by vibrating objects . . . pitch can be varied by changing rate of vibration . . ."

Follow-up Questions:
Ask your child what the force of air pushing up on a wing is called (lift).
Ask your child to name one thing that can affect the amount of lift a wing has (shape).
Ask your child to give examples of things that use lift to fly (anything similar to the correct illustrations above).

188 · PHYSICAL   Copyright ©2006 The Concerned Group, Inc. All rights reserved.

Food For Thought

A related "Scripture Object Lesson" you can share with your students.

James 4:10

We've learned that whenever something moves, there is a force involved. When it comes to flying, the force that scientists call "lift" is what keeps a plane flying high.

This Scripture talks about another kind of force, but one that is much more powerful. It reminds us that when we humble ourselves before God, when we bow down and worship Him, recognizing that we are completely dependent on Him for our every need, then He will "lift us up."

Why not thank God right now for all He has done for you? Daily prayer can bring you closer to God's mighty power, so He can lift you up and keep you flying high!

Expand - Day 4

Begin **Day 4** with a review of **Day 3**, then have students answer "part 2" questions.

What I Learned (part 2)

These are higher-level cognitive questions (explain, compare, predict). Student answers will vary, but suggested responses may include:

1 the upward push of air was stronger than the downward pull of gravity

2 answers will vary but should include comments on height, distance, accuracy, etc. or variations in structure of loops

3 a) would not fly b) without the proper shape, there is no lift

Assess - Day 5

Suggestions for modifying assessments to reflect reading levels can be found under ASSESSMENT METHODS on page 12.

Show What You Know 1
(general assessment in Student Worktext)

Blanks: 1) gravity 2) lift 3) shape
Also the airplane, flying loop, and flying disc should be circled

Show What You Know 2
(optional test master in Teacher Guide)

1) gravity   2) shape   3) lift
4) force   5) air

To The Parent

Included at the bottom of all assessment tests, "To The Parent" provides a great way to solicit parent involvement. It not only gives parents an overview of the lesson, but also provides follow-up questions for home use.

NAME _____

Show What You Know 2

Unscramble the letters below to make words. Use the correct word to fill in the blank in each sentence.

ityagrv   ahpes   tlfi   reofc   ria

1. The force that pulls things downward on Earth is _____.

2. The _____ of a wing can affect the amount of lift.

3. The force of air pushing up on a wing is called _____.

4. Nothing moves without some kind of _____ (push/pull).

5. Slower _____ under a wing has higher pressure.

To the Parent . . .   **Scripture Connection:** James 4:10

Lesson Focus:
Flight

Lesson Objective:
To explore how forces relate to flight

National Science Education Standards:
Standard B2 — *"All students should develop an understanding of position and motion of objects . . . (both) can be changed by pushing or pulling . . . sound is produced by vibrating objects . . . pitch can be varied by changing rate of vibration . . ."*

Follow-up Questions:
Ask your child what the force of air pushing up on a wing is called (lift).
Ask your child to name one thing that can affect the amount of lift a wing has (shape).
Ask your child to give examples of things that use lift to fly (answers will vary).

Simple Machines
Lesson 30

FOCUS   Simple Machines

OBJECTIVE   To explore how a simple machine can change the direction of a force

OVERVIEW   Simple machines (like levers, pulleys, and wheels) can be used to change the direction of a force. We use many kinds of simple machines every day.

WHAT TO DO

With your team, carefully follow each step below.

Observe

Look at the pinwheel, the ruler, the spool, and the dowel. Think about the shape of each item. Talk about things you might do with each one.

Describe

Describe each item. What does it look like? What does it feel like? What color is it? What shape is it? How is it similar to or different from the other items?

Discuss

What is needed to make anything move? force
What can change direction of a force? machine
What can simple machines help us do? work

PHYSICAL · 189

Lesson 30

National Standards
Focus: B2

Related: A1, A2, B1, E1, E2

Category
Physical Science

Focus
Simple Machines

Objective
To explore how a simple machine can change the direction of a force

Overview
Read the overview aloud to your students. The goal is to create an atmosphere of curiosity and inquiry.

Say: *"Simple machines like levers, pulleys, and wheels can be used to change the direction of a force. We use many kinds of simple machines every day."*

Additional Notes

To introduce this lesson, ask your students if they've ever seen a "seesaw." This unique piece of playground equipment has begun disappearing in recent years, but once was so common that many parts of the country had different names for it!

Southeast New Englanders call it a "tilt"; in northeast New England it's called a "teedle board."

Narragansett Bay uses the term "dandle." "Teeterboard" is common in the rest of the Northeast, while "teeter-totter" is familiar to the rest of the country.

Regardless of its name, this outdoor toy is actually a simple machine (a lever). As students work through this lesson, challenge them to figure out what kind of simple machine it represents.

What To Do

Once students are seated in "research teams" with materials in front of them, read the first section (OBSERVE) aloud.

Say, *"To start this lesson, we're going to **observe** some things. Good scientists always carefully examine the things they will be working with before beginning. First, I will read the instructions to you. Then you can follow the instructions as you **observe** the items in front of you."*

Monitor teams closely as they follow instructions. When teams are finished with this section, repeat the process with the DESCRIBE section. Conclude with the DISCUSS section.

Options

Expand the DISCUSS section by having students trace dotted "key words" using crayons or markers. Trace the word **force** in red, the word **machine** in yellow, and the word **work** in green.

FOCUS   Simple Machines

OBJECTIVE   To explore how a simple machine can change the direction of a force

OVERVIEW   Simple machines (like levers, pulleys, and wheels) can be used to change the direction of a force. We use many kinds of simple machines every day.

WHAT TO DO

With your team, carefully follow each step below.

Observe

Look at the pinwheel, the ruler, the spool, and the dowel. **Think** about the shape of each item. **Talk** about things you might do with each one.

Describe

Describe each item. What does it **look** like? What does it **feel** like? What **color** is it? What **shape** is it? How is it **similar** to or **different** from the other items?

Discuss

What is needed to make anything move? force

What can change direction of a force? machine

What can simple machines help us do? work

PHYSICAL · **189**

Teacher to Teacher

Most scientists refer to *six* simple machines: the lever, the pulley, the inclined plane, the wedge, the wheel and axle, and the screw.

Some scientists, however, group them more simply. In their view, a pulley is actually a group of wheels and axles working together; a wedge is really two inclined planes back to back; and a screw is just an inclined plane wrapped around a center.

When two or more simple machines work together, it creates a *compound* machine. A hand-operated can opener is a good example. It uses levers, a wedge, and a wheel and axle to open the can. Imagine trying to open a simple can without one!

Simple Machines

Simple machines can change the direction of force.
Nothing can move without some kind of force. Simple machines can change the direction of a force. This makes many kinds of work much easier to do.

This is a lever.
Push one end down, the other goes up.
When you push down on one end of a lever, the other end goes up. Levers can help raise heavy objects.

There are many kinds of levers.
A paint can opener is a lever. So is a crowbar, the handle of a hammer, and many other tools. Even a seesaw is a lever!

This is a pulley.
Pull one end down, the other goes up.
When you pull down on a rope attached to a pulley, the other end of the rope goes up. Pulleys can help lift heavy loads.

There are many kinds of pulleys.
Flag poles have pulleys to raise and lower flags. There are tiny plastic pulleys in mini-blinds, and huge steel pulleys in cranes.

This is a wheel and axle.
The wheel goes around. The bike moves forward.
The wheels of a moving bicycle turn round and round, pushing backward against the ground. This makes the bike go forward.

There are many kinds of wheels and axles.
Wheels and axles are everywhere — bikes, planes, wagons, trains — even in pizza cutters, doorknobs, and pencil sharpeners!

190 · PHYSICAL

Extended Teaching

1. To expand vocabulary, discuss the concept of a "machine" as a device for changing force, usually to do work. Emphasize that some machines have motors (washing machine, lawn mower, etc.), but other machines do not (crowbar, wedge, etc.). Talk about various machines and how they make our lives easier.

2. To help students appreciate the power of a lever, bring a bag of unshelled pecans or walnuts to class. Have students try to open a nut using just their hands. Now show them how to open a nut using a nutcracker. After all of them have had a turn, point out that this "simple machine" is actually a kind of lever.

Inform - Day 2

Read The Story
Read the story aloud with your students. (See READING LEVELS on page 12.) After reading, monitor teams as they discuss what was read. Once you feel students have mastered the basic concepts, have them answer the comprehension questions (**What I Learned** - part 1) on the next page.

To introduce the story, say:

"The title of this story is 'Simple Machines.' Look at your story and follow along as we read it together."

If you wish, encourage Emergent readers to point to words and pictures as you read.

What I Learned (part 1)
These are basic fact-based comprehension questions. Student answers will vary, but suggested responses include:

① a) lever, pulley, wheel and axle
b) answers will vary, but should reflect examples in story

② a) both simple machines; both change direction of force b) lever uses push; pulley uses pull

③ answers will vary, but should include the idea that many kinds of work would be much harder

Field Trip
Visit a museum that has a collection of antique tools. Ask your guide to explain how these tools were used. Discuss how these tools made people's lives easier.

Guest Speaker
Invite a carpenter or plumber to visit your class and bring his/her tools. Have him/her demonstrate their use, and talk about how much easier a job is when you are using the right kind of tool.

Materials Needed*

ruler	spool
string	pinwheel
turtle	dowel rod

Safety Concerns

4. Other

Remind students to behave like scientists. There is no room for horseplay!

Do the Activity

Read the activity in advance so you understand it thoroughly. (If time allows, try it yourself.) Before students begin, carefully go over the **Safety Concerns** together.

Pass out materials, then have your students follow along as you read the instructions for **Step 1**. Monitor teams closely as they complete this step.

Once teams have completed **Step 1**, read instructions for **Step 2**. Monitor teams as before. Repeat for **Step 3** and **Step 4**.

After the activity, allow time for each team to share their observations. To encourage higher-level thinking, encourage teams to not only share their observations with each other, but also with other teams.

Special Instructions

Step 1 - Have one team member hold the spool so it doesn't move. (Sticking the dowel rod in it can help.) Remind students to push the ruler down *slowly*! Turtles are not designed to fly!

Step 2 - Have two team members hold the dowel while another team member wraps the string around the spool. The "pulley" works best if the string is wrapped one complete time around the spool.

Step 3 - Make sure the pinwheel is facing the team member who is blowing. Otherwise it is difficult to see the hole in the blade.

DO THE ACTIVITY
Working with your research team, carefully follow each step below. Before you start, be sure you know the **safety rules** for this activity.

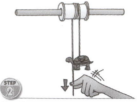

STEP 1 — Place the ruler across the spool. Place the turtle on the blue dot. Now observe the turtle's motion as you slowly push down on the red dot. Record the results.

STEP 2 — Slip the dowel through the spool. Wrap the string around the spool. Tape one end to the turtle. Pull the other end and observe the turtle's motion. Record the results.

STEP 3 — Hold the pinwheel as shown. Push air toward the pinwheel by blowing at it softly. Observe the motion of the hole as you blow. Record the results.

STEP 4 — Review each step in this activity. Discuss how each machine changed the direction of force. Compare your team's findings with other research teams.

What Happened?

Immediately following the activity, help your students understand what they observed.

Say: *"In this activity you created and tested three different types of simple machines.*

In Step 1, you discovered that a lever can change a downward force into an upward force. You pushed down on one end of the lever and the turtle on the other end went up.

In Step 2, you discovered that a pulley can also change a downward force into an upward force. You pulled down on the string, and the turtle went up.

In Step 3, you discovered that a wheel and axle can also change the direction of a force. You blew forward, but the pinwheel went around and around.

Finally in Step 4, you shared your findings with other research teams."

---

* *Bold-faced items supplied in kit.*

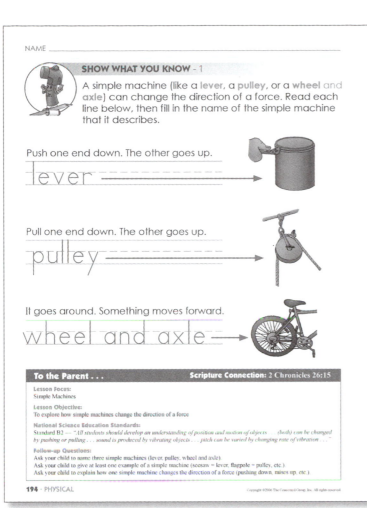

NAME _____

SHOW WHAT YOU KNOW - 1

A simple machine (like a **lever**, a **pulley**, or a **wheel** and **axle**) can change the direction of a force. Read each line below, then fill in the name of the simple machine that it describes.

Push one end down. The other goes up.

lever

Pull one end down. The other goes up.

pulley

It goes around. Something moves forward.

wheel and axle

To the Parent . . .   Scripture Connection: 2 Chronicles 26:15

Lesson Focus:
Simple Machines

Lesson Objective:
To explore how simple machines change the direction of a force

National Science Education Standards:
Standard B2 — "...All students should develop an understanding of position and motion of objects . . .   (both) can be changed by pushing or pulling . . . sound is produced by vibrating objects . . . pitch can be varied by changing rate of vibration . . ."

Follow-up Questions:
Ask your child to name three simple machines (lever, pulley, wheel and axle).
Ask your child to give at least one example of a simple machine (seesaw = lever, flagpole = pulley, etc.).
Ask your child to explain how one simple machine changes the direction of a force (pushing down, raises up, etc.).

194 · PHYSICAL

Food For Thought

A related "Scripture Object Lesson" you can share with your students.

2 Chronicles 26:15

In this lesson, we discovered that machines can make our lives much easier. Many marvelous inventions have been designed to keep us happy and comfortable.

Sometimes people look at all the clever machines that surround us and they become proud. They may even think that we no longer need God in our modern world.

But remember, God is the source of all good things. Not only does He supply the knowledge to invent useful machines, but He also gives us the wisdom to use them to help others.

Don't let the machines in your life change your *spiritual* direction! Keep your eyes and your heart focused on God, the greatest inventor of all.

Expand - Day 4

Begin **Day 4** with a review of **Day 3**, then have students answer "part 2" questions.

What I Learned (part 2)
These are higher-level cognitive questions (explain, compare, predict). Student answers will vary, but suggested responses may include:

1   a) lever b) pulley c) wheel and axle

2   a) both use downward force to raise something on the other end   b) answers will vary

3   answers will vary but should reflect the concepts learned in this activity

Assess - Day 5

Suggestions for modifying assessments to reflect reading levels can be found under ASSESSMENT METHODS on page 12.

Show What You Know 1
(general assessment in Student Worktext)

Blanks: a) lever b) pulley c) wheel and axle

Show What You Know 2
(optional test master in Teacher Guide)

1) lever   2) wheel and axle   3) lever
4) pulley 5) wheel and axle

Note: When your students eventually take high school physics, they'll discover that 2) is also a "3rd class lever" and 4) is also a "2nd class lever."

To The Parent
Included at the bottom of all assessment tests, "To The Parent" provides a great way to solicit parent involvement. It not only gives parents an overview of the lesson, but also provides follow-up questions for home use.

Show What You Know 2

Look at each item listed below. Think about how the object functions, then fill in the blank with the word or phrase that best describes the machine it represents.

lever   **pulley**   **wheel** and **axle**

1. paint can opener   _____

2. wheelbarrow   _____

3. crowbar   _____

4. industrial crane   _____

5. roller skates   _____

To the Parent . . .   **Scripture Connection:** 2 Chronicles 26:15

Lesson Focus:
Simple Machines

Lesson Objective:
To explore how simple machines change the direction of a force

National Science Education Standards:
Standard B2 — *"All students should develop an understanding of position and motion of objects . . . (both) can be changed by pushing or pulling . . . sound is produced by vibrating objects . . . pitch can be varied by changing rate of vibration . . ."*

Follow-up Questions:
Ask your child to name three simple machines (lever, pulley, wheel and axle).
Ask your child to give at least one example of a simple machine (seesaw = lever, flagpole = pulley, etc.).
Ask your child to explain how one simple machine changes the direction of a force (pushing down raises up, etc.).

FOCUS   Refraction

OBJECTIVE   To explore how light is bent by a lens

OVERVIEW   To see anything, we need light. Light usually travels in straight lines. But some things can make light bend (refract). When light refracts, strange things can happen!

WHAT TO DO

With your team, carefully follow each step below.

Observe

Look at the large coin. Look at it again through the magnifying lens. How does it look different? Observe other coins and small objects using the lens.

Describe

Describe the large coin. What does it look like? What does it feel like? What shape is it? How does it change when you look at it through the magnifying lens?

Discuss

What is needed for us to see anything? *light*

What word can mean "to bend light"? *refract*

What word can mean "to make larger"? *magnify*

PHYSICAL · 195

Introduction

National Standards
Focus: B3

Related: A1, A2, B1, B2, E1, E2

Category
Physical Science

Focus
Refraction

Objective
To explore how light is bent by a lens

Overview
Read the overview aloud to your students. The goal is to create an atmosphere of curiosity and inquiry.

Say: *"To see anything, we need light. Light usually travels in straight lines. But some things can make light bend. This is called 'refraction.' When light refracts, strange things can happen!"*

Additional Notes

To introduce this lesson, darken your classroom. Shine a flashlight at a book placed on top of a desk. Have students observe and discuss the path the light takes from the flashlight to the book.

Now have a student place the book behind the desk. Without moving, shine the flashlight toward the book again. Ask students why the light can't get to the book. (The desk is in the way.) Discuss what this tells us about the path light usually takes. (It goes straight from one point to another.)

Say, *"We've just seen how light usually follows a straight path. But in this lesson, we'll discover that sometimes light can bend! Scientists call this 'refraction'."*

What To Do

Once students are seated in "research teams" with materials in front of them, read the first section (OBSERVE) aloud.

Say, *"To start this lesson we're going to **observe** some coins. By using a magnifying lens, we can look even more closely at the details. First, I will read the instructions to you. Then you can follow the instructions as you **observe** the items in front of you."*

Monitor teams closely as they follow instructions. When teams are finished with this section, repeat the process with the DESCRIBE section. Conclude with the DISCUSS section.

Options

Expand the DISCUSS section by having students trace dotted "key words" using crayons or markers. Trace the word **light** in yellow, the word **refract** in blue, and the word **magnify** with a black marker.

FOCUS   Refraction

OBJECTIVE   To explore how light is bent by a lens

OVERVIEW   To see anything, we need light. Light usually travels in straight lines. But some things can make light bend (refract). When light refracts, strange things can happen!

WHAT TO DO
With your team, carefully follow each step below.

Observe

Look at the large coin. Look at it again through the magnifying lens. How does it look different? Observe other coins and small objects using the lens.

Describe

Describe the large coin. What does it **look** like? What does it **feel** like? What **shape** is it? How does it **change** when you look at it through the magnifying lens?

Discuss

What is needed for us to see anything? *light*

What word can mean "to bend light"? *refract*

What word can mean "to make larger"? *magnify*

PHYSICAL · 195

Teacher to Teacher

Anton van Leeuwenhoek (1632-1723) is considered by many to be the father of microscopy. As an apprentice in a dry goods store, he used magnifying glasses to count the threads in cloth. Not satisfied with these crude magnifiers, he created new ways to grind tiny curved lenses, creating the finest magnifiers of the day. Soon he was building microscopes and was the first to see and describe bacteria, yeast plants, and the teeming life in a drop of water.

During his long life, Leeuwenhoek used his lenses to study an incredible variety of living and non-living things. He also reported his findings in over a hundred letters to the Royal Society of England and the French Academy.

READ THE STORY

Light usually travels in a straight line. But some things can make light bend (refract). Read the story below to find out what happens when light bends.

Bending Light

Sometimes light bends. Scientists call this "refraction."
Light usually travels in a straight line. But sometimes light can bend (refract). When light refracts, it can makes objects look different. It can even make colors appear!

Refraction can magnify.

A lens can cause refraction.
The curved surface of a lens causes light passing through it to refract. Objects seen through a lens usually look bigger.

Many devices use a lens to magnify.
A camera uses a lens to magnify. So do things like telescopes, microscopes, reading glasses, and binoculars.

Refraction can make illusions.

Water can cause refraction.
If you push a straight stick halfway into a pool of still water, refraction makes it seem to bend where it enters the water.

A mirror can cause refraction.
If a mirror's surface is curved, it causes light to refract. This can make the reflection you see look very strange!

Refraction can make rainbows.

A water drop can cause refraction.
The curved surface of a water drop can bend light, too. When light is bent different amounts, it can make different colors.

Raindrops make rainbows!
If the angle of the sunlight is just right, raindrops refract light into all its basic colors. That's when we see a beautiful rainbow!

196 · PHYSICAL

Extended Teaching

Here are some great cross-curricular connections for this lesson:

Vocabulary: The word "lens" comes from "lenticula," the Latin word for lentil. (A lentil is a small, round, convex shaped bean with the same shape as a simple lens.)

History: Magnifiers are ancient devices. References to "burning glasses" or "magnifying glasses" are found in the writings of Seneca and Pliny the Elder (first century Roman philosophers). These devices, however, were considered more as curiosities than for any practical use.

Science: In the late 1500s, a Dutch spectacle maker was experimenting with several lenses in a tube. He discovered that nearby objects appeared greatly enlarged. A few years later, Galileo (father of physics and astronomy) heard about this discovery, figured out the principles involved, and created early forerunners of modern microscopes and telescopes.

Read The Story

Read the story aloud with your students. (See READING LEVELS on page 12.) After reading, monitor teams as they discuss what was read. Once you feel students have mastered the basic concepts, have them answer the comprehension questions (**What I Learned** - part 1) on the next page.

To introduce the story, say:

"The title of this story is 'Bending Light.' Look at your story and follow along as we read it together."

If you wish, encourage Emergent readers to point to words and pictures as you read.

What I Learned (part 1)

These are basic fact-based comprehension questions. Student answers will vary, but suggested responses include:

1 a) bending light b) magnify, make illusions, make rainbows

2 a) both magnify b) telescope makes things far away seem closer; microscope makes tiny things seem larger

3 The angle of the sunlight must be just right

Field Trip

Go on a hike with binoculars. (Encourage students who have them to bring binoculars from home.) Let students take turns looking at far away objects and describing what they see.

Guest Speaker

Invite a science teacher from a local college to visit your class. Ask him/her to bring a microscope and several slides your students can examine under the lens.

Materials Needed*
magnifying lens
coins - 2   pipette
paper towels   water

Safety Concerns

4. Slipping
There is a potential for spilled liquids. Remind students to exercise caution.

Do the Activity

Read the activity in advance so you understand it thoroughly. (If time allows, try it yourself.) Before students begin, carefully go over the **Safety Concerns** together.

Pass out materials, then have your students follow along as you read the instructions for **Step 1**. Monitor teams closely as they complete this step.

Once teams have completed **Step 1**, read instructions for **Step 2**. Monitor teams as before. Repeat for **Step 3** and **Step 4**.

After the activity, allow time for each team to share their observations. To encourage higher-level thinking, encourage teams to not only share their observations with each other, but also with other teams.

Special Instructions

Step 1 - Give each team a small cup of water. Demonstrate how to use the pipette: squeeze it, place the tip in the water, then relax your grip so the water is drawn into the bulb. Now squeeze gently to release a single drop of water.

Allow students to practice this by writing their name on a paper towel strip, then dropping one drop of water on each letter.

Step 2 - Differences in motor skills development may make it difficult for some teams to "stack" water drops on the coins. If you see problems, join the group and demonstrate. This will shift the focus from the skill to the observation process.

DO THE ACTIVITY
Working with your research team, carefully follow each step below. Before you start, be sure you know the **safety rules** for this activity.

STEP 1 Place the large coin on the paper towel. Carefully observe its surface. Now fill the pipette with water. Place one drop of water in the center of the coin.

STEP 2 Continue adding drops (one at a time) until the coin is full. Now look through the water at the coin's surface. Compare this with how it looked in step 1.

STEP 3 Repeat steps 1 and 2 using both sides of the second coin. Record your observations. Make sure that everyone on your team has had a turn.

STEP 4 Review each step in this activity. Discuss how the water changed the way the coins looked. Compare your team's findings with those of other research teams.

198 · PHYSICAL

What Happened?

Immediately following the activity, help your students understand what they observed.

Say: *"In this activity, you were able to see how light can bend. Scientists call this 'refraction.' You also discovered that refraction can magnify.*

*In **Steps 1** and **2**, you* *added drops to the large coin until it was covered with water. You saw the water form a lens that magnified the image on the coin.*

*Then you checked your discovery by repeating the process with another coin in **Step 3**, and comparing your findings with other teams in **Step 4**."*

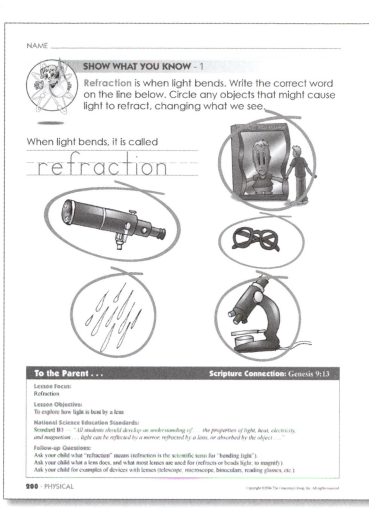

NAME _____

SHOW WHAT YOU KNOW - 1

Refraction is when light bends. Write the correct word on the line below. Circle any objects that might cause light to refract, changing what we see.

When light bends, it is called

refraction

To the Parent . . .   Scripture Connection: Genesis 9:13

Lesson Focus:
Refraction

Lesson Objective:
To explore how light is bent by a lens

National Science Education Standards:
Standard B3 — "All students should develop an understanding of . . . the properties of light, heat, electricity, and magnetism . . . light can be reflected by a mirror, refracted by a lens, or absorbed by the object . . ."

Follow-up Questions:
Ask your child what "refraction" means (refraction is the scientific term for "bending light").
Ask your child what a lens does, and what most lenses are used for (refracts or bends light; to magnify).
Ask your child for examples of devices with lenses (telescope, microscope, binoculars, reading glasses, etc.).

200 · PHYSICAL

Food For Thought

A related "Scripture Object Lesson" you can share with your students.

Genesis 9:13

We've learned that refraction can magnify images, make illusions, and even create rainbows.

Scientists tell us that rainbows are the result of sunlight hitting raindrops at just the right angle. But that's not the whole story. To Christians, the beautiful colors of the rainbow mean so much more. Scripture tells us that God placed a rainbow in the sky as a sign of His promise to never flood the entire earth again. Whenever we see a rainbow, it should remind us that God always keeps his promises.

God expects us to keep our promises too! Think about promises you've made — to God and to others. Ask Him to give you the courage to keep your promises.

Expand - Day 4

Begin **Day 4** with a review of **Day 3**, then have students answer "part 2" questions.

What I Learned (part 2)
These are higher-level cognitive questions (explain, compare, predict). Student answers will vary, but suggested responses may include:

1 it made the images on the coins look bigger; it bent or "refracted" the light

2 a) both curved, both can magnify, etc. b) water drop is liquid, lens is usually glass or plastic; water drop is temporary, lens lasts much longer; etc.

3 a) a lens b) more permanent, clearer focus, etc.

Assess - Day 5

Suggestions for modifying assessments to reflect reading levels can be found under ASSESSMENT METHODS on page 12.

Show What You Know 1
(general assessment in Student Worktext)

Blank: refraction
Also, ALL the objects should be circled.

Show What You Know 2
(optional test master in Teacher Guide)

1) light   2) straight   3) refraction
4) rainbow   5) magnify

To The Parent
Included at the bottom of all assessment tests, "To The Parent" provides a great way to solicit parent involvement. It not only gives parents an overview of the lesson, but also provides follow-up questions for home use.

Show What You Know 2

Read each sentence below. Using the "word bank" choose the best word to complete each sentence, then write it on the line. (Some words will not be used.)

1. To see anything, we need to have _____ .

2. Light usually travels in a _____ line.

3. Sometimes light can bend. Scientists call this _____ .

4. A _____ can happen when raindrops refract sunlight.

5. When a lens refracts light, it can _____ an image.

WORD BANK:

   magnify   rainbow   freeze   camera   refraction   light   square   straight

---

To the Parent . . .   **Scripture Connection:** Genesis 9:13

Lesson Focus:
Refraction

Lesson Objective:
To explore how light is bent by a lens

National Science Education Standards:
Standard B3 — *"All students should develop an understanding of . . . the properties of light, heat, electricity, and magnetism . . . light can be reflected by a mirror, refracted by a lens, or absorbed by the object . . ."*

Follow-up Questions:
Ask your child what "refraction" means (refraction is the scientific term for "bending light").
Ask your child what a lens does, and what most lenses are used for (refracts or bends light; to magnify).
Ask your child for examples of devices with lenses (telescope, microscope, binoculars, reading glasses, etc.).

FOCUS   Reflection and Refraction

OBJECTIVE   To explore two basic properties of light

OVERVIEW   Light usually bounces off things (reflects). But sometimes light also bends (refracts). There are many useful ways to use these special properties of light.

Mirror Magic
Lesson 32

WHAT TO DO
With your team, carefully follow each step below.

Observe

Look at the front of the mirror. Think about what you see. Now look at the back of the mirror. How does this view differ from what you saw in the front of the mirror?

Describe

Describe the mirror. What does it look like? What does it feel like? What shape is it? What color is it? How is it like other mirrors that you've seen? How is it different?

Discuss

What do we need in order to see anything? light
What word can mean "to bounce off"? reflect
What word can mean "to bend light"? refract

PHYSICAL · 201

National Standards
Focus: B3

Related: A1, A2, B1, B2, E1, E2

Category
Physical Science

Focus
Reflection and Refraction

Objective
To explore two basic properties of light

Overview
Read the overview aloud to your students. The goal is to create an atmosphere of curiosity and inquiry.

Say: *"Light usually bounces off things (reflects). But sometimes light also bends (refracts). There are many useful ways to use these special properties of light."*

Additional Notes

To introduce this lesson, ask a student to stand with you in front of the class. Toss a playground ball (dodgeball) to them and have them catch it. Now toss the ball again, only this time make it bounce once on the floor before they catch it. Ask the class what was different. (The ball bounced off something.)

Say, *"You can see how the ball bounces off the floor and changes directions before it is caught."* Bounce the ball back and forth a few more times, then say, *"Do you know light can bounce off things, too? Sometimes light even bends! Light bouncing off something is called* **reflection**. *Light being bent by something is called* **refraction**. *In this lesson, we'll explore how light behaves."*

What To Do

Once students are seated in "research teams" with materials in front of them, read the first section (OBSERVE) aloud.

Say, *"To start this lesson, we're going to look closely at a mirror. Good scientists always carefully examine the things they will be working with before beginning. First, I will read the instructions to you. Then you can follow the instructions as you **observe** the mirror and think about each question."*

Monitor teams closely as they follow instructions. When teams are finished with this section, repeat the process with the DESCRIBE section. Conclude with the DISCUSS section.

Options

Expand the DISCUSS section by having students trace dotted "key words" using crayons or markers. Trace the word **light** in yellow, the word **reflect** in red, and the word **refract** in blue.

FOCUS   Reflection and Refraction

OBJECTIVE   To explore two basic properties of light

OVERVIEW   Light usually bounces off things (reflects). But sometimes light also bends (refracts). There are many useful ways to use these special properties of light.

WHAT TO DO

With your team, carefully follow each step below.

Observe

Look at the front of the mirror. Think about what you see. Now look at the back of the mirror. How does this view differ from what you saw in the front of the mirror?

Describe

Describe the mirror. What does it look like? What does it feel like? What shape is it? What color is it? How is it like other mirrors that you've seen? How is it different?

Discuss

What do we need in order to see anything? light

What word can mean "to bounce off"? reflect

What word can mean "to bend light"? refract

PHYSICAL · **201**

Teacher to Teacher

Although light is very complex, its behavior can be understood with simple models based on rays (see next page). A ray is a small beam of light traveling in a straight line.

For smooth-surfaced objects like mirrors, light rays travel in one direction and are reflected (or bounced back) from the object in another direction.

But when light rays travel from one medium (like air) through another (like glass), the speed of the light changes. Instead of being reflected, the ray of light goes through the material —but its path is deflected or "bent."

The "law of reflection" and "index of refraction" help scientists predict specific behaviors of light.

READ THE STORY

Light bouncing off something is called reflection. Light being bent by something is called refraction. Read the story below to discover more about light.

Changing Light

Light changes directions in interesting ways.
Light usually bounces off of things. Scientists call this "reflection." Light can also be bent by certain things. Scientists call the bending of light "refraction."

Light can reflect.

We need reflection to see.
To see anything, we need light. Unless it gives off light itself, an object can only be seen because of the light it reflects.

Reflection can bounce back images.
Mirrors are great reflectors. They reflect the light shining on things. Mirror images are usually right-side up, but reversed!

Light can refract.

Refraction can create illusions.
Refraction makes light change its path. If you place a pencil in water, refraction can make the pencil look broken or bent!

Refraction can make rainbows.
The curved surface of raindrops can bend light. If the angle of sunlight is just right, raindrops refract light into its basic colors.

Light is used in many ways.

Reflection can be helpful.
The most common "reflectors" are mirrors. They are used for everything from combing hair, to driving a car, to fixing teeth!

Refraction can be helpful.
The most common "refractors" are lenses. Lenses are used in devices like cameras, telescopes, lasers, and microscopes.

202 · PHYSICAL

Extended Teaching

1. To expand vocabulary, explain that "reflect" means to bounce light back, and "refract" means to deflect or change the path of light. Illustrate this by drawing the simple models below.

2. Play "Reflection Detection." Have each team list as many items as possible that use mirrors in some way. Common examples include hand mirrors and bathroom mirrors — but mirrors are also found in searchlights, flashlights, and telescopes! Have each team share their findings, then compile a "master list" on the board.

3. Play "Refraction Action" by listing various objects that bend light.

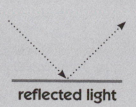

reflected light

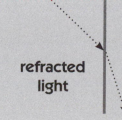

refracted light

Read The Story

Read the story aloud with your students. (See READING LEVELS on page 12.) After reading, monitor teams as they discuss what was read. Once you feel students have mastered the basic concepts, have them answer the comprehension questions (**What I Learned** - part 1) on the next page.

To introduce the story, say:

"The title of this story is 'Changing Light.' Look at your story and follow along as we read it together."

If you wish, encourage Emergent readers to point to words and pictures as you read.

What I Learned (part 1)

These are basic fact-based comprehension questions. Student answers will vary, but suggested responses include:

1) a) reflection = various kinds of mirrors
b) refraction = anything with a lens

2) answers will vary, but should include the idea that reflection bounces light back, but refraction changes light's path

3) a) no b) it takes light to make a rainbow

Field Trip

Visit a local glass shop. Ask the owner to describe and show various kinds of mirrors. Show students what happens when the backing is scraped off a piece of mirror scrap (it no longer reflects).

Guest Speaker

Invite an optometrist, dentist, or doctor to visit your class. Have him/her bring various medical tools that are made with mirrors. Ask him/her to demonstrate their use.

Materials Needed*

mirror   plastic jar
flashlight   water
paper towels

Safety Concerns

4. Slipping

There is a potential for spilled liquid. Remind students to exercise caution.

4. Other

Remind students to handle the mirror carefully to avoid breakage.

Do the Activity

Read the activity in advance so you understand it thoroughly. (If time allows, try it yourself.) Before students begin, carefully go over the **Safety Concerns** together.

Pass out materials, then have your students follow along as you read the instructions for **Step 1**. Monitor teams closely as they complete this step.

Once teams have completed **Step 1**, read instructions for **Step 2**. Monitor teams as before. Repeat for **Step 3** and **Step 4**.

After the activity, allow time for each team to share their observations. To encourage higher-level thinking, encourage teams to not only share their observations with each other, but also with other teams.

Special Instructions

Step 1 - If mirror is placed correctly, the students should see the ceiling. Make sure every student has a turn.

Step 2 - *(Darken room for Steps 2 and 3.)* A white light should appear on the ceiling. Make sure every student gets a turn to hold the flashlight.

Step 3 - A faint rainbow should appear on the ceiling. If it doesn't, simply have students change the angle of light from the flashlight. Keep some paper towels on hand for immediate cleanup of spills.

* Bold-faced items supplied in kit.

DO THE ACTIVITY

Working with your research team, carefully follow each step below. Before you start, be sure you know the **safety rules** for this activity.

Place the mirror in the jar so that the glass side is facing you and the top is tilted back. **Look** into the mirror from table level and **describe** what you see.

Shine the flashlight directly at the mirror (touching the jar). **Look** up and **observe** the ceiling. **Move** the flashlight around to vary the reflected light.

Fill the jar with water. **Repeat** step 2. Look at the ceiling and **observe** how the "refracted" light differs from the "reflected" light that you saw in step 2.

Review each step in this activity. **Discuss** how the light changed in steps 2 and 3. **Compare** your team's findings with those of other research teams.

What Happened?

Immediately following the activity, help your students understand what they observed.

Say: *"In this activity, you explored two properties of light — reflection and refraction.*

*In **Step 1**, you saw how a mirror makes a good reflector.*

*In **Step 2**, you reflected light off the mirror onto the ceiling. Since the light* only went through air, the light did not change.

*In **Step 3**, however, the light had to go through water. This changed the light's speed, creating an illusion — a rainbow on the ceiling! The curved surface of the water in the jar bent the light, refracting the light into its basic colors.*

*Finally in **Step 4**, you compared your observations with other teams."*

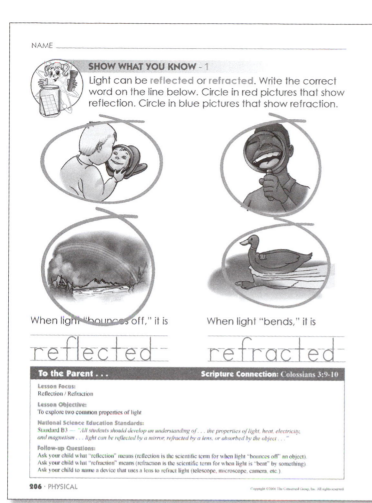

NAME _____

SHOW WHAT YOU KNOW - 1
Light can be **reflected** or **refracted**. Write the correct word on the line below. Circle in red pictures that show reflection. Circle in blue pictures that show refraction.

When light "bounces off," it is

reflected

When light "bends," it is

refracted

To the Parent . . .   **Scripture Connection:** Colossians 3:9-10

Lesson Focus:
Reflection / Refraction

Lesson Objective:
To explore two common properties of light

National Science Education Standards:
Standard B3 — "All students should develop an understanding of . . . the properties of light, heat, electricity, and magnetism . . . light can be reflected by a mirror, refracted by a lens, or absorbed by the object . . ."

Follow-up Questions:
Ask your child what "reflection" means (reflection is the scientific term for when light "bounces off" an object)
Ask your child what "refraction" means (refraction is the scientific term for when light is "bent" by something)
Ask your child to name a device that uses a lens to refract light (telescope, microscope, camera, etc.)

206 · PHYSICAL   Copyright ©2006 The Concerned Group, Inc. All rights reserved.

Food For Thought

A related "Scripture Object Lesson" you can share with your students.

Colossians 3: 9-10

When we look in a mirror, it reflects our image, letting us see what we look like. A mirror provides a very truthful picture of what we look like.

But if we use a bent mirror, our appearance is much different! It might make us look disproportionate and all bent out of shape. A bad mirror can seriously distort what we really look like.

God wants us to be a good mirror, clearly reflecting a true picture of Him. But sometimes we distort God's image by making bad decisions. If we lie or cheat or steal, it doesn't give others a true picture of God.

To reflect God's love means to live as Jesus lived. Why not ask God to help you always reflect the true light of Jesus!

Expand - Day 4

Begin **Day 4** with a review of **Day 3**, then have students answer "part 2" questions.

What I Learned (part 2)
These are higher-level cognitive questions (explain, compare, predict). Student answers will vary but suggested responses may include:

1. a) in the flashlight b) on the ceiling

2. a) both used light, both used mirror
b) in step 2, the light only went through air; in step 3, it also went through water

3. a) it would be brighter b) more light

Assess - Day 5

Suggestions for modifying assessments to reflect reading levels can be found under ASSESSMENT METHODS on page 12.

Show What You Know 1
(general assessment in Student Worktext)

Blanks: a) reflected b) refracted
Also, the baby and the duck should be circled in red; the boy and the rainbow should be circled in blue.

Show What You Know 2
(optional test master in Teacher Guide)

1) reflection   2) refraction   3) reflection
4) refraction   5) refraction

To The Parent
Included at the bottom of all assessment tests, "To The Parent" provides a great way to solicit parent involvement. It not only gives parents an overview of the lesson, but also provides follow-up questions for home use.

NAME _____

Show What You Know 2

Look at the list of items below. If the item reflects light, then circle the word **reflection**. If the item refracts light (usually with a lens), then circle the word **refraction**.

1. the rear-view mirror on a truck   reflection   refraction

2. a small, portable camera   reflection   refraction

3. the mirror in your bathroom   reflection   refraction

4. a small, hand-held telescope   reflection   refraction

5. the microscope in the school lab   reflection   refraction

---

To the Parent . . .   Scripture Connection: Colossians 3: 9-10

Lesson Focus:
Reflection and Refraction

Lesson Objective:
To explore two common properties of light

National Science Education Standards:
Standard B3 — *"All students should develop an understanding of . . . the properties of light, heat, electricity, and magnetism . . . light can be reflected by a mirror, refracted by a lens, or absorbed by the object . . ."*

Follow-up Questions:
Ask your child what "reflection" means. (Reflection is the scientific term for when light "bounces off" an object.)
Ask your child what "refraction" means. (Refraction is the scientific term for when light is "bent" by something.)
Ask your child to name a device that uses a lens to refract light (telescope, microscope, camera, etc.).

Finding Friction
Lesson 33

FOCUS Friction

OBJECTIVE To explore some of the characteristics of friction

OVERVIEW Friction can produce heat or slow moving things down. Rough surfaces usually cause more friction. Reducing friction usually makes things easier to move.

WHAT TO DO

With your team, carefully follow each step below.

Observe

Look at the sandpaper. Look at the wheels on the car. Rub your finger on the sandpaper. Now spin one of the car's wheels. Think about how the friction felt different.

Describe

Describe the sandpaper and the car wheels. What do they look like? What do they feel like? Describe how it feels to slide your finger along each one.

Discuss

What does rubbing things together cause? friction

What is one thing that friction can produce? heat

What type of surface causes more friction? rough

PHYSICAL · 207

Lesson 33

Introduction

National Standards
Focus: B3

Related: A1, A2, B1, B2, E1, E2

Category
Physical Science

Focus
Friction

Objective
To explore some of the characteristics of friction

Overview
Read the overview aloud to your students. The goal is to create an atmosphere of curiosity and inquiry.

Say: *"Friction can produce heat or slow moving things down. Rough surfaces usually cause more friction. Reducing friction usually makes things easier to move."*

Additional Notes

To introduce this lesson, give your students a hypothetical problem.

Say, *"Suppose I have a large box that I have to move across the room. It's the weekend and there's no one to help me. The box is so big that I can't carry it by myself. It's far too heavy to slide across the floor. What could I use to help me move this big box?"*

Have students discuss the problem with their team members, then collect their suggestions. Focus on solutions that use a device with wheels (wagon, dolly, etc.).

Now ask, *"Why was the job so hard? What do wheels do to make it easier? In this lesson, we'll explore how friction affects the way things move."*

What To Do

Once students are seated in "research teams" with materials in front of them, read the first section (OB-SERVE) aloud.

Say, *"To start this lesson, we're going to **observe** some items. Good scientists always carefully examine the things they will be working with before beginning. First, I will read the instructions to you. Then you can follow the instructions as you **observe** the items in front of you."*

Monitor teams closely as they follow instructions. When teams are finished with this section, repeat the process with the DE-SCRIBE section. Conclude with the DISCUSS section.

Options

Expand the DISCUSS section by having students trace dotted "key words" using crayons or markers. Trace the word **friction** in yellow, the word **heat** in orange, and the word **rough** in red.

Finding Friction
Lesson 33

FOCUS   Friction

OBJECTIVE   To explore some of the characteristics of friction

OVERVIEW   Friction can produce heat or slow moving things down. Rough surfaces usually cause more friction. Reducing friction usually makes things easier to move.

WHAT TO DO
With your team, carefully follow each step below.

Observe

Look at the sandpaper. Look at the wheels on the car. Rub your finger on the sandpaper. Now spin one of the car's wheels. Think about how the friction felt different.

Describe

Describe the sandpaper and the car wheels. What do they look like? What do they feel like? Describe how it feels to slide your finger along each one.

Discuss

What does rubbing things together cause? friction

What is one thing that friction can produce? heat

What type of surface causes more friction? rough

PHYSICAL · 207

Teacher to Teacher

The wheel is one of mankind's oldest and most important inventions.

Archaeologists tell us that wheels are descended from an early tool called the sledge — a kind of platform rolled across logs. Over time, the rollers of the sledge would develop wide grooves and someone noticed that the grooved rollers actually worked better!

This led to cutting and smoothing the wood in the grooves, creating the first axle. Next, pegs were added under the platform (so the axle and wheels did all the movement), creating the first carts.

Eventually, someone cut the ends off the logs, drilled holes to insert the axles, and thus created the first true wheel!

READ THE STORY

Usually the more friction there is between two objects, the hotter they get, and the more they will slow down. Read the story below to find out more.

Friction

Friction happens all around us!
Friction occurs whenever two objects rub together, or when an object rubs against some other surface. Friction can be harmful or helpful depending on the situation.

Friction can be harmful.

Friction takes energy.
Friction slows everything down. To overcome friction when riding a bike, you must apply energy by pedaling harder.

Friction produces heat.
Energy lost to friction can turn to heat. Too much heat can be harmful. For instance, sliding against carpet may "burn" you.

Friction can be helpful.

Friction helps us move.
If you've ever tried to walk on ice, you know too little friction can be a problem! It takes some friction just to move around.

Friction keeps thing in place.
Friction also helps keep things from moving. For instance, a little friction can keep your glasses from sliding off your nose!

Friction can be changed.

Friction can be reduced.
Lubricants (like oil) help reduce friction in machines. Wheels or rollers also help reduce friction, making things easier to move.

Friction can be increased.
Special materials and special shapes can increase friction. Look at the bottom of shoes or at different kinds of car tires.

Extended Teaching

1. To expand vocabulary, point out that the word "rubbing" always implies a certain amount of pressure. As the pressure increases, so will the friction between the two objects. This leads to heat. Students can experience this by rubbing their hands together and varying both the pressure and speed.

2. Allow students to experience the variations in friction on a tiled floor. Have them walk down an empty hallway in their shoes. Tell them to think about the friction involved. Now have them *carefully* walk down the same hallway in their socks. Discuss the difference in friction.

3. Have students remove their shoes and compare the soles. Discuss which types of shoes might produce the greatest amount of friction, and which types might produce the least. Ask, *"Why aren't all shoes the same?"* As you discuss this, make comparisons between athletic shoes, dress shoes, hiking boots, etc.

Inform - Day 2

Read The Story

Read the story aloud with your students. (See READING LEVELS on page 12.) After reading, monitor teams as they discuss what was read. Once you feel students have mastered the basic concepts, have them answer the comprehension questions (**What I Learned** - part 1) on the next page.

To introduce the story, say:

"The title of this story is 'Friction.' Look at your story and follow along as we read it together."

If you wish, encourage Emergent readers to point to words and pictures as you read.

What I Learned (part 1)

These are basic fact-based comprehension questions. Student answers will vary, but suggested responses include:

① Friction can be *reduced* by oil, wheels, or rollers; Friction can be *increased* by special materials or shapes

② a) takes energy; produces heat b) helps us move around; helps keep things in place

③ tall grass; more friction makes it harder to move

Field Trip

Take a walk on various surfaces (gym floor, parking lot, dirt, gravel, tall grass, short grass, etc.). Have teams make notes about how each surface produces different amounts of friction. Discuss why different surfaces are needed for different areas.

Guest Speaker

Invite an experienced athletic shoe salesperson to visit your class. Ask him/her to bring several different kinds of shoes and to explain the reason for the different surfaces on each shoe's sole.

FINDING FRICTION · 215

Materials Needed*

toy car   books - 2
sandpaper strip   tape

Safety Concerns

4. Sharp Objects
Remind students to exercise caution if scissors are used.

Do the Activity

Read the activity in advance so you understand it thoroughly. (If time allows, try it yourself.) Before students begin, carefully go over the **Safety Concerns** together.

Pass out materials, then have your students follow along as you read the instructions for **Step 1**. Monitor teams closely as they complete this step.

Once teams have completed **Step 1**, read instructions for **Step 2**. Monitor teams as before. Repeat for **Step 3** and **Step 4**.

After the activity, allow time for each team to share their observations. To encourage higher-level thinking, encourage teams to not only share their observations with each other, but also with other teams.

Special Instructions

Step 2 - Lay one book (preferably thick) flat on the table with the narrow end toward the student. Turn the second book (preferably thinner) at 90 degrees to the first book with one end resting on the first book. Be sure to use hardback books since paperbacks tend to sag.

Step 3 - Tape should only go around the middle of the car. (Center the tape at right angles to the sandpaper strip, run it up along each door, and secure both ends to the roof.) Remind students to use the minimum amount of tape. They're testing the friction of the *sandpaper,* not the tape! Also, they must be sure the wheels are free to turn, but that the sandpaper is touching the ramp.

DO THE ACTIVITY
Working with your research team, carefully follow each step below. Before you start, be sure you know the **safety rules** for this activity.

STEP 1
Rub your hands together rapidly. **Discuss** how they feel. **Rub** one hand against your leg rapidly. **Discuss** how this feels. Why did the temperature change?

STEP 2
Make a ramp from two hardback books (see illustration). **Place** the car at the top of the ramp. **Release** the car. **Observe** and **record** the results.

STEP 3
Tape a strip of sandpaper to the bottom of the car. (Make sure it is rough side down and will touch the ramp.) Now **repeat** step 2 using the modified car.

STEP 4
Review steps 2 and 3. **Discuss** how added friction changed the way the car performed. **Compare** your findings with those of other research teams.

What Happened?

Immediately following the activity, help your students understand what they observed.

Say: *"In this activity, you explored some of the key characteristics of the force called friction.*

*In **Step 1**, you saw how friction between two objects can produce heat.*

*In **Steps 2** and **3**, you were able to compare the difference in friction between a rough surface and a smooth one. You discovered that the toy car went much faster when it was not slowed down by the friction of the sandpaper dragging against the book.*

*Finally, in **Step 4**, you compared and discussed your observations with other research teams."*

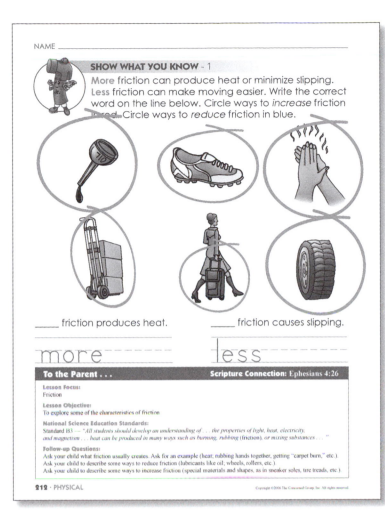

NAME _____

SHOW WHAT YOU KNOW - 1

More friction can produce heat or minimize slipping. Less friction can make moving easier. Write the correct word on the line below. Circle ways to *increase* friction in red. Circle ways to *reduce* friction in blue.

_____ friction produces heat.   _____ friction causes slipping.

more   less

To the Parent . . .   Scripture Connection: Ephesians 4:26

Lesson Focus:
Friction

Lesson Objective:
To explore some of the characteristics of friction

National Science Education Standards:
Standard B3 — *"All students should develop an understanding of . . . the properties of light, heat, electricity, and magnetism . . . heat can be produced in many ways such as burning, rubbing (friction), or mixing substances . . ."*

Follow-up Questions:
Ask your child what friction usually creates. Ask for an example (heat; rubbing hands together; getting "carpet burn," etc.).
Ask your child to describe some ways to reduce friction (lubricants like oil; wheels, rollers, etc.).
Ask your child to describe some ways to increase friction (special materials and shapes, as in sneaker soles, tire treads, etc.).

212 · PHYSICAL   Copyright ©2006 The Concerned Group, Inc. All rights reserved.

Food For Thought

A related "Scripture Object Lesson" you can share with your students.

Ephesians 4:26

In this lesson, we discovered that friction occurs when two objects begin to rub together.

But did you know that objects aren't the only things that can have friction? Relationships between people can have friction, too.

Friction in a relationship can lead to anger and frustration. God does not want us to have this kind of problem. In fact, this Scripture says you should not let the Sun go down without dealing with your anger.

Are you feeling friction with anyone in your life right now? Go to them and make your relationship right again. Let God's love and power be the lubricant that turns friction back into peace.

Expand - Day 4

Begin **Day 4** with a review of **Day 3**, then have students answer "part 2" questions.

What I Learned (part 2)
These are higher-level cognitive questions (explain, compare, predict). Student answers will vary, but suggested responses may include:

1. produce heat; slow things down; etc.

2. a) same ramp, angle, car, etc.
b) surface under car was different in Step 2

3. a) sand b) ice provides little friction; the surface of sand has a lot of friction

Assess - Day 5

Suggestions for modifying assessments to reflect reading levels can be found under ASSESSMENT METHODS on page 12.

Show What You Know 1
(general assessment in Student Worktext)

Blank: 1) more 2) less
Also, the shoe and rubbing hands should be circled in red. The luggage, oil can, and dolly should be circled in blue. The tire can be circled with either color, depending on whether the student sees it as a "wheel" (reducing friction) or a better surface (increasing friction)

Show What You Know 2
(optional test master in Teacher Guide)

1) easier 2) can 3) can 4) reduce
5) heat

To The Parent
Included at the bottom of all assessment tests, "To The Parent" provides a great way to solicit parent involvement. It not only gives parents an overview of the lesson, but also provides follow-up questions for home use.

NAME _____

Show What You Know 2

Read each sentence below. Look at the two words in the brackets, then draw a circle around the word that best completes the sentence.

1. Reducing friction usually makes things [harder easier] to move.

2. Friction [can can't] take energy away and produce heat.

3. Friction [can can't] help keep things in place.

4. Lubricants like oil can [reduce increase] friction.

5. Energy lost to friction usually turns into [water heat].

To the Parent . . .   **Scripture Connection:** Ephesians 4:26

Lesson Focus:
Friction

Lesson Objective:
To explore some of the characteristics of friction

National Science Education Standards:
Standard B3 — *"All students should develop an understanding of . . . the properties of light, heat, electricity, and magnetism . . . heat can be produced in many ways such as burning, rubbing* (friction)*, or mixing substances . . ."*

Follow-up Questions:
Ask your child what friction usually creates. Ask for an example (heat; rubbing hands together, getting "carpet burn", etc.).
Ask your child to describe some ways to reduce friction (lubricants like oil; wheels, rollers, etc.).
Ask your child to describe some ways to increase friction (special materials and shapes, as in sneaker soles, tire treads, etc.).

FOCUS Static Electricity

OBJECTIVE To explore the relationship between atoms and static electricity

OVERVIEW Everything is made of atoms. Atoms have "positive" and "negative" particles. When these particles give atoms different "charges," the atoms can cause static electricity.

WHAT TO DO

With your team, carefully follow each step below.

Observe

Look at the salt. Look at the sawdust. Observe the size of the pieces. Look at the balloon. Compare the way it feels to the feel of the salt and the sawdust.

Describe

Describe the salt. What does it look like? What does it feel like? What does it smell like? What shape is it? How is it similar to sawdust? How is it different?

Discuss

What is everything on Earth made from? atoms
What is one thing an atom can have? charge
What is one simple form of electricity? static

PHYSICAL **213**

Lesson 34

National Standards
Focus: B3

Related: A1, A2, B1, B2, E1, E2

Category
Physical Science

Focus
Static Electricity

Objective
To explore the relationship between atoms and static electricity

Overview
Read the overview aloud to your students. The goal is to create an atmosphere of curiosity and inquiry.

Say: *"Everything is made of atoms. Atoms have positive and negative particles. When these particles give atoms different charges, the atoms can cause static electricity."*

Additional Notes

To introduce this lesson, hand a flashlight (without batteries) to a student and ask them to turn it on. When it doesn't work, ask the class why it's not working.

When someone suggests that it needs batteries, install batteries in the flashlight incorrectly, then ask the student to turn it on again. When it doesn't work a second time, ask, *"What's wrong now?"*

After discussion, show students that the batteries are not installed correctly. Point out the positive and negative markings.

Say, *"Atoms have positive and negative charges, too. In this lesson, we'll discover one thing that happens when they interact."*

What To Do

Once students are seated in "research teams" with materials in front of them, read the first section (OB-SERVE) aloud.

Say, *"To start this lesson, we're going to **observe** some items. Good scientists always carefully examine the things they will be working with before beginning. First, I will read the instructions to you. Then you can follow the instructions as you **observe** the items in front of you."*

Monitor teams closely as they follow instructions. When teams are finished with this section, repeat the process with the DE-SCRIBE section. Conclude with the DISCUSS section.

Options

Expand the DISCUSS section by having students trace dotted "key words" using crayons or markers. Trace the word **atoms** in yellow, the word **charge** in red, and the word **static** in blue.

FOCUS	Static Electricity
OBJECTIVE	To explore the relationship between atoms and static electricity
OVERVIEW	Everything is made of atoms. Atoms have "positive" and "negative" particles. When these particles give atoms different "charges," the atoms can cause static electricity.

Shaking Salt
Lesson 34

WHAT TO DO

With your team, carefully follow each step below.

Observe

Look at the salt. **Look** at the sawdust. **Observe** the size of the pieces. **Look** at the balloon. **Compare** the way it feels to the feel of the salt and the sawdust.

Describe

Describe the salt. What does it **look** like? What does it **feel** like? What does it **smell** like? What **shape** is it? How is it similar to sawdust? How is it different?

Discuss

What is everything on Earth made from? *atoms*

What is one thing an atom can have? *charge*

What is one simple form of electricity? *static*

PHYSICAL · **213**

Teacher to Teacher

It's important to understand that the information for the story in this lesson is based on an over-simplification that is necessary for this age group.

When your students eventually take high school physics or chemistry, they'll discover that an atom's charge is not just based on the total number of electrons. The charge actually depends on whether the specific atom in question has *more* or *less* electrons than it normally has. They'll also discover that there are "neutral" atoms.

One more point: When an atom (or group of atoms) acquires a net electric charge by gaining or losing electrons, then scientists refer to it as an "ion."

Everything is made of atoms. Atoms with different "charges" can cause static electricity. Read the story below to find out more.

Static Electricity

Atoms can cause static electricity.
Everything is made of atoms. Atoms have "positive" and "negative" particles. When these particles give atoms different "charges," the atoms can cause static electricity.

This is an atom.
Everything is made of atoms.
Atoms are tiny particles of matter that are far too small to see. Everything on Earth is made from a combination of atoms.
Atoms are made from tiny parts.
The atom's center is tightly-packed "protons" and "neutrons." They are surrounded by fast-moving particles called "electrons."

Atoms can be "charged."
Atoms can be positive or negative.
Atoms with fewer electrons have a "positive" (+) charge. Atoms with more electrons have a "negative" (-) charge.
Charges can attract or repel.
Atoms with opposite charges (+ -) pull toward each other. Atoms with the same charge (+ + or - -) move away from each other.

Charges make static electricity.
Electrons try to balance opposite charges.
Static electricity happens when the positive and negative charges of atoms are not equal. Electrons try to move to restore balance. They may even jump from one object to another.
Walk across thick carpet and you pick up electrons. To restore balance, they may jump from your hand to a doorknob. Ouch!

Extended Teaching

Note: This lesson has a lot of new vocabulary. Take time to make sure your students master the concepts of atoms and their parts, and electrons seeking balance.

1. Remind students that household current is *very different* from static electricity. It can be very dangerous! Never use any kind of electricity without adult supervision.

2. There are many simple experiments you can do to create static electricity: Have students comb their hair with a plastic comb, pull a sweater over their head, rub wool yarn over a balloon, or rub their feet against carpeting. Once they've collected a "charge," have them move their index finger close to a grounded metal object (like a metal doorknob). Point out the tiny spark of electrons trying to bring the charge back into balance.

3. Ask students if they've ever seen a spark of static electricity in the sky. Ask what this is called. (Lightning, of course!)

Inform - Day 2

Read The Story

Read the story aloud with your students. (See READING LEVELS on page 12.) After reading, monitor teams as they discuss what was read. Once you feel students have mastered the basic concepts, have them answer the comprehension questions (**What I Learned** - part 1) on the next page.

To introduce the story, say:

"The title of this story is 'Static Electricity.' Look at your story and follow along as we read it together."

If you wish, encourage Emergent readers to point to words and pictures as you read.

What I Learned (part 1)

These are basic fact-based comprehension questions. Student answers will vary, but suggested responses include:

① a) tiny particles of matter too small to see b) everything is made of atoms

② atoms with fewer electrons have a positive charge; atoms with more electrons have a negative charge

③ a) less (or none) b) static electricity occurs when charges are not equal

Field Trip

Visit a school auditorium or similar facility with video projection capabilities. Arrange to show your students a video about lightning — National Geographic's *When Lighting Strikes* (1977) or similar.

Guest Speaker

Invite a college physics teacher to visit your class. Ask him/her to bring a Leyden Jar or Van de Graff Generator and to demonstrate how it works. (Both devices can produce huge sparks of static electricity!)

Materials Needed*

salt   sawdust
balloon

Safety Concerns

4. Other

Balloons can pose a choking hazard. Also, remind students that household current is *very different* from static electricity. It is dangerous! They must never experiment with any kind of electricity without adult supervision.

Do the Activity

Read the activity in advance so you understand it thoroughly. (If time allows, try it yourself.) Before students begin, carefully go over the **Safety Concerns** together.

Pass out materials, then have your students follow along as you read the instructions for **Step 1**. Monitor teams closely as they complete this step.

Once teams have completed **Step 1**, read instructions for **Step 2**. Monitor teams as before. Repeat for **Step 3** and **Step 4**.

After the activity, allow time for each team to share their observations. To encourage higher-level thinking, encourage teams to not only share their observations with each other, but also with other teams.

Special Instructions

Step 1 - A "small pile" means about the size of a quarter. Depending on developmental readiness, you may need to assist with inflating or tying balloons.

Step 2 - For hygiene reasons, only one student should touch the balloon to his/her hair in steps 2 and 3. Other team members can help by counting together aloud to thirty (one one thousand, two one thousand, three one thousand, etc.).

DO THE ACTIVITY
Working with your research team, carefully follow each step below. Before you start, be sure you know the **safety rules** for this activity.

STEP 1 Pour a small pile of salt on the desktop. **Inflate** a balloon and tie it off. **Move** the balloon just above the salt and **observe** what happens.

STEP 2 Have a team member "charge" the balloon by **rubbing** it on his/her hair for 30 seconds. Quickly **move** the balloon just above the salt and **observe** what happens.

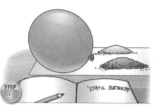

STEP 3 **Compare** what happened in steps 1 and 2 and record your observations. Now **repeat** step 2 using a pile of sawdust instead. **Record** the results.

STEP 4 **Review** each step. **Discuss** what you did to change how the salt and sawdust reacted. **Compare** your findings with those of other research teams.

What Happened?

Immediately following the activity, help your students understand what they observed.

Say: *"In this activity, you explored the relationship between static electricity and atoms.*

*In **Step 1**, the salt and the balloon had equal charges, and so nothing happened.*

*In **Step 2**, you "charged"* the balloon by rubbing it on your hair. When you moved it over the salt, the salt began to shake. Some pieces even jumped onto the balloon!

*In **Step 3**, the sawdust also reacted to the charge. Like the salt, the lighter pieces may have even stuck to the balloon.*

*Then in **Step 4**, you compared observations with other research teams."*

---

* Bold-faced items supplied in kit.

NAME _____

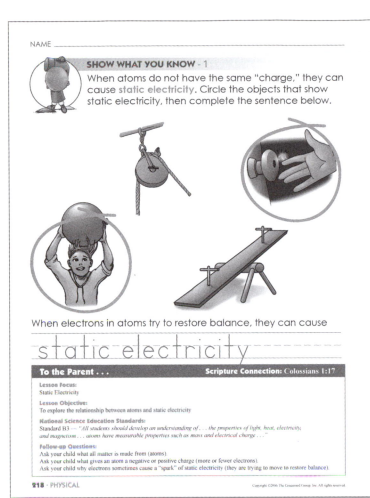

SHOW WHAT YOU KNOW - 1

When atoms do not have the same "charge," they can cause **static electricity**. Circle the objects that show static electricity, then complete the sentence below.

When electrons in atoms try to restore balance, they can cause

static electricity

To the Parent . . .   Scripture Connection: Colossians 1:17

Lesson Focus:
Static Electricity

Lesson Objective:
To explore the relationship between atoms and static electricity

National Science Education Standards:
Standard B3 — *"All students should develop an understanding of . . . the properties of light, heat, electricity, and magnetism . . . atoms have measurable properties such as mass and electrical charge . . ."*

Follow-up Questions:
Ask your child what all matter is made from (atoms).
Ask your child what gives an atom a negative or positive charge (more or fewer electrons).
Ask your child why electrons sometimes cause a "spark" of static electricity (they are trying to move to restore balance).

Food For Thought

A related "Scripture Object Lesson" you can share with your students.

Colossians 1:17

The ancient Greeks thought that atoms were the smallest particles of matter. But today's scientists tell us that the core of an atom is filled with even tinier particles!

Scientists know the name, the weight, the size, and the charge of each kind of particle. However, they still don't know what keeps all these charged particles in place.

But Scripture tells us *God* holds all creation together. You can count on it!

Sometimes it feels like your whole world is jumping around like the electrons in an atom. But remember, if God can hold all the atoms in the world together, He can hold your world together too. Put your trust in the Creator of everything — put your trust in God!

Expand - Day 4

Begin **Day 4** with a review of **Day 3**, then have students answer "part 2" questions.

What I Learned (part 2)

These are higher-level cognitive questions (explain, compare, predict). Student answers will vary, but suggested responses may include:

(1) rubbed it against someone's hair

(2) a) both small particles, both react to the charged balloon, etc. b) can eat salt but not sawdust; salt white, sawdust brown; etc.

(3) a) same as salt and sawdust
b) answers will vary, but should include the idea that they are small particles like sawdust, so should probably react in much the same way

Assess - Day 5

Suggestions for modifying assessments to reflect reading levels can be found under ASSESSMENT METHODS on page 12.

Show What You Know 1

(general assessment in Student Worktext)

Blank: static electricity
Also, the pictures of the hand/doorknob, and the girl with flying hair, should both be circled

Show What You Know 2

(optional test master in Teacher Guide)

1) T   2) T   3) T   4) F   5) T

To The Parent

Included at the bottom of all assessment tests, "To The Parent" provides a great way to solicit parent involvement. It not only gives parents an overview of the lesson, but also provides follow-up questions for home use.

Show What You Know 2

Read each sentence below. If the sentence is true, circle the letter **T**. If the sentence is false, circle the letter **F**.

T F 1. Everything is made from atoms.

T F 2. An atom can have a positive or negative charge.

T F 3. Atoms with fewer electrons have a positive (+) charge.

T F 4. Atoms with the same charge pull toward each other.

T F 5. Unbalanced electrons can cause static electricity.

To the Parent . . .   **Scripture Connection:** Colossians 1:17

Lesson Focus:
Static Electricity

Lesson Objective:
To explore the relationship between atoms and static electricity

National Science Education Standards:
Standard B3 — *"All students should develop an understanding of . . . the properties of light, heat, electricity, and magnetism . . . atoms have measurable properties such as mass and electrical charge . . ."*

Follow-up Questions:
Ask your child what all matter is made from (atoms).
Ask your child what gives an atom a negative or positive charge (more or fewer electrons).
Ask your child why electrons sometimes cause a "spark" of static electricity (they are trying to move to restore balance).

FOCUS   Magnetism

OBJECTIVE   To explore some properties of magnets and magnetism

OVERVIEW   All materials have characteristics called "properties." Magnets have a property called magnetism. Magnetism affects how magnets relate to each other and to other materials.

Attracting Iron
Lesson 35

WHAT TO DO

With your team, carefully follow each step below.

Observe

Look at the magnets. Look at the iron filings. Look at the sawdust. Think about ways these items are similar. Think about ways they are different.

Describe

Describe the iron filings. What do they look like? What do they feel like? What color are they? How do the iron filings compare to the sawdust?

Discuss

What's another name for characteristic? *property*
What property do magnets have? *magnetism*
What is one thing magnets can do? *attract*

PHYSICAL · 219

Introduction

National Standards
Focus: B3

Related: A1, A2, B1, B2, E1, E2

Category
Physical Science

Focus
Magnetism

Objective
To explore some properties of magnets and magnetism

Overview
Read the overview aloud to your students. The goal is to create an atmosphere of curiosity and inquiry.

Say: *"All materials have certain characteristics that are called 'properties."* Magnets have a property called magnetism. Magnetism affects how magnets relate to each other and to other materials."*

Additional Notes

To introduce this lesson, ask a student to stand with you in front of the class. Describe a personal quality that he/she has (friendly, funny, polite, well-mannered, kind, talented, helpful, etc).

Say, "(child's name) *has what some people call a 'magnetic personality'."* Explain that this phrase is used to describe someone who has characteristics that attract us to them. Repeat this activity with a few more students. (Be sure to emphasize some characteristics of less outgoing students.)

Say, *"We all have characteristics that attract others. In this lesson, we'll discover that some materials have special characteristics that attract other materials, too!"*

What To Do

Once students are seated in "research teams" with materials in front of them, read the first section (OB-SERVE) aloud.

Say, *"To start this lesson, we're going to **observe** some items. Good scientists always carefully examine the things they will be working with before beginning. First, I will read the instructions to you. Then you can follow the instructions as you **observe** the items in front of you."*

Monitor teams closely as they follow instructions. When teams are finished with this section, repeat the process with the DE-SCRIBE section. Conclude with the DISCUSS section.

Options

Expand the DISCUSS section by having students trace dotted "key words" using crayons or markers. Trace the word **property** in black, the word **magnetism** in red, and the word **attract** in their favorite color.

FOCUS   Magnetism

OBJECTIVE   To explore some properties of magnets and magnetism

OVERVIEW   All materials have characteristics called "properties." Magnets have a property called magnetism. Magnetism affects how magnets relate to each other and to other materials.

WHAT TO DO

With your team, carefully follow each step below.

Observe

Look at the magnets. Look at the iron filings. Look at the sawdust. Think about ways these items are similar. Think about ways they are different.

Describe

Describe the iron filings. What do they look like? What do they feel like? What color are they? How do the iron filings compare to the sawdust?

Discuss

What's another name for characteristic? *property*

What property do magnets have? *magnetism*

What is one thing magnets can do? *attract*

PHYSICAL · **219**

Teacher to Teacher

The first known magnets were chunks of stone made of magnetite or lodestone.

An ancient legend (unsubstantiated) says that a shepherd on the Island of Crete was the first to notice lodestone. Whenever he passed a certain large stone, the iron-tipped end of his shepherd's crook was pulled downward!

The shepherd's name was "Magnes" — hence the term "magnetism" to describe this unique phenomenon.

Early mariners used the properties of lodestone to help them navigate. They discovered that when a length of lodestone was suspended from a thread, it always came to rest in a North/South direction.

READ THE STORY
Magnets have a characteristic called magnetism. This affects how magnets react to each other and to other materials. Read the story below to find out more.

Magnetism

Magnets have "magnetism."
All magnets have a characteristic called "magnetism." Magnetism affects how these magnets react to each other. It also controls how they react to other materials.

These are magnets.

Magnets can attract.
Magnets have a north pole and a south pole. If you place opposite poles near each other, the magnets will pull together.

Magnets can also repel.
If you place poles that are the same together, the magnets will push apart. They will turn so opposite poles are touching.

These are iron bolts.

Iron is "magnetic."
Iron is called "magnetic" because magnets stick to it. (A note magnet stuck to a refrigerator is a good example.)

Few materials are magnetic.
Although some common metals are magnetic (iron, cobalt, nickel), many other metals (like copper and aluminum) are not.

These are wood chips.

Wood is "non-magnetic."
Wood is a "non-magnetic" material because it is not attracted by magnets. A magnet will not stick to a wooden door.

Most materials are non-magnetic.
Materials like glass, plastic, and paper are non-magnetic. To test any material for magnetism, simply touch it with a magnet.

220 · PHYSICAL

Extended Teaching

1. To expand vocabulary, explain that this use of the word "properties" means "attributes, qualities, features, or traits." To enhance understanding, ask students to list some properties of pencils (long, round, made from wood, has lead in the center, used for making marks, etc.).

2. Explore the history of magnetism. The magnetic properties of iron-rich rocks (lodestone) were described by Greek philosophers as early as 600 B.C. Electromagnets were invented in 1825.

These led to inventions like the telegraph and telephone. Magnetism is also closely related to the development of electricity and electric motors.

3. Give each research team a small magnet and challenge them to find items in the room that are or are not magnetic. Have them keep a detailed list. Encourage them to also explore how magnets react to each other. (Warning: Keep magnets away from computers. They can erase valuable data!)

Read The Story

Read the story aloud with your students. (See READING LEVELS on page 12.) After reading, monitor teams as they discuss what was read. Once you feel students have mastered the basic concepts, have them answer the comprehension questions (**What I Learned** - part 1) on the next page.

To introduce the story, say:

"The title of this story is 'Magnetism.' Look at your story and follow along as we read it together."

If you wish, encourage Emergent readers to point to words and pictures as you read.

What I Learned (part 1)

These are basic fact-based comprehension questions. Student answers will vary, but suggested responses include:

1 a) repel b) attract

2 Iron bolts are attracted by magnets; wood chips are not.

3 The nails would stick to the magnet, but the sawdust would not.

Field Trip

Visit a salvage yard that uses a large electromagnet to sort and move scrap metal.

Guest Speaker

Invite a high school physics teacher to visit your class. Ask him/her to show your students how to build a simple electromagnet, and to demonstrate how it works.

Materials Needed*

magnet   iron filings
plastic spoon   sawdust
sealable bags - 2

Safety Concerns

4. Slipping

There is a potential for spilled material. Remind students to exercise caution.

4. Other

If not handled properly, iron filings can prick fingers. Keep filings and sawdust away from mouth and eyes at all times. Keep magnets away from computer equipment. Also, sawdust and filings are flammable.

Do the Activity

Read the activity in advance so you understand it thoroughly. (If time allows, try it yourself.) Before students begin, carefully go over the **Safety Concerns** together.

Pass out materials, then have your students follow along as you read the instructions for **Step 1**. Monitor teams closely as they complete this step.

Once teams have completed **Step 1**, read instructions for **Step 2**. Monitor teams as before. Repeat for **Step 3** and **Step 4**.

After the activity, allow time for each team to share their observations. To encourage higher-level thinking, encourage teams to not only share their observations with each other, but also with other teams.

Special Instructions

Step 1 - Have one team member hold the bag while another pours. If students need help sealing bags, offer assistance.

Step 2 - Remind students to separate materials gently to avoid tearing the bags.

Step 3 - Have students wash their hands thoroughly after completing this activity to remove sawdust or iron filing residue.

* Bold-faced items supplied in kit.

DO THE ACTIVITY
Working with your research team, carefully follow each step below. Before you start, be sure you know the **safety rules** for this activity.

STEP 1
Pour a spoonful of iron filings into each plastic bag. Seal the bags carefully. Hold one bag by the top and move a magnet close to it. Record the results.

STEP 2
Stick the magnet to the bag. Add the other bag to make a "magnet sandwich." Record the results. Now remove the magnet and observe what happens.

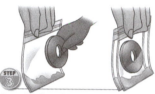 

STEP 3
Pour the iron filings back into their bottle. Repeat steps 1 and 2 using sawdust instead of iron filings. Record the results. Pour the sawdust back into its bag.

STEP 4
Review each step in this activity. Discuss how the materials reacted to the magnet. Compare your team's findings with those of other teams.

What Happened?

Immediately following the activity, help your students understand what they observed.

Say: *"In this activity, you explored some of the properties of magnets and magnetism.*

*In **Steps 1** and **2**, you saw how iron filings reacted to a magnetic field. You discovered that iron is attracted by a magnet.*

*In **Step 3**, you repeated the activity using sawdust. You discovered that unlike iron, wood is not affected by a magnet.*

*Then in **Step 4**, like good scientists, you compared observations with other research teams."*

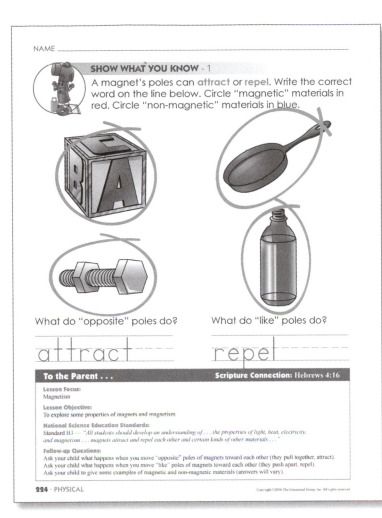

NAME _____

SHOW WHAT YOU KNOW - 1
A magnet's poles can **attract** or **repel**. Write the correct word on the line below. Circle "magnetic" materials in red. Circle "non-magnetic" materials in blue.

What do "opposite" poles do?

attract

What do "like" poles do?

repel

To the Parent . . .   **Scripture Connection:** Hebrews 4:16

Lesson Focus:
Magnetism

Lesson Objective:
To explore some properties of magnets and magnetism

National Science Education Standards:
Standard B3 — "All students should develop an understanding of . . . the properties of light, heat, electricity, and magnetism . . . magnets attract and repel each other and certain kinds of other materials . . ."

Follow-up Questions:
Ask your child what happens when you move "opposite" poles of magnets toward each other (they pull together, attract).
Ask your child what happens when you move "like" poles of magnets toward each other (they push apart, repel).
Ask your child to give some examples of magnetic and non-magnetic materials (answers will vary).

224 · PHYSICAL

Food For Thought

A related "Scripture Object Lesson" you can share with your students.

Hebrews 4:16

In this lesson, we learned that magnets have a special relationship with each other. Depending on how they turn, they can attract or repel.

In a way, God is the ultimate magnet! He is constantly pulling us with His great love.

But we "little magnets" can be attracted or repelled by God's love.

If we turn away, then God's love will not draw us closer. We may move far from His loving protection and power.

But if we choose to trust God, spending time getting to know Him better each day, then we will be pulled closer and closer to Him!

Turn to God and feel the attraction of His love!

Expand - Day 4

Begin **Day 4** with a review of **Day 3**, then have students answer "part 2" questions.

What I Learned (part 2)
These are higher-level cognitive questions (explain, compare, predict). Student answers will vary, but suggested responses may include:

① it stuck to the iron filings, but not to the sawdust

② a) both small particles, both in bags, etc. b) iron filings attracted to magnet, sawdust was not

③ a) it would stick to the pan b) iron is attracted to magnets

Assess - Day 5

Suggestions for modifying assessments to reflect reading levels can be found under ASSESSMENT METHODS on page 12.

Show What You Know
(general assessment in Student Worktext)

Blanks: a) attract b) repel
Also, the skillet and bolt should be circled in red; the block and bottle should be circled in blue

Show What You Know 2
(optional test master in Teacher Guide)

1) F   2) T   3) T   4) F   5) F

To The Parent
Included at the bottom of all assessment tests, "To The Parent" provides a great way to solicit parent involvement. It not only gives parents an overview of the lesson, but also provides follow-up questions for home use.

NAME _____

Show What You Know 2

Read each sentence below. If the sentence is true, circle the letter **T**. If the sentence is false, circle the letter **F**.

T F 1. Magnets have a characteristic called "materialism".

T F 2. Magnets have both a north pole and a south pole.

T F 3. Iron and nickel are magnetic materials.

T F 4. Aluminum and copper are magnetic materials.

T F 5. Wood, glass, and plastic are magnetic materials.

To the Parent . . .   **Scripture Connection:** Hebrews 4:16

Lesson Focus:
Magnetism

Lesson Objective:
To explore some properties of magnets and magnetism

National Science Education Standards:
Standard B3 — *"All students should develop an understanding of . . . the properties of light, heat, electricity, and magnetism . . . magnets attract and repel each other and certain kinds of other materials . . ."*

Follow-up Questions:
Ask your child what happens when you move "opposite" poles of magnets toward each other (they pull together, attract).
Ask your child what happens when you move "like" poles of magnets toward each other (they push apart, repel).
Ask your child to give some examples of magnetic and non-magnetic materials (answers will vary).

Managing Magnetism
Lesson 36

FOCUS Magnetism

OBJECTIVE To explore some practical applications of magnetism

OVERVIEW Knowing magnets are attracted to certain metals is "science." Applying that knowledge to sort trash, lock doors, or run electric motors is "technology."

WHAT TO DO

With your team, carefully follow each step below.

Observe

Look at the iron filings. Look at the sawdust. Look at the salt. Think about some ways these items are similar. Think about some ways they are different.

Describe

Describe each of the materials you observed. What do they look like? What do they feel like? What are some places you might find materials like these?

Discuss

What is one thing magnets usually attract? metal
What is knowing about materials called? science
What is applying science called? technology

PHYSICAL · **225**

Lesson 36

Introduction

National Standards
Focus: B3

Related: A1, A2, B1, B2, E1, E2

Category
Physical Science

Focus
Magnetism

Objective
To explore some practical applications of magnetism

Overview
Read the overview aloud to your students. The goal is to create an atmosphere of curiosity and inquiry.

Say: *"Knowing magnets are attracted to certain metals is 'science.' Applying that knowledge to sort trash, lock doors, or run electric motors is 'technology'!"*

Additional Notes

To introduce this lesson, hold up a magnetic paper clip holder filled with paper clips. Turn it upside down. Ask students, *"Why aren't the paperclips falling out?"* (The holder has a magnet in it that holds the paper clips in place.)

Explain that knowing all about magnets and how they work is interesting information. But such knowledge by itself doesn't do much. When scientific knowledge is used to create something useful, however, (like the generators that produce electricity), we all reap the benefits!

That's why it's important to study science. The more we learn and apply good science, the better our world can become.

What To Do

Once students are seated in "research teams" with materials in front of them, read the first section (OB-SERVE) aloud.

Say, *"To start this lesson, we're going to **observe** some items. Try to think of very specific words to describe what you're seeing. First, I will read the instructions to you. Then you can follow the instructions as you **observe** the items in front of you."*

Monitor teams closely as they follow instructions. When teams are finished with this section, repeat the process with the DE-SCRIBE section. Conclude with the DISCUSS section.

Options

Expand the DISCUSS section by having students trace dotted "key words" using crayons or markers. Trace the word **metal** in silver or gray, the word **science** in blue, and the word **technology** in yellow or gold.

FOCUS   Magnetism

OBJECTIVE   To explore some practical applications of magnetism

OVERVIEW   Knowing magnets are attracted to certain metals is "science." Applying that knowledge to sort trash, lock doors, or run electric motors is "technology."

Managing Magnetism
Lesson 36

WHAT TO DO

With your team, carefully follow each step below.

Observe

Look at the iron filings. **Look** at the sawdust. **Look** at the salt. **Think** about some ways these items are similar. **Think** about some ways they are different.

Describe

Describe each of the materials you observed. What do they **look** like? What do they **feel** like? What are some places you might find materials like these?

Discuss

What is one thing magnets usually attract? metal

What is knowing about materials called? science

What is applying science called? technology

PHYSICAL · 225

Teacher to Teacher

There are four known types of forces in the universe: strong nuclear, weak nuclear, electromagnetic, and gravity.

Strong nuclear force holds atoms together. It's the most powerful force of all, but it only works at extremely small distances.

Weak nuclear force helps elements change. It even drives the fusion power of the Sun!

Electromagnetic force combines electricity and magnetism. It's a force we use every day.

Gravity is the attraction between all matter. While it can affect things at very great distances, it's still the weakest of the four.

Extended Teaching

1. To expand vocabulary, explain that "managing" means "controlling" — in this case, controlling the power of magnets. Scientists' ability to control magnetic power has led to many useful devices, including everything that uses electricity!

2. An electric motor is a machine that uses magnetism and electric current to perform useful work. Ask students to name some common devices with electric motors and describe the work they do. (Examples include vacuum cleaners, refrigerators, sewing machines, washers, power drills, electric saws, ceiling fans, microwaves, blow dryers, etc.)

3. Ask students if they have ever seen a "dimmer switch" on a light. Explain that this is an example of managing (controlling) technology. A dimmer switch allows us to reduce the electric current to the light, reducing light. The volume control on a TV or radio is another simple device to help us manage technology.

Read The Story
Read the story aloud with your students. (See READING LEVELS on page 12.) After reading, monitor teams as they discuss what was read. Once you feel students have mastered the basic concepts, have them answer the comprehension questions (**What I Learned** - part 1) on the next page.

To introduce the story, say:

"The title of this story is 'Managing Magnetism.' Look at your story and follow along as we read it together."

If you wish, encourage Emergent readers to point to words and pictures as you read.

What I Learned (part 1)
These are basic fact-based comprehension questions. Student answers will vary, but suggested responses include:

1 answers should reflect examples from the story, or similar uses

2 answers will vary

3 answers will vary, but a common theme would be difficulties related to the lack of electricity

Field Trip
Visit a veterinarian that has a "large animal" practice. Ask him/her to explain how a cow magnet works.

Guest Speaker
Invite a "treasure hobbyist" to visit your class. Ask him/her to bring their metal detector and samples of things they've found. If possible, have them give a demonstration of the device on the playground.

Materials Needed*

craft stick   iron filings
salt   sawdust
magnet   sealable bag
petri dish

Safety Concerns

4. Slipping

There is a potential for spilled material. Remind students to exercise caution.

4. Other

If not handled properly, iron filings can prick fingers. Keep filings and sawdust away from mouth and eyes at all times. Keep magnets away from computer equipment. Also, filings and sawdust are flammable.

Do the Activity

Read the activity in advance so you understand it thoroughly. (If time allows, try it yourself.) Before students begin, carefully go over the **Safety Concerns** together.

Pass out materials, then have your students follow along as you read the instructions for **Step 1**. Monitor teams closely as they complete this step.

Once teams have completed **Step 1**, read instructions for **Step 2**. Monitor teams as before. Repeat for **Step 3** and **Step 4**.

After the activity, allow time for each team to share their observations. To encourage higher-level thinking, encourage teams to not only share their observations with each other, but also with other teams.

Special Instructions

Step 4 - Have students wash their hands to remove sawdust or iron filing residue. When the magnet is removed from the bag, the iron filings will drop off. Take special care not to let them come in contact with the magnet — they can be hard to remove!

DO THE ACTIVITY
Working with your research team, carefully follow each step below. Before you start, be sure you know the **safety rules** for this activity.

STEP 1
Pour the iron filings, salt, and sawdust into the petri dish. **Stir** them together with the craft stick. **Discuss** ways you might separate these materials.

STEP 2
Place the magnet in the bag. Slowly **drag** the bag across the mixture of iron filings, salt, and sawdust in the petri dish. **Record** the result.

STEP 3
Continue dragging the bag back and forth through the pile until one material is completely removed. **Discuss** how you used "technology" to sort materials.

STEP 4
Review each step. Discuss how each material reacted to the magnet. What "science" was used? Compare your findings with those of other teams.

What Happened?

Immediately following the activity, help your students understand what they observed.

Say: *"In this activity, you explored one way a magnet's power can be applied to do useful work.*

In **Step 1**, *you created a pile of mixed materials.*

In **Steps 2** *and* **3**, *you used your knowledge of how magnets work to remove all the iron filings from the pile. (Imagine how difficult this would have been without a magnet!)*

Then in **Step 4**, *you compared and discussed your observations with other research teams."*

NAME _____

SHOW WHAT YOU KNOW - 1
Magnets are all around us. Magnetic technology helps us perform many useful tasks. Circle objects with magnets in red. Circle objects without magnets in blue.

Using a science like magnetism to perform practical tasks is called

technology

Food For Thought

A related "Scripture Object Lesson"
you can share with your students.

2 TIMOTHY 3:14

In this lesson, we learned that magnets are very useful. Many inventions are the result of deep study in the science of magnetism. Most of these have made our world a much better place to live. And new things are discovered in science every day.

Do you think God is unhappy when we learn more about His creation? Of course not!

God wants us to study and to use the knowledge we gain to help others. But God also wants us to remember that He is the one who created all of these marvels, the one who fills our world with wonder.

Always enjoy the excitement of discovering new things in science. But be sure to give credit where credit is due – to God, the Creator of everything!

Expand - Day 4

Begin **Day 4** with a review of **Day 3**, then have students answer "part 2" questions.

What I Learned (part 2)
These are higher-level cognitive questions (explain, compare, predict). Student answers will vary, but suggested responses may include:

1 iron filings stuck to magnet; salt and sawdust did not

2 a) all three are small particles, dry or powdery, etc. b) iron filings are magnetic, salt and sawdust are not

3 they can pull magnetic materials (like iron and steel) out of the pile, leaving non-magnetic materials (like plastic, paper, and glass) behind

Assess - Day 5

Suggestions for modifying assessments to reflect reading levels can be found under ASSESSMENT METHODS on page 12.

Show What You Know 1
(general assessment in Student Worktext)

Blank: technology
Also, the motor, toy, and paperclip holder should be circled in red; the feather duster, skillet, and salt shaker should be circled in blue

Show What You Know 2
(optional test master in Teacher Guide)

1) N   2) Y   3) N   4) Y   5) Y

To The Parent
Included at the bottom of all assessment tests, "To The Parent" provides a great way to solicit parent involvement. It not only gives parents an overview of the lesson, but also provides follow-up questions for home use.

NAME _____

Show What You Know 2

Read each sentence below. If a magnet would be helpful for this task, circle **Y** for "yes". If a magnet would NOT be helpful for this task, circle **N** for "no."

Y   N   1. You are sticking a poster on the classroom wall.

Y   N   2. You are placing a note on the refrigerator door.

Y   N   3. You are separating rock salt from a pile of sawdust.

Y   N   4. You are picking up loose nails at a construction site.

Y   N   5. You are safely collecting bits of metal inside a cow.

This **"Shopping List"** is provided for your convenience. It contains all the items that are not common classroom supplies (paper, pencil, scissors, etc.) or components found in your Materials Kit.

Lesson 2
food coloring (blue)

Lesson 6
pictures of moths

Lesson 7
newspaper

Lesson 9
vegetable oil

Lesson 16
lamp

Lesson 17
lamp

Lesson 20
vinegar

Lesson 21
bubble solution

Lesson 22
liquid soap

Lesson 23
liquid soap
food coloring (blue)
food coloring (yellow)
whole milk

Lesson 24
vegetable oil

Lesson 28
stopwatch (optional)

Lesson 29
measuring tape

This Black-line Master is for use with Lesson 6 - **Mighty Moth**.